India and
South Asia

D1160866

India and South Asia

A Short History

DAVID LUDDEN

ONEWORLD

OXFORD

INDIA AND SOUTH ASIA: A SHORT HISTORY

Oneworld Publications
(Sales and Editorial)
185 Banbury Road
Oxford OX2 7AR
England
www.oneworld-publications.com

ISBN 1–85168–237–6

Cover design by Design Deluxe
Typeset by LaserScript, Mitcham, UK
Printed and bound in Britain by Clays Ltd, St Ives plc

For Mohona Sara Siddiqi

Contents

List of Maps, Tables, and Figures

Preface and
Acknowledgements

In writing this book, I have tried to incorporate more information from local and regional histories than is normally contained in survey histories. I have also tried to compose a narrative that indicates the complexity of social change over long periods of time and of historical knowledge in the present day. Selected Readings provide next steps for the study of particular topics. In addition, online companion materials can be found on my website, which also contains an array of visual accompaniments to the text (www.sas.upenn.edu/~dludden).

I have used ideas and information from many people. I want to thank the following people by name without implicating them in any errors of fact or interpretation that remain in the text. In alphabetical order, they are Itty Abraham, Bina Agarwal, Muzaffar Alam, G. Aloysius, Arjun Appadurai, Carol Breckenridge Appadurai, Amiya Kumar Bagchi, Christopher Baker, Christopher Bayly, Vivek Bhandari, Neeladri Bhattacharya, Sugata Bose, James Boyce, Brian Caton, Binay Bhushan Chaudhuri, Bernard S. Cohn, A.R. Desai, Nicholas B. Dirks, Richard Eaton, Sandria Freitag, Paul Greenough, Sumit Guha, H.A.R.L. Gunawardana, C.R. De Silva, Irfan Habib, Ayesha Jalal, Sanjay Joshi, Madhavi Kale, Tom Kessinger, Dharma Kumar, Michelle Maskiell, Barbara Metcalf, Savita Nair, Robert Nichols, Gail Omvedt, Pratyoush Onta, Gyanendra Pandey, M.S.S. Pandian, Michael Pearson, Sheldon Pollock, Gyan Prakash, Pamela Price, John Rogers, David Rudner, Ashok Rudra, Amartya Sen, Dina Mahnaz Siddiqi, Sanjay Subrahmanyam, Romila Thapar, Daniel Thorner,

Peter van der Veer, David Washbrook, Anand Yang, and Eleanor Zelliot.

Thanks also to David Nelson for his constant bibliographic assistance; and to Jeremie Dufault, Teresa Watts, Linda Oh, Sue Yi, Richard Mo, Anna Cullotti, and Vivek Arora for their help on various phases of this project. Lori Uscher and Brooke Newborn merit special thanks for her detailed reading, perceptive comments and insightful suggestions. Victoria Warner and Rebecca Clare have been steadfast at Oneworld Publications; I have needed all their encouragement.

Introduction: An Approach to Social History

This survey of history covers the part of the world that now includes the national states of Bangladesh, Bhutan, India, the Maldives, Nepal, Pakistan, and Sri Lanka. (See Country Profiles.) The book compiles useful information for readers who want to use the past to understand contemporary affairs and also provides an introduction to South Asian history for students and teachers in colleges and universities.

This book differs from other surveys in several important ways. Though its chronology is mostly political, its central subject matter is the historical process of social change, including economic, cultural, and political aspects. To introduce readers to the very long history of social change in South Asia, each chapter concentrates on major innovations in each period of time that most clearly indicate how change occurred in social conditions that ordinary people experienced in everyday life.

Each chapter describes the major connections between large-scale trends in the wide world of history and changing patterns of social routine in South Asian localities. The vast scale of South Asian history makes it inappropriate for readers to imagine that any one set of peoples or places represents the whole of South Asia's past. With this in mind, the book pays considerable attention to diversity. Rather than telling one single story, the book presents a series of strategic simplifications that sketch the bare contours of very complex historical trends, in order to provide a useful framework for organizing factual information and to establish a reliable starting point for further study.

1

Thematically, the book centres on the problem of collective identity. It traces the historical invention and reinvention of group definitions, associations, and solidarities that have shaped peoples' experience, feeling, and thinking about where they live, where they belong, who belongs with them, and who and what are foreign, separate, and different.

Scholars approach the study of collective identity in different ways and this book combines two conflicting approaches. One approach can be called 'essentialist.' It begins by assuming that people inherit social identity as a cultural attribute analogous to a genetic trait. Individuals *have* an inherent identity as members of a group. Scholars who employ this approach interpret social activity as an expression of pre-existing group sentiments and mentalities. In applying this view to history, we would say that a social group – defined by nationality, ethnicity, religion, language, race, gender, caste, class, or other trait – expresses its essential character through the activity of its members, particularly of leaders who represent collective sentiments and interests publicly.

The other approach can be called 'constructivist'. It begins by assuming that human identities are inherently malleable, multiple, ambiguous, shifting, and contextual. Powerful elements in society construct social identity as an experienced reality and make some identities feel more important than others at particular places and times. In this view, the activity of prominent people does not so much reflect pre-existing collective identity as it promotes the feeling of solidarity. Historically, social identities are always available for redefinition and recombination because they are always unstable products of social power in specific sites, under contestation as the various powers of identity-formation push and pull this way and that.

Both approaches have strengths and weaknesses. Essentialists have as much trouble explaining change as constructivists have explaining continuity. This book combines ideas from both approaches but leans heavily toward constructivism. Social historians today most often adopt a flexible attitude toward social identity to combine various elements. Madhu Kishwar provides a crystal clear image of the kind of biographical mentality that underlies the social history in this book, as she describes the mixing and sorting of identities in her own life:

Every human being is the product of many cross-cutting, multi-layered identities. For instance, a vital part of my identity is defined by my gender. But I am also (among other things) a daughter, a sister, a college teacher, a writer, a Punjabi, a Hindu, a resident of a particular neighbourhood, and a citizen of India. Most identities (e.g., those based on nationality, religion, language) are acquired or mutable. A few are fixed and immutable, such as biological parentage. Identities based on native land, village, or locale where a person is born and reared are also fixed.

For the most part, people take these identity layers for granted and they find expression in their appropriate realms at different points of time. However, a group or person may begin to assert a particular identity with greater vigour if it provides greater access to power and opportunities, as happens with caste or gender-based job reservations. Alternately, a person begins to assign a high priority to a particular basic identity if she or he perceives it as threatened or suppressed, especially if that identity is essential to the person's personal, economic or social well-being. For instance, if the government implemented censorship laws that forbade me as a writer to publish and disseminate my work freely, I would be forced to give greater emphasis to my identity as a writer, and to devote a good deal of my time and efforts to fighting against the censors. This struggle may require working in alliances with other writers, though our other identities and commitments may have very little in common.

When I travel down South, I become aware of my identity as a North Indian, because most people there do not understand the languages I speak, and as a result I feel handicapped. By contrast, I feel culturally much closer to and communicate much better with Punjabis from Pakistan, even though they are citizens of a state that has a long history of enmity with India. I become acutely aware of my identity as an Indian only when I travel abroad, especially in the West, because of the frequent incidents of racial prejudice and cultural arrogance I routinely encounter there.

Similarly, I become conscious of my identity as a woman only on those few occasions when I am discriminated against or feel special disabilities on account of my gender, for example, when facing sexual harassment or discrimination in employment. Otherwise, my gender identity is only one of my multiple overlapping and cross-cutting identities which peacefully coexists with other identities.[1]

1. Madhu Kishwar, 'Who Am I? Living Identities vs Acquired Ones', *Manushi*, 94, May–June 1996.

This book provides a very long term perspective on present-day social identities. In this perspective all the contemporary identities that Madhu Kishwar describes appear as changing historical phenomena. For individuals in each generation, identities often *feel* inherited. This feeling emerges in a changing society, as do the contrary feelings that identities are transient, imposed, or ill-fitting. As Madhu Kishwar says, the experience of identity arises from the recognition that a person is a part of a group. This group may have not existed at all in earlier times. Its relevance for personal identity might have sat quietly in the shadows before being illuminated. Public cultural activists promote and develop social identity by making identities more visible and potent. Activists also resist the imposition of identities and assert alternatives that create new possibilities. Gautama Buddha's activity in ancient times can be interpreted in this way, as resistance and visionary counter-construction. We will see that ethnic, religious, linguistic, regional, and national identities have all been constructed by the accumulation of innovative interventions in social history. Such interventions are still being made as history continues into the unpredictable future.

Here we trace long-term patterns of change in social environments where social activities of various kinds have made collective identities into essential facts for individuals in everyday life, creating the combinations that Kishwar calls 'layers'. In the long view of history, we begin to see how modern identities have been invented and old identities have been reproduced. I would suggest that collective identity feels like a natural inheritance when it has been institutionalized in systems of power that effectively organize social experience in everyday life. South Asia has emerged as a world region in modern times, separated from other regions, because a particular constellation of social identities has become essential for people living there through the operation of powerful social institutions. Geographical boundaries around South Asia have changed over centuries. They are still changing today. Identities are still being contested and reconstructed. National identities have become predominant in modern times. The contemporary condition nationality constitutes a central problem for modern historical studies, and thus for this book.

ONE

Inventing Ancient Civilization

South Asian history has no one beginning, no one chronology, no single plot or narrative. It is not a singular history, but rather many histories, with indefinite, contested origins and with countless separate trajectories that multiply as we learn more about the past. In recent decades, history's multiplicity, antiquity, and ambiguity have become more complicated as scholars have opened new perspectives on the past and made new discoveries.

Not long ago, it seemed that South Asian history began at a singular moment in the second millennium BCE, when the oldest known texts, the Vedas, were composed. A clear, continuous stream of cultural tradition once seemed to flow from Vedic to modern times, allowing modern scholars to dip into ancient texts to savour the original essence of a culture that we can still see around us today. The early flow of culture seemed to swell into a fully developed classical civilization under the ancient empires of the Mauryas (321–181 BCE) and Guptas (320–520 CE), which arose on the banks of the sacred river Ganga. Classical societies seemed to follow Vedic norms, and seemed to preserve sacred traditions recorded in other ancient Sanskrit texts that also prescribed the division of society into ritual strata, called *varna*, containing social groups called *jati*. Classical tradition seemed to provide a blueprint for caste society down to modern times. After the Gupta Empire collapsed, apparently under the impact of foreign invasions, political fragmentation was seen to have characterized medieval times; but despite a long series of foreign conquests, the clear stream of cultural tradition seemed to flow on continuously. After the end of the ancient empire, history brought political turmoil and social and economic change, but ancient cultural tradition seemed to maintain its purity, responding and adapting to the challenges of history.

In this now antiquated view of ancient history, we hear echoes of modern nationalism resounding in the idea that indigenous resistance to foreign invasion spurred the early formation of ancient empires. It is indeed true that in the wake of victories by Darius, king of Persia, who conquered Sind and Gandhara in the sixth century BCE, and after several early efforts at empire building by rulers along the banks of the Ganga, the Maurya empire rose at the same time as Alexander the Great entered Punjab from Persia in 327 BCE. But now we can see that modern national identities had projected themselves into the distant past to imagine that Mauryan armies were defending their homeland against foreign invaders from Greece and Persia. This same idea of defensive response was also used to explain the later rise of the Guptas, who finally managed to unify the Ganga basin once again after centuries of conquest by Indo-Greeks, Sakas, Indo-Parthians, and Kushanas, who came from Central Asia and marched down the Hindu Kush into the Indus valley lowlands. The same idea was used again to show how invading Hunas (Huns) from Central Asia broke up the Gupta empire, in the fifth century. But then, political fragmentation inside India was seen to have prevented imperial unity, and internal fragmentation continued to prevent unity against many later invaders. In the eighth century, Arabs came by sea to conquer Sind. From the twelfth century onwards, invading conquerors included Afghans, Turks, Mongols, Persians, and, finally, Europeans. From 1290 until 1947, Muslims and Christians ruled most of the land of Indic civilization. The British were the last foreign rulers, from 1757 to 1947. Thus it fell to modern nationalism to unify native peoples against foreign conquerors once and for all.

This grand narrative of history in South Asia – based on the idea of an original, indigenous culture facing foreign invasions – provided the first framework for modern historical studies. It informed national cultures and national identities. It perpetuated the idea that Hindus, Buddhists, Muslims, and Christians represent different civilizations, each with their own ancient, native territories. Thus it helped to bolster the modern association of national polities with separate domains of world history in Europe, the Middle East, and South Asia.

New discoveries and new perspectives now provide many different avenues for exploring South Asia's ancient, medieval, and modern history. We now see that rather than having one singular origin, South Asia has always included many peoples and cultures, which had different points of departure and followed distinctive historical trajectories. What once seemed like a single tree of Indic culture, rooted in the Vedas, with many branches spreading out over centuries, has come to look more like a vast forest of many cultures filled with countless trees of various sizes, ages, and types, constantly cross-breeding to fertilize one another. The profusion of cultures blurs the boundaries of the forest. Cultural boundaries drawn by modern scholars in and around South Asia have come to be seen more as artefacts of modern national cultures than as an accurate reflection of pre-modern conditions. Prehistoric cities in the Indus river valley much older than the Vedas participated in a vast prehistory of urbanism that ran across southern Eurasia and they also participated in the indigenous evolution of agro-pastoral societies in South Asia. Pre-Vedic cultures should not be assigned exclusively to the prehistory of modern South Asia, West Asia, India, or Pakistan: they participate in all of these at the same time. The singers of the Vedas also moved among prehistoric pastoral cultures of Central and West Asia as they informed cultures in ancient South Asia. A mingling and fusion of cultures has always crossed the boundaries that today divide national states in and around South Asia.

With all this in view, it becomes obvious that we must now separate the academic study of pre-modern history from contemporary efforts to construct modern cultural boundaries. We need to separate the study of collective identities and everyday experience in the distant past from our current cultural politics of national identity. As we will see, pre-modern history does indeed help us to understand the present, not by its immanent foreshadowing of the present or by its revelation of classical truths to guide modern life, but rather by its indication that distinctively modern modes of social existence came into being in the nineteenth and twentieth centuries, setting them apart from

TABLE 1. A CHRONOLOGICAL FRAMEWORK FOR ANTIQUITY

I. Prehistory BCE

To 2500	Stone age, microlithic tool cultures; Mehrgarh.
2500–1500	Harappa and Indus valley urban culture.

II. Earliest history to 600 BCE

1200–400s	Early Vedas, late Vedas and *Brahmana*s.
1000s	Iron smelting and tools
900s	Period of wars recounted in *Mahabharata*.
700s	Prominence of *janapada* and *mahajanapada* territories in the Ganga basin.

III. Ancient Transformation

a. The original states, *circa* 600–327 BCE

600s–500s	Rise of Kuru, Panchala, Kosala, Magadha.
500s	Persian King Darius occupies Sind and Gandhara; life of Mahavira.
400s	Life of Buddha; composition of *Ramayana* and *Mahabharata*.
327	Alexander the Great enters Punjab.

b. The original empire, 300s-185 BCE

Late 300s	Chandragupta Maurya founds Maurya empire; composition of Pannini's grammar, possible first version of *Arthasastra*.
268–233	Ashoka Maurya.
185	Last Mauryas. Founding of Sunga dynasty in Pataliputra.

c. Imperial competition, 250 BCE to 250 CE

250 BCE to 250 CE	North-west: Indo-Greeks, northern Sakas, Indo-Parthians, Kushanas.
55 BCE to 500s CE	South: Satavahana and Vakataka dynasties in Pratisthana and Vidarbha.
70–409 CE	West: Sakas in Malwa Ujjaini–Rajasthan–Gujarat.
100 BCE to 100 CE	Early Siva and Vishnu worship; Buddhist stupas prominent in north-west, south-east, Sri Lanka; early Sangam literature; composition of Manu's *Dharmasastra*, *Bhagavad Gita*.

TABLE 1. *CONTINUED*

d. Dynastic territories, *circa* 200 BCE to 600 CE

320–840s CE	Ganga basin: Guptas and Pusyaputis.
400s–500s CE	North-west: southern Hunas.
100 BCE–400 CE	Southern peninsula: Cheras, Cholas, and Pandyas.
200s–500s	Maharashtra: Vakatakas, Kalacuris, and Rashtrakutas.
500s–750s CE	Karnataka: Chalukyas.
200s BCE–1200s CE	Sri Lanka: Lambakannas.

medieval and ancient histories that came before. Using ancient and medieval evidence to validate modern boundaries, identities, and cultures obscures more than it reveals about pre-modern histories in South Asia, which moved across all the regions of southern Eurasia and were unique to their own time.

South Asia was a radically different world during the millennia before it took on its modern character. The first basic lesson of this book is that travelling back into the distant past reveals cultures, identities, and environments that are as distant from those of today as are their physical surroundings. The landscapes in which pre-modern populations lived would be very unfamiliar to people today. For most of its history, South Asia was thinly populated. Its countless small communities were widely scattered. In ancient and medieval times, much more of the land was covered by forests full of wild animals than by farms, villages, towns, and cities. Entering into the history of this vast pre-modern world provides us with a critical perspective on the novelty of modernity.

LAND AND WATER

Eons ago in the geological past, a triangle of rocky land broke off from East Africa, drifted north in the Indian Ocean, and crashed into Eurasia. The upheaval produced the Himalayas; its violence still visits the pivotal point of geological merger when earthquakes rock Gujarat, as they did in January 2001. Merging tectonic plates produced volcanoes that spewed ash across the new peninsula that they formed. Monsoon rains washed this fertile black volcanic soil into wide seams along peninsular rivers. Rain and melting ice and

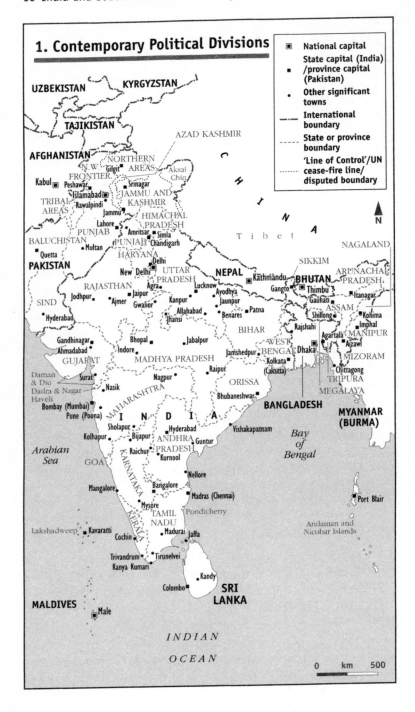

1. Contemporary Political Divisions

▣	National capital
■	State capital (India) /province capital (Pakistan)
●	Other significant towns
— —	International boundary
- - - -	State or province boundary
....	'Line of Control'/UN cease-fire line/ disputed boundary

UZBEKISTAN

KYRGYZSTAN

TAJIKISTAN

AZAD KASHMIR

AFGHANISTAN

NORTHERN
AREAS

N.W. Gilgit
FRONTIER.
Kabul ▣ Peshawar

Aksai
Chin

C H I N A

Srinagar

TRIBAL Islamabad ▣
AREAS Rawalpindi

JAMMU AND
KASHMIR

Jammu

Lahore

BALUCHISTAN

PUNJAB

HIMACHAL
PRADESH

Amritsar Simla

Tibet

NAGALAND

● Quetta

Multan

PUNJAB Chandigarh

HARYANA

PAKISTAN

Delhi

SIKKIM

ARUNACHAL
PRADESH

New Delhi UTTAR
PRADESH

NEPAL Kathmandu

BHUTAN

SIND

RAJASTHAN

Agra
Jaipur

Lucknow
Ayodhya

Gangto Thimbu
Gauhati

Itanagar

● Hyderabad

Jodhpur
Ajmer Gwalior

Kanpur
Jaunpur

ASSAM

Kohima

Allahabad Benares
Jhansi

Patna

Shillong MANIPUR

BIHAR

Rajshahi

Imphal

Gandhinagar
Ahmadabad

Bhopal

Jabalpur

WEST

Agartala Aizawl

Jamshedpur BENGAL Dhaka

MIZORAM

GUJARAT

INDORE

MADHYA PRADESH

Daman
& Diu

Surat

Raipur

Kolkata
(Calcutta)

Chittagong
TRIPURA

Dadra & Nagar Nasik
Haveli

Nagpur

ORISSA

MEGALAYA

Bombay (Mumbai)

Bhubaneshwar

Pune (Poona)

I N D I A

BANGLADESH

MYANMAR
(BURMA)

MAHARASHTRA

Sholapur
Kolhapur

Hyderabad
Bijapur

ANDHRA Guntur
PRADESH

Vishakapatnam

Bay
of
Bengal

Arabian
Sea

Raichur
Kurnool

GOA

KARNATAKA

Mangalore

Bangalore

Nellore

Port Blair

Mysore
Madras (Chennai)

TAMIL Pondicherry
NADU

Andaman and
Nicobar Islands

Lakshadweep Kavaratti

KERALA

Madurai Jaffa

Cochin

Trivandrum Tirunelvei

Kanya Kumari

Kandy

MALDIVES

Male

Colombo

SRI
LANKA

INDIAN

OCEAN

0   km   500

N

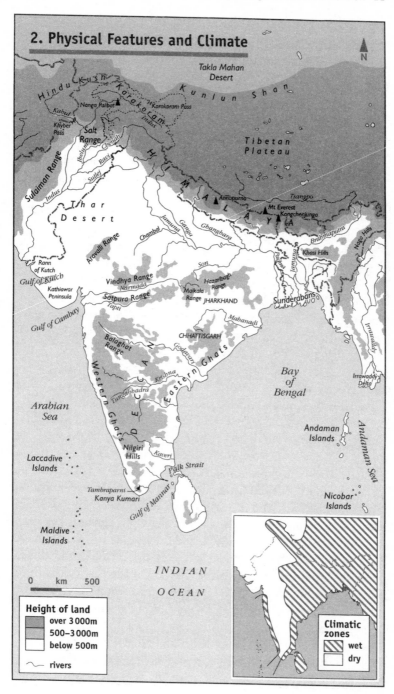

2. Physical Features and Climate

N

Takla Mahan Desert

Hindu Kush

Karakoram

Kunlun Shan

Kabul
Nanga Parbat
Karakoram Pass
Indus

Khyber Pass
Salt Range
Jhelum
Chenab
Ravi

Tibetan Plateau

Sulaiman Range

Indus
Sutlej

Thar Desert

H I M A L A Y A
Annapurna
Tsangpo
Mt Everest
Kongchenjunga

Jamuna
Ganga
Ghaghara
Chambal

Brahmaputra
Tista
Jamuna

Khasi Hills

Naga Hills

Aravali Range

Son

Rann of Kutch
Gulf of Kutch

Vindhya Range
Narmada

Hazaribagh Range
Malkala Range
JHARKHAND

Sunderabans

Kathiawar Peninsula

Satpura Range
Tapti

Mahanadi

Gulf of Cambay

CHHATTISGARH

Balaghat Range

D E C C A N

Godavari

Eastern Ghats

Irrawaddy

Western Ghats

Krishna
Tungabhadra

Bay of Bengal

Arabian Sea

Andaman Islands

Irrawaddy Delta

Andaman Sea

Laccadive Islands

Nilgiri Hills
Kaveri

Tambraparni
Kanya Kumari

Palk Strait

Gulf of Mannar

Nicobar Islands

Maldive Islands

INDIAN OCEAN

0   km   500

Height of land
over 3 000m
500–3 000m
below 500m
~ rivers

Climatic zones
wet
dry

snow scoured Himalayan slopes to make the great rivers, Indus, Ganga, and Brahmaputra. These rivers washed Himalayan silt across the plains and still dump it continuously into the Bengal delta; and today, silt visible in satellite photos is washing along the floor of the Indian Ocean almost as far south as Sri Lanka. Over millennia, flowing silt has routinely changed the course of Indo-Gangetic rivers. In Bengal, the Ganga shifted steadily eastward and by the eighteenth century, the Ganga and Brahmaputra merged in what is now Bangladesh. Silt routinely forms new islands, called *char*, in Bangladesh, where the rivers just as routinely wash land along their banks out to sea.

South Asia lies in the south-western expanse of monsoon Asia. Embracing the Himalayas and Sri Lanka, it stretches from Afghanistan to Burma, between five and forty degrees north latitude. It is hot at mid-day all year round, but temperatures do vary between winter and summer, especially in the north, where winters are quite cold, even severe at high altitudes, and the peak summer heat is brutally extreme. Yet the seasons are marked more by rainfall than by temperature. When Central Asia heats up each spring, rising hot dry air draws in wet cooler air from oceans and generates barometric disparities that spark storms of varying scope and ferocity all across Asia, from Baluchistan to Korea. These seasonal rainstorms are called *monsoons*.

Rain is always the big weather news in South Asia and there is usually very little rain to report from January to June. At the peak of the hot season in May, the mid-day sun can fry an egg on the ground. Then the monsoon hits. Its starting date varies but its arrival normally falls at the beginning of June. First, the monsoon rains soak the coast and the east, which comprise South Asia's wet half, where rainfall normally exceeds eighty centimetres per year, and peaks in Assam, Bangladesh, and the north-east mountains at three metres per year. In these wet regions, cyclones and floods normally bring the worst weather news. On the east coast, from Madras to Chittagong, killer cyclones strike every few years. A 'super cyclone' hit Orissa in 1999, washing away villages hundreds of miles inland. In Bengal, storms from the sea often combine with flooding. In the eastern Ganga basin and all along the Brahmaputra, severe flooding is a constant threat. In Bangladesh, much of the land floods annually; the area covered by water exceeds that covered by land in the live delta regions; and fish are as essential in the diet as waterways are in transport. The meaning of flooding has changed dramatically over centuries. In the eighteenth century, sea-going ships were built in the Sylhet mountains above the Bengal plains and floated out to sea across a hundred miles of flooded forest; but now that same land is full of farms, villages, towns, and cities, including Dhaka, with ten million people, so that today flooding causes death and destruction.

The monsoon arrives later in the western dry half of South Asia, as late as the end of July in Baluchistan and Multan in what is now Pakistan. In the dry west and in the dry central peninsula, the bad weather news is normally drought, though flash floods do occur when swollen rivers wash suddenly over hard parched land, as they did in Hyderabad, Andhra Pradesh in 2000. The monsoon is often late and stingy in dry South Asia, full of hot air. All of the interior peninsula and western plains from Gujarat north to the Khyber Pass and from Baluchistan east to Malwa and Delhi are parched and dusty most of the year. Most rivers are bone dry in the summer. Rain rarely measures more than eighty centimetres annually, often less than twenty, and in the Thar Desert, in Rajasthan, less than ten. Desert winds from Rajasthan blow dust storms across Delhi in the late summer. The long-term climatic trend seems to be toward aridity. The drying up of the Saraswati river, which once flowed from the Himalayas into Rajasthan across eastern Punjab, was one of the major ecological events of prehistoric times. The great prehistoric Indus valley cities probably declined in part because they could not get enough water to survive; as did Fatehpur Sikri, the first major Mughal fortress capital, which was built a little too far west, too far into the desert. Modern deforestation has been broadly blamed for increasing aridity. Current trends in global warming may be dooming South Asia's dry plains to increasing desertification and its wet coastal lowlands to submersion beneath the sea.

OPEN GEOGRAPHY

Human living environments span a wider range of climatic variation in South Asia than anywhere else in the world at these latitudes. Continental environments to the west (in the Middle

East and Africa) are uniformly dry; and to the east (in South-East Asia and China), uniformly wet. South Asia has both extremes. South Asia's dry half is climatically part of a vast geographical zone that covers western Asia and northern Africa: the natural ground cover is thin scrub forest; nomadic tribes and pastoral economies have been historically prominent; millet and wheat are ancient staple grains; irrigation is the key to agrarian wealth; and old oasis towns dot sandy expanses of thinly populated land like port cities on the sea coast. South Asia's wet half is instead climatically part of a humid climatic zone running along the eastern Indian Ocean rim, from Bombay to Sri Lanka and through Bangladesh and Burma south to Indonesia, where heavy rain, cloudy humid days, dense tropical jungles, slash-and-burn farming, rice paddy cultivation, fishing, and seafaring have historically been prominent features of everyday life. The people who live at high altitudes inhabit other environments altogether, which in the arid west shade off into Central Asia and in the north resemble Tibet more than South Asia's wet or dry lowlands. High mountain rain forests in the north-east resemble interior South-East Asia much more than Rajasthan or Gujarat. Places along the coast physically resemble coastal Indonesia more than arid inland or high altitude South Asia.

Environmental similarities among regions that straddle today's political boundaries also embrace ancient human terrains. South Asia has always been open geographically for movement and communication across all its current borderlands. To and from its dry half, routes of migration, trade, and resettlement lead to and from Asia's dry west and north, into the arid home of the Central Asian Silk Road. Human cultivation of millet and wheat began somewhere along these routes; where, exactly, is unknown. Recent carbon dates for pollen found in dry lakes in Rajasthan indicate that a period of increasing moisture occurred in Asia's dry zone at the time of the earliest known grain cultivation in the Middle East, around 7500 BCE; this means that archaeological finds at Mehrgarh and elsewhere may represent a roughly simultaneous origination of dry grain cultivation in South Asia and the Middle East. In Himalayan localities, settlers, herders, and migrants have moved regularly across borders with Tibet. Tibetan Buddhism is as deeply entrenched as Hinduism in Nepal. Borders with Burma are open in Assam and Bengal even today. The earliest evidence of rice cultivation in South Asia is roughly contemporary with evidence from South-East Asia. In the eighteenth century, migrants from Arakan did much of the most arduous new land clearance in southern Bengal. In Shillong, now in India's north-eastern state of Meghalaya, people speak Mon-Khmer, Tibeto-Burman, and Indo-European languages. The coastal regions are also intimately connected: the Sinhala and Bangla languages are closely related; southern India has sent many waves of migrants to Sri Lanka; and coastal sites have long been their own best trading partners, including those in South-East Asia, where a major historical period of so-called 'Indianization' occurred during the first millennium CE, when merchants from Gujarat arrived regularly in Java. In 1800, fishing ships from many towns along India's east and west coast brought workers and equipment for digging pearls from the ocean floor in the Gulf of Manaar off the coast of Sri Lanka.

From ancient times, cultural elements of all sorts have spilled in all directions across what are today national borders separating and enclosing state territories. We find Hindu temples and Sanskrit texts in Cambodia and Indonesia. Buddhism flourished more in East and South-East Asia than in its birthplace in northern India. Japanese Buddhists today tour holy sites in India the way Christians visit Jerusalem. Christians and Jews came by sea to settle on the Kerala coast in the early centuries of the Common Era. Islam spread across southern Asia by land among inland regions, and by sea among Indian Ocean ports, until the majority of the world's Muslims lived east of Iran. The definitive linguistic components of South Asian languages are found in languages that are spread all across Central, North, and West Asia. Examples are endless of cultural mobility and dispersion along the inland and coastal routes of southern Eurasia. In addition, as we will see, the boundaries of historical activity and networks of interaction that determined the character of change in everyday life in South Asia have never corresponded to the boundaries constructed by modern cultural authorities or by modern states.

To understand history inside South Asia, we must escape the confines of modern boundaries that enclose and separate civilizations to explore a wider world within which these boundaries have been invented, contested, defended, and redrawn historically. As we will see, the political boundaries of South Asia have changed dramatically at various points in time. It is therefore most appropriate to study South Asia as a huge open geographical space in southern Eurasia, rather than imagining it to be a fixed historical region with a single territorial definition.

PREHISTORIC SOCIETIES

Humans may have lived in South Asia for half a million years. Relics of their activity for much of that time are preserved in so many places that we can surmise that the earliest human settlers lived in virtually every feasible ecological niche. They all would have migrated from somewhere else at some point in time, but some places have been continuously occupied since the eighth millennium BCE, when agro-pastoral settlements were established. Mehrgarh, in central Baluchistan, is now the oldest site where archaeology can show that a microlithic tool-using people produced a complex farming society; it is in the dry, mountainous borderlands between the Indus valley and Afghanistan, where physical remains survive much better than they do in wet lands. From the seventh to the fourth millennium BCE, Mehrgarh underwent an indigenous process of technological development that was connected to but apparently not dependent on migratory trade with West and Central Asia.

Similar sites dating to about 3000 BCE also reflect a culture that is now named after a later Indus valley site at Harappa, which included large, solid buildings, pottery, wool and cotton textiles, copper ware, seals, and female figurines. Along the Indus valley, large cities were built by about 2500 BCE at Mohenjo-Daro and Harappa; but five hundred years later, they were being depopulated; and a few centuries later, they were abandoned completely. As they and other Indus urban settlements declined, other smaller sites containing similar cultural material multiplied in adjacent Gujarat and Punjab. Recent findings suggest that Harappan cultural production may have continued into the first millennium BCE alongside settlements that are distinguished by later archaeological finds of Painted Grey Ware pottery. The famous prehistoric cities along the Indus emerged within a very old, resilient cultural complex that covered a vast area of dry land and river valleys stretching from Afghanistan to Sind, Punjab, and the western Gangetic plain. These cities engaged in long distance trade and their material culture was at the same time indigenous to South Asia.

If we toured South Asia around 2000 BCE, we would certainly want to begin with its impressive cities along the Indus, which boasted advanced hydrology and architecture. But we would soon find that South Asia's scant prehistoric human population was composed primarily of hunters, gatherers, herders, and farmers, who lived in tiny and, typically, temporary settlements. Wild animals – including elephants, tigers, deer, and buffalos – outnumbered humans many times over. Dry, wet, high altitude, and coastal climates offered different kinds of opportunities for human communities.

In the wet regions, dense tropical jungles were naturally endowed with food supplies for humans but also with wild animals (notably snakes and tigers) and micro-organisms (notably water-borne parasites) that killed humans. To create stable living environments in tropical settings, people had to clear jungles to create farming communities, arduous work that needed to be done repeatedly because the jungle growth was tenacious. Before the advent of iron tools around 1200 BCE, jungles constantly defeated human efforts to create permanent farming settlements; shifting cultivation was the only agricultural option, which combined with hunting, gathering, and fishing provided ample human diets. Rice, originally a swamp grass, was first domesticated on temporary fields. Slash-and-burn farming remained the norm long after agrarian societies began to cut, burn, and build permanent fields and settlements. This agrarian transformation of the wet lowlands began in the first millennium BCE.

In dry lands, prehistoric migratory life typically moved over wider spaces. Where water failed to come to the land, people and animals moved to water. Animal herding and nomadism combined naturally with extensive hunting, warfare, and trade; these all developed productive but often conflict-ridden synergies with sedentary farming. Nomads bred animals that settled farming communities used for manure and ploughing, for edible meat and milk, and for skins, fur, and wool. Pastoral nomads also engaged in trade and carried craft products and implements among settled communities far from one another. Animal-herding pastoral peoples exchanged goods with farmers who provided them with staple grains (millets and wheat), fruits, vegetables, and manufactures, including metal tools and weapons. To sustain their animals, herders needed water and grass that often lay on land controlled by farmers. Farmers and herders were also hunters and hunting skills were often turned toward human competitors for land and water. Nomads herding and riding horses became the most successful warriors ranging over wide distances. Agropastoral communities combining the skills and resources of herders, farmers, and craft workers built the small prehistoric homelands that we see scattered in archaeological remains in dry regions from Baluchistan to Punjab and the Deccan.

Mixtures of hunting, gathering, herding, farming, manufacturing, and trade supported prehistoric communities that combined sedentary and migratory ways of life and whose human geography was thus both intensely local and extensively widespread. Archaeological remains from Gujarat in the second millennium BCE indicate that pastoral circuits of animal grazing and nomadic migration ran through sedentary farming communities like thread through beads on a necklace.

Elements of sedentary cultures moved along circuits of migration and trade that connected and sustained small, separate communities. Cultural assemblages thus emerged that were composed of various symbolic and material elements, which we see in archaeological evidence. As elements dispersed geographically they formed distinct cultural areas that changed shape and overlapped. The cultural complex that includes Mehrgarh and Harappa is now the oldest we know. Physical remains indicate that a different but perhaps related Banas culture characterized by white pottery painted black and red developed in Rajasthan and Malwa in the millennium after 2500 BCE. At the same time, another Malwa culture was spreading south in central India, as a Savalda complex formed in Maharashtra, and as other areas of settlement marked by distinctive pottery and metal tools developed in the eastern Vindhyas and southern Deccan. Other cultural areas of comparable antiquity are also visible in the southern peninsula, which contained megalithic tombs, urns, cists, rock-cut caves, cairns, sarcophagi, and stone tombs that resemble hats, called *topi kals*. Especially in the wetter regions, most of the evidence of cultural activity in prehistory returned to nature and is invisible today, though later evidence indicates many cultural contributions from prehistoric forest dwellers.

In Punjab, a dry region whose grasslands received water from five rivers draining the western Himalayas (hence the name: *panch-ab*), one prehistoric culture left no material remains but produced ritual texts that priests preserved over millennia. This culture is called Aryan. Evidence in its texts indicates that it slowly spread southeast, following the course of the Yamuna and Ganga rivers. Its elite called itself Arya ('pure') and led kin groups organized into nomadic horse-herding tribes. Aryan ritual texts are called Vedas; their language, Sanskrit. Vedic Sanskrit is recorded only in the hymns that were sung in Vedic rituals for Aryan gods. To be Aryan apparently meant to be a member of an elite among pastoral tribes. The texts that record Aryan culture cannot be dated precisely, but they seem to emerge around 1200 BCE in four collections of Vedic hymns (*Rg*, *Sama*, *Yajur*, and *Artharva*).

The textual evidence of the expanding use of Sanskrit and Vedic rituals is spread unevenly across the next millennium. Six hundred years after the first Vedas, ritual texts called Brahmanas and numerous mystical and philosophical Aranyakas and Upanishads appear that describe activity farther and farther east in the Ganga basin. Two epic poems, *Ramayana* and *Mahabharata*, probably refer to wars among tribes in the first half of the first millennium BCE in the watershed between the Indus and Ganga and in the western part of the Ganga basin; but these epics were composed many centuries after the wars they recount and they were added to and revised many times over the centuries that followed. The major ancient grammatical text of the Sanskrit language, Pannini's *Astadhyayi* (with a geographical appendix, *Ganapatha*), is datable to the late fourth century BCE by references to contemporary events and personalities. By this time, the corpus of ancient Sanskrit texts comprised a culture of Vedic Brahmanism. In this textual culture, social rituals prescribed that rulers should protect and enforce stratified ranks among four *varnas*: Brahman (priest), Kshatriya (warrior), Vaisya (merchant), and

Sudra (workers). Ritual texts also describe the territory of Aryan culture, called *Madhyama Dis* or *Madhya Desh*, 'the central country'. By about 500 BCE, Aryan cultural evidence had spread east from Gandhara (in the hills above Punjab, where Pannini composed his grammar), across the plains of Kurukshetra (around Delhi), where the *Mahabharata* war occurred), as far east as the confluence of the Ganga and Yamuna at Pratisthana or Prayaga (around Allahabad). Sanskrit geographical knowledge was wider than this, however. Rama, the hero of the *Ramayana*, travelled south across the peninsula and over the water to *Lanka* (Sri Lanka) to save his wife, Sita, from her captor, Ravana. Even so, Pannini indicates in his detailed list of peoples and places that ancient Sanskrit authors were at home in Punjab, Haryana, and the Ganga-Yamuna Doab. Their culture was only one among several in these regions, though we know much less about others.

ANCIENT TRANSFORMATION

Prehistory shades into history as ancient documentation becomes firmly datable. This begins to occur in the sixth century BCE, during the reign of the Magadha kings in the eastern Ganga basin, when Buddhist texts can be dated along with recorded activity by Achaemenid Greek rulers in Persia and Afghanistan. Early historical texts come into being during major changes in the human landscape that become more visible over the next millennium as documentary evidence becomes ever richer in descriptive detail and chronological specificity.

During the first thousand years of recorded history in South Asia, an ancient transformation produced entirely new social environments. Prehistoric societies were many but small and they had no institutions holding them together. In the sixth century BCE, history's curtain rises on a dramatic scene of political invention as powerful people begin to make powerful states. By 300 BCE, societies in the Ganga basin were part of vast networks of politics, economy, and culture; settlements stretching from Afghanistan to Bengal were connected to one another by regular flows of ideas and goods that ran through cities that became central sites for imperial society. By 100 CE, competing imperial armies ranged from Central Asia to Sri Lanka. By 500 CE, complex regions of social change all across South Asia were connected intricately to one another and to the wider world.

The vast epoch of ancient transformation from *circa* 500 BCE to *circa* 500 CE produced a new order that would be called 'classical' in later times. The changes that occurred in this millennium are so vast, complex and poorly documented that we may never be able to explain them adequately. The arrival of iron-making technologies around the time of the Vedas certainly made a major impact. Chopping and digging with iron tools gave new advantages to the people who struggled against the forest, for they could now burn trees to make farms and keep new jungle growth away with arduous manual labour. In the Ganga basin, land clearance to make permanent farms spread from west to east and created a new productive landscape that spanned wet and dry regions of monsoon Asia for the first time. Rice-growing societies in the eastern basin could sustain larger populations with their more productive agriculture, and they also had closer access to iron ores and other minerals in mountains south of the Ganga in Jharkhand. River routes into and out of the eastern mountains provided rapid entry into the Gangetic transport system for people working the uplands north and south of the Ganga. Iron tools increased agricultural output everywhere but made a much bigger difference in the east, where iron weapons also strengthened armies. People with iron tools made the boats that travelled the highway of the Ganga and the carts that plied roads along the Ganga basin. It was thus in the east that early states arose.

Major routes ran along the river basins from Bihar to Gujarat and to the Hindu Kush. People living in the western dry regions had superior access to most of the length of these routes and they took full advantage of trading opportunities. Kautilya's *Arthasastra* indicates that by the start of the Common Era, long-distance trade sustained widely known sites of commodity specialization stretching from Central Asia and Sind to Assam. Horses came from Punjab; pearls from Sind; cotton and sandalwood from Malwa; elephants, stones, and minerals from the southern mountains; cotton and silk from Bengal; and sandalwood from Assam. Cotton, silk, and wool cloth came from many places along the Ganga. Iron and silver came from mines in Jharkhand.

Connected localities spanning lands from Kabul to Gujarat and Assam formed one of the largest integrated economic regions in the ancient world. By 300 BCE, production and trade in this region generated enough profit, taxation, tribute, and consumption to sustain a burst of social invention, most visibly along the highway of the Ganga, especially in the east. The first big cities built after the fall of Harappa arose around Pataliputra (now Patna in Bihar). They had a distinctive urban culture, elites, and expressive arts. Social stratification became more complex. The first recorded political elites were lineage elders in agro-pastoral domains called *janapada* and *maha* (great) *janapada*. These small domains were named after their dominant clans and are described in epics, in Pannini's grammar, in Buddhist texts, and in other sources. Pannini indicates that in 300 BCE, *janapada*s and *mahajanapada*s were the most prominent political features of the Indo-Gangetic flatlands from Punjab to Bengal. By this time, however, new ruling elites and institutions had also appeared in eastern regions, where new rulers came to power in political systems that embraced many kin groups. Some of these early polities are called 'republics' because elite lineages shared power inside them. Others are called 'kingdoms' because single ruling dynasties became supreme. In these new political territories, urban capital cities emerged at strategic military and commercial sites, where rising elites changed the face of the land forever.

INVENTING EMPIRE

Chandragupta Maurya was born into this changing ancient land, near Pataliputra, where, in the sixth century BCE, Magadha rulers had raised armies to conquer widely and create the first large state in the region. From the obscure Moriya clan, Chandragupta may have owned some land around Magadha before he led Magadha armies to conquer *janapada*s as far west as Punjab and Sind. In doing so, he had crossed a cultural divide. Agro-pastoral warrior lineages controlling various *janapada*s had diverse cultural identities, but later Vedic sources indicate that some had embraced Aryan culture as far east as Prayaga (Allahabad). Magadha lay further east on the outer fringe of Aryan culture, and it was here in the east that Buddha Gautama had composed a spiritual and ethical path that diverged from Aryan Brahmanism. Having conquered local competitors, the armies of Magadha expanded west. Victorious commanders subordinated *janapada*s under an imperial authority whose main work was to maintain its own military strength. This rudimentary imperial scaffolding provided a framework for Chandragupta's ambition.

In the far west, Magadha troops faced Achaemenid Greek armies marching across Persia. As Greek soldiers marched east and Magadha troops marched west, they both knew they were following old routes of long-distance travel, but they did not know that they were creating a new world of politics that would stretch from Greece to Assam. Routes from Europe to the Orient and from Magadha to Persia met in Punjab; thus the Indus became the symbolic western border of a region that Greeks called 'India'. The original division of Asia and Europe, East and West, Orient and Occident derived from military competition over routes and resources flowing across ancient Eurasia. Ancient empires thus invented cultural boundaries that we still live with today; how these territorial identities came down to the present is a long story that we will follow in the coming chapters.

Chandragupta won wars for Magadha in Sind and may have fought Alexander the Great in Punjab before Alexander's army mutinied to force a Greek retreat down the Indus in 327 BCE. Alexander then sailed to Mesopotamia and died in Babylon at age thirty-four. Chandragupta marched east, conquered his overlords, and became South Asia's first emperor. He launched his Maurya imperial dynasty by building on Magadha victories to incorporate *janapada*s in a structure of military command that eventually deployed nine thousand elephants, thirty thousand cavalry, eight thousand chariots, and several hundred thousand soldiers on its many battlefields. Supporting its war machine with taxes, troops, provisions, commanders, and victories preoccupied the Maurya state, which sustained an official elite that was the first of its kind. Elite intellectuals became the brains of empire. One legendary figure was Kautilya, known as the author of the *Arthasastra*, a manual of statecraft and administration. This text was not completed until the Gupta age, six hundred years later, and thus it constitutes one of many links between the two classical empires of the Ganga basin.

Mauryan armies conquered widely from 321 until 260 BCE. Chandragupta marched west to the Hindu Kush and Kashmir. His son, Bindusara, turned south to the Deccan. After a four-year war of succession, the emperor Ashoka conquered Kalinga, on the Orissa coast, where imperial conquest finally outstripped imperial resources. Subduing Kalinga cost one hundred thousand lives and displaced twice as many people. This suffering apparently stunned Ashoka into embracing Buddhism. Ashoka's intellectual elite invented a new, ethical imperialism. By Ashoka's time, the teachings of Gautama Buddha and Mahavira had defined distinctive strains of cultural activity that we know under the names of Buddhism and Jainism; they shared many elements with Aryan Brahmanism but opposed its sacred division of caste society and established another set of values for rulers, including universal ethical norms that made salvation a moral quest. Rulers could support this righteous vision by becoming great alms-givers for the learned monks who preached harmonious moral order and showed the way to enlightenment in their piety and learning. Buddhist righteousness (*dhamma*) became a moral compass for Ashoka's empire. Ashoka used his vast winnings at war to support Buddhist monks, ritual centres (stupas), preachers, and schools. Rather than conquering kingdoms south of Kalinga, Ashoka brought them under his spiritual patronage, supporting Buddhist kings in Sri Lanka and Buddhist centres in Andhra, Karnataka, and the Tamil country. Jain missions also prospered in his domain.

Thus Maurya dynastic elites invented imperial culture, including new social identities that were attached to imperial expansion, integration, and authority. In addition to supporting its war machine, the empire constituted an ethical ideology and infrastructure. In addition to commanding armies and gathering wealth for war, generals announced the arrival of good governance wherever they conquered. In addition to collecting tribute, imperial officers established a local presence to keep roads open, to adjudicate disputes, and to supersede the local authority of *janapada*s. Building on the legacy of Magadha and initially travelling the same routes, the Maurya regime protected merchants who were major patrons of Buddhism and Jainism. Empire increased the concentration of wealth at central places of imperial authority. It attracted ambitious lineage leaders and their disgruntled local competitors who allied with imperial officers and identified themselves with imperial authority. Imperial culture fostered a new elite cosmopolitanism, which elevated its own people and ideas and also reduced localities and local identities to the status of rustic parochialism. Empire institutionalized high and low culture at the same time.

INVENTING CIVILIZATION

In new territories of empire and elite formation, Brahmanism, Buddhism, and Jainism represented three solutions to fundamental problems of human existence and political order. Their proponents obtained royal patronage in the circuits of urbane cosmopolitanism. All three became more prominent in dispersed localities on the tracks of imperial expansion. They had much in common, including their vast cosmology and complex ideas about reincarnation and *karma* (the effect of acts in past lives on future lives). They all emerged in the Ganga basin from the mixing of Aryan culture with other cultures during social changes underway in the first millennium BCE. Their intellectuals also shared the creative spirit of the Upanishads, later Vedic texts that elaborated the nature of power in the fires of Vedic sacrifice, which could be internalized by humans through spiritual discipline, renunciation, contemplation, and mysticism.

By the later centuries BCE, elements of Aryan ideology were adapted to local conditions by elites in diverse agrarian societies. The Brahmanas codified Vedic ritual in the changing contexts where learned Brahmans embodied and translated Aryan tradition. Newly emerging social elites found valuable assets in Sanskrit texts, Vedic rituals, and learned Brahmans, which they used to elevate themselves above others and to mark ranks of privilege in their domains. One hymn from the *Rg Veda* became particularly useful. It describes the origin of the world in the sacrificial dismemberment of the Lord of Being, Prajapati, into four *varna*s or human essences: his mouth became the Brahman priest; his arms became the warrior (Rajanya or Kshatriya); his thighs became the Vaisya (farmer and merchant); and his feet became the Sudra (worker and servant). Ancient landowners, merchants, warriors, army commanders, rulers, kings, and emperors used

Brahmanical interpretations of *varna* to raise and validate their social status. Thus many elites became at least partially Aryanized by patronizing Brahman knowledge and rituals. Various aspiring groups collaborated with Brahmans to create higher status for themselves. Brahmanism allowed kin groups to form caste groups (*jati*) by assigning each kin group to a *varna*. Among the *dharmasastra* texts that defined the emerging Brahmanical social order, *The Laws of Manu*, composed *circa* 100 BCE, explained in great detail how every marriage that mixed *jati*s produced a new *jati* with a definite status in the *varna* scheme. This was a recipe for taking the infinite complexity of ancient society and reducing it to a single schematic ideological order in which everyone knew their place.

Jains and Buddhists opposed the fixed social stratification of Vedic Brahmanism, the authority of Brahmans, and the all-pervasive power of Vedic ritual. Jainism and Buddhism arose around Magadha, where Mahavira (born *circa* 550) and Gautama Buddha (born *circa* 480) both originally preached. It is reasonable to surmise that these schools of thought represented restless spiritual aspirations among new elites who challenged Vedic ideas about social rank. Merchants relegated to lower *varna* ranks were clearly influential patrons for Buddhist and Jain monks who propagated the spiritual power of learning, piety, merit, discipline, and ethical values, and who rejected the idea that the highest spiritual purity is attainable only by Brahmans. The Buddhist or Jain path of liberation was open to anyone.

Supporters of Brahmanism, Buddhism, and Jainism moved along routes of physical mobility and communication that extended their scope under Mauryan authority. Imperial cultural activists circulated among localities and settled locally to become local representatives of imperial authority and high culture. Locally, their elite status could attract patronage from aspiring donors who sought prized intermediary roles in imperial society. Locally, too, most people could only appreciate high culture when it was translated into local terms, in the local vernacular. Most local religious feelings, practices, and ideas could never attain wide currency; they remained local until they were translated into terms that could travel. A three-tiered cultural hierarchy thus developed. At the top, high culture emerged among imperial elites who communicated with one another across great distances at the apex of political authority. Intermediary elites arose in regions of political power as they translated and mixed imperial and local cultures. Many local cultural elements remained purely local, outside imperial circuits of power, though many others were incorporated and subordinated. Thus 'great' and 'little' traditions came into being with the expansion of empire and with efforts by aspiring local elites to lift themselves out of their local status. The interaction of these three levels of culture became a basic feature of social life. They are visible even today, though the centuries have changed their significance. In ancient times, local cultures were overwhelmingly predominant for people in everyday life. Very few people had access to high culture or elite traditions. Elite culture made its impact locally in proportion to the power of patrons in local society.

Buddhism exemplifies ancient high culture. It spread widely as elite cultural elements sank local roots from town to town in the ambit of Mauryan power and along routes of mobility running into Central Asia, the southern peninsula, and Sri Lanka. Buddhists always confronted proponents of Jainism and Brahmanism, and everywhere patronage from various sources decided the outcome. Ashoka's patronage indicates that rulers in his day devised ingenious means for making empire into civilization. Giving financial and moral support to high culture ideas, practices, and intellectuals like Buddhist monks enabled rulers to attract literate elites to their service and to bring cosmopolitan cultural activists into localities of ethical empire. At the same time, this strategy enabled conquerors to turn tribute extracted from vanquished local warriors into pious generosity. Religious patronage enhanced political supremacy and incorporation. Instead of suffering humiliating military defeat, a weaker rival could embrace imperial subordination by negotiating an acceptable contribution to charitable cultural projects endorsed by the emperor.

Such ingenious cultural politics suffused social struggles for power and rank. For rulers, patronizing religious leaders and institutions became indispensable for gaining local support that turned coercive force into public spirit. In everyday life, religious institutions that shaped social identities thrived in competitions for imperial patronage. Spiritual leaders became socially prominent as they cultivated patronage and turned wealth into moral authority. In local society, financing cultural institutions and religious activities like festivals and rituals became an indicator of social status. Social ranks thus took aesthetic, spiritual forms. The highest status people were those who participated in imperial rituals and commanded the language and culture of the imperial religion. The lowest status people were those who spoke only local tongues and worshipped local deities. Social mobility moved among tiers of culture as local people moved up in regional societies by incorporating themselves into elite culture, giving it local roots.

The project of civilizing conquered peoples proceeded within empire as influential people established religious institutions across wide spaces inside local societies. Buddhists and Jains seem to have been most successful among merchants. The Greek king of Punjab, Menander, adopted Buddhism as he sought to bring more merchants into his realm. Ashoka made Buddhism a moral compass that made his realm more attractive for merchants. In Mauryan times, kings, monks, and landed elites on the island of Sri Lanka came together under the banner of *dhamma* to create one of the world's longest-lasting Buddhist polities. Elsewhere, too, religious institutions became central in cultural politics by bringing disparate groups together in new, more extensive regional communities. Pious donors sanctified their own wealth with spending on festivals, shrines, stupas, or pious education; and they used public religious rituals to announce their own beneficence. Religious communities formed as emerging social elites pursued their common interests to forge shared identities in public piety.

Donations to Jains and Buddhists became increasingly popular among merchants who travelled routes protected by Mauryan armies. Merchant wealth flowed into religious centres in market towns, where it combined with royal patronage to finance a spiritual realm of public sentiment that brought together local elites and imperial officers, itinerants and residents, civilians and army commanders, and many other people in various professions. Buddhist and Jain sculpture became public art. Gigantic stone sculptures and buildings embodied the physical presence of spiritual and imperial power. Technologies of artistic beauty became media for the everyday experience of spirituality, transcendence, and political stability. A creative explosion in all the arts was a most remarkable feature of the ancient transformation for later generations. Mauryan territory was marked out visibly on the ground in its day by awesome armies and dreadful war, but future inhabitants saw instead its beautiful pillars, inscriptions, coins, sculptures, buildings, ceremonies, and textual accounts, particularly those by Buddhist writers.

Ancient imperialism created a new kind of social space, an imperial landscape. But all around it, most people lived in agro-pastoral communities, and lineages like those in *janapada*s dominated most localities. The geography of Mauryan empire resembled a spider with a small dense body and long spindly legs. The highest echelons of imperial society lived in the inner circle composed of the ruler, his immediate family, other relatives, and close allies, who formed a dynastic core. Outside the core, Mauryan empire ran along stringy routes dotted with armed cities. Outside the palace, in capital cities, the highest ranks in the imperial elite were held by military commanders whose active loyalty and success in war determined imperial fortunes. Wherever these men failed or rebelled, dynastic power crumbled. In the provincial urban centres of imperial authority, administrators applied official rules, merchants cherished law and order, elites gathered wealth, and pious people received patronage: all these groups carried imperial identities into everyday life.

Imperial society flourished where these elites mingled; they were its backbone; its strength was theirs. Kautilya's *Arthasastra* describes imperial elite power in the Maurya core, in old Magadha, where some key institutions seem to have survived for about seven hundred years, down to the age of the Guptas. Here, Maurya state institutions ruled local society. But not elsewhere. In provincial towns and cities, officials formed a top layer of royalty; under them, old conquered royal families were not removed, but rather, subordinated. In most *janapada*s, the Mauryas' empire consisted of strategic urban sites connected loosely to vast hinterlands through lineages and local institutions that were already there when the Mauryas arrived and were still in control when they left.

ARYAVARTA AND IMPERIAL *BHARAT*

The Mauryas defined ancient *Bharat*. Following the contours of trade routes, the spidery empire took the geometrical shape of a tall triangle with a broad base, lying on its side with its apex in Magadha. One long northern leg ran west up the Ganga, across Punjab, into the Hindu Kush; and one long, jagged, leg ran south-west from Pataliputra, up the Son river valley, down the Narmada river, into Berar, Maharashtra, and Gujarat. The broad base of imperial space spanned Punjab, the Indus, Rajasthan, Gujarat, and western Maharashtra. The north-western frontier revolved around Gandhara and Kashmir; the south-western frontier, around Nasika in Maharashtra. North of Kashmir and west of the Khyber Pass, Greek dynasties held sway. South of Nasika, the Mauryan presence consisted primarily of diplomatic missions. Buddhist activity was particularly prominent in the east, from Bengal down the Orissa coast to Amaravati, Kanchipuram, Madurai, and Sri Lanka. Buddhism and Jainism both became most deeply rooted on the outer imperial fringe: Buddhism in the east, in the Himalayas, and on routes into Central Asia; Jainism in the west, in Rajasthan and Gujarat, and along trade routes in the southern peninsula.

Four hundred years after the last of the Mauryas, the Gupta dynasty reinscribed the same spaces of ancient *Bharat* with Brahmanical cultural supremacy. The new imperial dynasty's founder, Chandragupta, apparently renamed himself after Chandragupta Maurya. He began his imperial career by marrying a daughter of the Licchavi clan, which had controlled the Terai uplands between Magadha and Nepal since before Mauryan times and which would later go on to form a powerful dynasty in the Kathmandu valley. Using this strategic alliance, he conquered westward along the path of the Mauryas. In the late fourth century, his son, Samudragupta, declared himself *maharaja adhi raja* (great king of kings) and boldly recounted his conquests on a pillar in Prayaga (Allahabad) that dated back to the Mauryas. The Allahabad inscription divides Gupta lands into four categories. At the centre is *Aryavarta*, including all the Ganga plain, Naga domains in Bundelkhand and Malwa, Kota lands around Delhi, and Pundravardhana and Vanga in Bengal. Inside *Aryavarta*, conquered rulers were said to have been brought under direct

Gupta administration. Outside this imperial territory, in southern regions of *Dakshinapatha*, twelve conquered kings were left on their thrones. In the mountains, unconquered rulers paid tribute. In the north and west, distant Kushanas and Mundas offered their obeisance, as did Sinhala kings in Sri Lanka.

Since Pannini's time, cultural elites had worked assiduously to describe and mark geographical space so as to give places identities defined by imperial societies. Places became visible in a wide world etched with a cultural design that encompassed localities. The region of highest privilege in Gupta classicism came into being with conscious efforts to create an imperial heartland with a timeless identity. It was called *Aryavarta*. Texts that depict this new imperial territory describe the homeland of Gupta elites whose cultural privilege set an enduring standard for classical civilization.

Samudragupta built the Gupta imperial system, first by using his army to throw another canopy of conquest over *janapada*s and then by displacing many *janapada*s with a more powerful administration than the Mauryas could have imagined. The Gupta imperial heartland was like a banyan tree with strong roots in cities, towns, rituals, and holy places – a solid structure as awesome as the rivers, mountains, and heavens among which it formed a mythical and ritual universe. *Aryavarta* invoked imperial eternity as cosmic reality. In addition to Gupta arms, a Brahman intellectual elite wielding the magic of Sanskrit constructed this classical domain. Indian classicism became by definition Sanskritic and Brahmanical.

Gupta imperial society concentrated in the Gangetic lowlands. Its core region was much larger than the Mauryas', extending west to Mathura, and its cultural impact was deeper and more permanent. In *Aryavarta*, Samudragupta performed Vedic rituals on a grand scale and pursued a widely publicized policy of donating land to Brahmans, funding temple construction, and financing temple rituals. Gupta power launched imperial Brahmanism. Not surprisingly, Brahman authors saw the fall of the Guptas in the sixth century as a sign of cosmic chaos and degradation, *Kali Yuga*; and many later generations of Sanskrit authors looked back on the Guptas' reign as their golden age. The Gupta core region in Uttar Pradesh still has the largest Brahman population in India and the most Brahman politicians.

Brahmanism spread outward from the Gupta core and evolved into a diverse but coherent Hindu cultural complex that scattered across South Asia in the first millennium. Exactly how this occurred is still far from fully understood, though textual evidence appears in widely dispersed texts in Sanskrit and other languages. Clearly, Sanskrit and its learned authors were critical cultural elements wherever Hindu cultures emerged. When Pannini codified Sanskrit, it was already archaic, and he effectively compiled a codebook for a Brahman secret tongue, a user's guide for Brahman cultural software. Buddhist and Jain authors used Pali, Prakrits, and other vernaculars. Local cults expressed themselves in local vernaculars. The influence of Sanskrit spread with the influence of learned Brahman men who were the only people who could officially know the language and convey its magic. Elements of Sanskrit – its sounds, words, grammar, and script – could be learned, used, and enjoyed by anyone, however, and over time entered most languages; and translations out of Sanskrit conveyed its influence into literature almost everywhere in South Asia. Until in the seventeenth century, when it was partially displaced by Persian as the premier elite imperial language, Sanskrit enjoyed a status like that of Latin in Western Europe as an elite language of law, ritual, science, philosophy, literature, and high culture generally.

Patronage for Brahman literati spread their influence far and wide and the Gupta classical age emerged retrospectively in Puranic literature. Puranas form a large corpus of texts that recount 'oldness' or 'venerability' in genealogies and tales of the misty past, combining myth, folklore, history, and historical fiction. A typical Purana begins with the creation of the world and narrates a genealogy leading from heavenly gods to earthly kings and saints in some present time that can be mythical but can also be historical, as it is in the Sthala Purana genre, which explains how a particular god came to reside a specific temple. Puranas have their mundane, factual counterpart in laudatory introductions to inscriptions called *prasasti*, which describe the royal personage making temple donations, land grants, and public proclamations.

Ashokan edicts and Samudragupta's inscriptions were prototypes for millions of texts carved in stone and etched in metal that begin to appear by Gupta times and proliferate from the sixth to the sixteenth centuries. *Prasasti*s recount genealogies and dynastic chronicles: though they often begin in the heavens in mythical times, they always come down to earth to the moment of the activity announced in the inscription. *Prasasti*s, like Puranas, are typically in Sanskrit, though Puranas were also composed in vernaculars, and inscriptions introduced by Sanskrit *prasasti*s typically include a vernacular text for the business or contractual portion of the record. Puranas and *prasasti*s are two major textual media for evoking relations among gods, rulers, and everyday folk, thus between cosmic and mundane power.

The Guptas invested heavily in Puranic mythology and inscriptional documentation. Later rulers all over South Asia followed their example to produce inscriptional records in all the major languages, including Arabic and Persian. These texts provide a clear sense of cultural geography. In the accumulation of Puranic texts, *Aryavarta* became the *desa*, the cultured land of civilization where Prayaga (Allahabad) and Kasi (Varanasi/ Benares) were the holiest places in the sacred geography of *Bharat*. The *desa* does not include the high mountains, Indus valley, Punjab, or western desert. The Puranic *desa* of *Bharat* are *Madhya desa* (the Ganga lowlands), *Purva desa* (Bengal and Assam), and *Aparanta desa* (including Avanti, Malwa, Gujarat, Konkan, and Nasik). Places outside the *desa* were frontiers and peripheries. The western plains, Punjab, high mountains, central mountains, and coast and interior peninsula outside Nasika-Konkana are not called *desa* in Puranas, but rather *asreya, patha*, and *pristha*. This Puranic geography travelled widely with migrating Brahman literati. Sanskrit cosmopolitanism made *Aryavarta* its cultural heartland. With the spread of Brahman influence in post-Gupta centuries, localities far and wide were named and located in relation to the Gangetic holy lands. Kings as far away as Java and Cambodia traced their genealogies to the Guptas and even to the early Aryans.

IMPERIAL REGIONS

Ancient imperialists in the Ganga basin were surrounded by competitors in other regions whose power increased over the centuries. The Mauryas faced no serious obstacles in their quest for control of major routes and centres east of the Hindu Kush. But when the last Maurya fell and Sungas took Pataliputra, in 185 BCE, new empires on Magadha's old western frontier foreshadowed a new future. In the south, in Maharashtra, Satavahanas (55 BCE to 250 CE) conquered the Deccan and the eastern peninsula south to Kanchipuram. In the western plains, Sakas (70–409) expanded south and west into Gujarat from their capital at Ujjaini in Malwa. In the north-west, the Kushanas (0–250) formed the greatest of the new empires. They came from Central Asia and had twin capitals at Purusapura and Mathura. They conquered Afghanistan and the Ganga basin east to Pataliputra; and Kanishka, their most powerful ruler, also conquered Sakas and Satavahanas. Non-Gangetic armies formed a strenuous opposition to Gupta expansion outside *Aryavarta*. Hunas, Sakas, and Vakatakas hemmed in the Guptas throughout their reign, and competitors tore their realm to bits when Hunas rampaged down the Ganga to end the aura of Gupta supremacy.

After the Guptas, empires ruling *Aryavarta* came from Maharashtra, Gujarat, Rajasthan, Punjab, Afghanistan, and Central Asia, which were markedly different from the Ganga basin as material and cultural environments. Agricultural land was not nearly as rich. Nomadic pastoral lineages were much more numerous, powerful, and prestigious. Elites were less sedentary and land-based; they depended more on trade, herds, and war for wealth; and their military control over routes between Delhi and Kabul and between Allahabad and Cambay provided a permanent strategic advantage in struggles for access to markets in Persia, Central Asia, and Indian Ocean ports. They often patronized Brahmans but they were eclectic, less inclined to Vedic ritual, and more respectful of nomadic warriors and itinerant merchants. Buddhism and Jainism flourished in their domains. Even Satavahanas, who were staunch Hindus, also patronized Buddhists. Jainism remained prominent in Gujarat and adjacent Rajasthan. All along the Indian Ocean coast, Zoroastrians, Christians, Arabs, and Jews became well established. Kushanas descended from Hsung-nu clans in China; and like Sakas and Hunas, they were aliens in *Aryavarta*. Kushanas represented a radical ethnic and ideological alternative to the Guptas. Buddhism travelled north along the routes of Kushana power into Central Asia and China.

When Chinese Buddhists toured India in the fifth and seventh centuries, they found that Buddhism had virtually disappeared in its Gangetic homeland, under the imperial force of Brahmanism, though it still thrived in Afghanistan and Central Asia. Outside the Ganga basin, however, cultures flourished across the length and breadth of South Asia that were markedly less Brahmanical. Culturally distinct regimes based outside the Brahmanical strong-holds in the Gupta heartland struggled constantly *against* Gangetic imperialism and *for* control over *Bharat*.

Aryavarta was one region among others in ancient, medieval, and early modern times. Outside the geographical confines of imperial *Bharat*, political histories and collective identities flowing from them followed different trajectories. In the south, in the Deccan, in ancient *Dakshinapatha*, south of the Vindhyas, dynasties of Satavahanas, Vakatakas, Kalacuris, Rashtrakutas, and Yadavas conquered and defined cultural regions in central India; and in the seventeenth century, the Marathas followed suit, as we will see. In the west, in Rajasthan, Gurjara-Pratihara lineages launched five hundred years of military colonization in the ninth century when Rajput clans conquered all across the Ganga basin, into the Himalayas, and into central India, to form a long-lasting, far-reaching political and cultural force. In the north-west, in the land that straddles Punjab, Kashmir, and Afghanistan, Kushanas and later Turks and Afghans produced imperial spaces that repeatedly encompassed the Ganga basin and laid the historic basis for the sixteenth-century Mughal empire, whose land ran from Samarkand to Assam.

MEDIEVAL TRANSITIONS

Post-Gupta regimes produced another new mosaic of social environments; in recognition of this, historians treat the centuries from *circa* 550 to 1556, between the empires of the Guptas and Mughals, as a reasonably coherent, though very diverse, medieval epoch. One dominant feature of this epoch is documentation in dozens of languages and regions. By comparison with earlier times, medieval history is very well documented, and its principle actors are better known, because inscriptions, travel accounts, chronicles, literature, and other sources multiply with each passing century. In the first millennium, the most visible actors appear in the texts of inscriptions that were produced by medieval dynasties. Hundreds of thousands of inscriptions have been traced, transcribed, stored, translated, and studied by scholars; but they still have not received the attention they deserve. The medieval millennium needs many more historians.

Epigraphy indicates that royal Gupta lineages were still settling in the western frontiers of *Aryavarta* in the sixth century, when the empire crumbled. They carried with them the apparatus of Gupta power. They used royal gifts to finance temples and Brahmans, and such gifts became a hallmark of medieval dynastic authority. Marking the end of Gupta supremacy, a new Maukhari dynasty made grants in the western edge of the Gupta heartland, around Kanyakubja (Kanauj), in the Doab (Awadh). Then Pusyabutis did the same farther west along the Yamuna and in Haryana. In the seventh century, the Pusyabuti king Harsha moved his capital to Kanyakubja and celebrated the event with a land grant to two Brahmans. The grant was to be administered personally by one of his commanders under the official protection of *janapada*s in his realm. This indicates that *janapada* lineages were still in business and that Harsha relied for his authority on the wealth and power of subordinates supported by local community leaders.

Inscriptions announce the formation of more than forty new dynasties in the sixth and seventh centuries across the length and breadth of South Asia. Typical *prasasti*s include elaborate genealogies that trace dynastic origins to mythical progenitors and sanctify royal domains by harking back to ancient regional kings. Regional societies become more historically visible in these centuries and many medieval dynasties laid foundations for long-lasting regional political cultures. The complexity of medieval political geography can be rendered by locating major dynasties in fifteen modern political regions (see Maps 3–5, pp. 38–9 & 109):

1. *Kashmir*: Karkotas (620s–850s) and Loharas (900s–1300s) were based in the Vale, around Srinagar.
2. *Nepal*: Licchavis (400s–700s) and Mallas (900s–1700s) ruled the Kathmandu valley.
3. *Punjab*: a contested terrain where Shahis (900s–1100s) built a major medieval domain.

4. *Rajasthan*: Gurjara-Pratiharas gave way to ruling dynasties of Paramaras (800s–1300s), Cahamanas (900s–1100s), and Rathors (1200s–1500s), in Ujjaini, Ajayameru (Ajmer), and Jodhpur, respectively.

5. *Gujarat*: Caulukyas (900s–1200s) were the dominant medieval dynasty.

6. *Uttar Pradesh*: major dynasties included Hunas (500s); Maukharis (500s) at Kanyakubja and Ayodhya; Pusyabhutis (500s–840s), whose most famous ruler was Harsha of Kanauj; Varmans (700s); and Gurjara-Pratiharas (700s–1150s), who spread from Gujarat to Bengal.

7. *Madhya Pradesh*: Candellas (800s–1300s) spread across a region including Khajuraho, Awadh, and Gorakpur; and Kalacuris (500s–1200s) covered land from Kheda and Ujjaini to Tripuri and Bengal.

8. *Maharashtra*: divided among Vakatakas (200s–500s) at Vidarbha (Nagpur), Kalacuris (500s–1200s) at Nasik, Rashtrakutas (600s–900s) at Vidarbha, and Yadavas (800s–1300s) at Devagiri.

9. *Orissa*: Gangas at Kataka Bhuvanesvara (300s–1400s) were the longest lasting dynasties.

10. *Bengal*: Palas (750s–1100s) and Senas (100–1200s) define the medieval epoch.

11. *Andhra Pradesh*: Eastern Chalukyas ruled from the Krishna-Godavari delta (620s–1000s); Kakatiyas ruled from the interior at Warangal, near Hyderabad (1000s–1300s).

12. *Karnataka*: Chalukyas (500s–750s) at Vatapi (Badami) gave way to the imperial Hoysalas (1000s–1300s), whose domain stretched to the east and west coasts; and later to the greatest southern empire at Vijayanagar (1336–1672).

13. *Tamil Nadu*: the Pallavas (300s–900s), Cholas (800s–1200s), and Pandyas (600s–1300s) ruled the northern, central, and southern regions of the coast at Kanchipuram, Tanjavur, and Madurai, respectively.

14. *Kerala*: the Cheras and Kulasekaras ruled the region around Trivandrum from the fourth to the twelfth century.

15. *Sri Lanka*: Lambakanna dynasties ruled from later Mauryan times to the twelfth century.

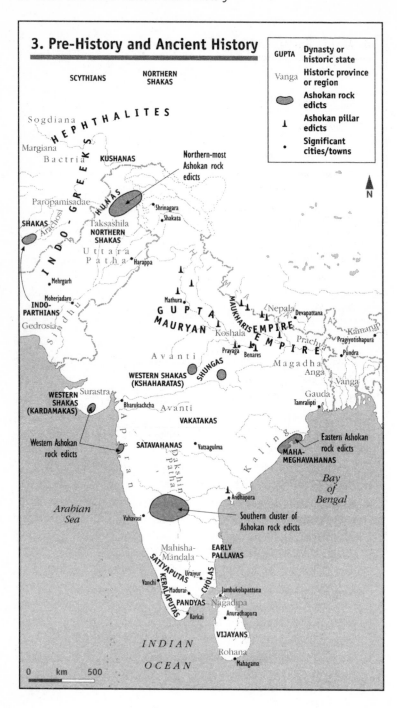

3. Pre-History and Ancient History

GUPTA	Dynasty or historic state
Vanga	Historic province or region
⬭	Ashokan rock edicts
⊥	Ashokan pillar edicts
•	Significant cities/towns

SCYTHIANS

NORTHERN SHAKAS

Sogdiana

HEPHTHALITES

Margiana

Bactria   KUSHANAS

Northern-most Ashokan rock edicts

Paropamisadae

HUNAS

INDO-GREEKS

SHAKAS

Arachosi

Taksashila

•Shrinagara
•Shakata

NORTHERN SHAKAS

Uttara Patha •Harappa

•Mehrgarh

Gedrosia

Moherjadaro

INDO-PARTHIANS

Sindhu

•Mathura

GUPTA
MAURYAN

MAUKHARIS

Nepala •Devapattana

EMPIRE

Kamarup

Koshala

Prachi •Pragiyotishapura

•Pundra

Avanti

•Prayaga •Benares

Magadha

Anga   *Vanga*

WESTERN SHAKAS (KSHAHARATAS)

SHUNGAS

Gauda
•Tamralipti

WESTERN SHAKAS (KARDAMAKAS)

Surastra

•Bharukachcha

Avanti

VAKATAKAS

Kalinga

Western Ashokan rock edicts

SATAVAHANAS •Vatsagulma

Dakshin Patha

Aparanta

MAHA-MEGHAVAHANAS

Eastern Ashokan rock edicts

Bay of Bengal

⊥ •Andhapura

Arabian Sea

•Vahavasi

Southern cluster of Ashokan rock edicts

Mahisha-Mandala

EARLY PALLAVAS

SATIYAPUTAS

•Uraiyur

•Vanchi •Madurai

CHOLAS

•Jambukolapattana

KERALAPUTAS

PANDYAS   Nagadipa

•Korkai

•Anuradhapura

VIJAYANS

INDIAN

Rohana

OCEAN   •Mahagama

0   km   500

N

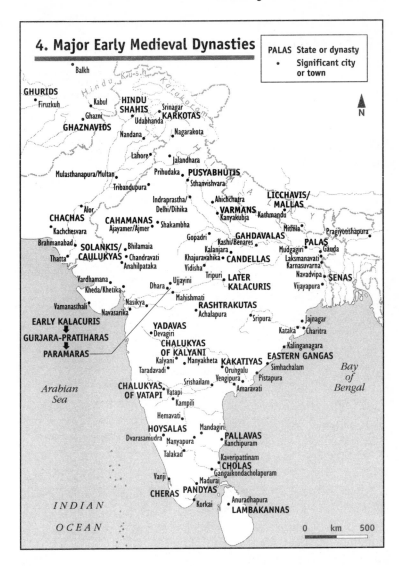

4. Major Early Medieval Dynasties

PALAS State or dynasty
• Significant city or town

Balkh

Hindu Kush
Karakoram

GHURIDS
Firuzkuh

HINDU SHAHIS
Kabul
Ghazni
Srinagar
Udabhanda
KARKOTAS

GHAZNAVIDS
Nandana
Nagarakota

Lahore
Jalandhara

Mulasthanapura/Multan
Prihudaka **PUSYABHUTIS**
Sthanvishvara

Tribandupura

Indraprastha/
Delhi/Dihika
Ahichchatra
LICCHAVIS/ MALLAS

CHACHAS
Alor
CAHAMANAS
Ajayamer/Ajmer
Shakambha
VARMANS
Kanyakubja
Kathmandu

Kachchesvara
Mithila
Pragjyotishapura

Brahmanabad
SOLANKIS/
Bhilamaia
Gopadri
Kashi/Benares **GAHDAVALAS**
Kalanjara
Mudgagiri
Gauda
PALAS

Thatta
CAULUKYAS
Chandravati
Anahilpataka
Khajuravahika **CANDELLAS**
Vidisha
Laksmanavati
Karnasuvarna

Vardhamana
Kheda/Khetika
Dhara
Ujjayini
Tripuri
LATER KALACURIS
Navadvipa **SENAS**
Vijayapura

Vamanasthali
Nasikya
Mahishmati

Navasarika
RASHTRAKUTAS
Achalapura
Sripura
Jajnagar

EARLY KALACURIS
GURJARA-PRATIHARAS
PARAMARAS
YADAVAS
Devagiri
Kataka
Charitra

CHALUKYAS OF KALYANI
Kalyani
Manyakheta **KAKATIYAS**
Orungalu
Simhachalam
Kalinganagara
EASTERN GANGAS

Arabian Sea
Taradavadi
CHALUKYAS OF VATAPI
Vatapi
Srishailam
Yengipura
Pistapura
Amaravati
Bay of Bengal

Kampili

Hemavati

HOYSALAS
Dvarasamudra
Manyapura
Mandagiri
PALLAVAS
Kanchipuram

Talakad
Kaveripattinam
CHOLAS
Gangaikondacholapuram

Vanji
Madurai
CHERAS PANDYAS
Korkai
Anuradhapura
LAMBAKANNAS

INDIAN OCEAN

0   km   500

The establishment of most medieval dynasties appears to represent emerging concentrations of wealth and power among agrarian warrior elites who controlled land and people in areas of agricultural expansion. These agrarian regimes were deeply rooted locally but they were also often politically expansive and they were all extensively connected to wide realms of trade, culture, and politics. Each dynasty had a strong territorial identity that concentrated in a specific core region, and when military expansion reached its limit, dynasties retreated into their homeland, unless they were driven out, which when it happened was often followed by the founding of a new homeland elsewhere. Over time, compact regional dynasties spread widely and they often produced permanent regional traditions preserved in monuments, literature, mythology, genealogies, and local rights and powers granted by medieval kings.

Many medieval dynasties emerged on routes from ancient *Bharat*. Ancient empires based inside and outside *Aryavarta* had produced networks of conquest, elite circulation, and cultural communication on long routes of human mobility that ran into and across the Ganga basin. Dispersed urban centres of late antiquity developed around army posts, administrative offices, markets, oases, ports, strategic mountain passes and river crossings, sacred sites, royal courts, lineage headquarters, stupas, monasteries, and other places valued by imperial elites. Human habitation and land use had intensified around cities where agropastoralism and shifting cultivation gave way to permanent farming, manufacturing, and commerce. When political leaders in imperial satellite towns challenged imperial elites for local leadership, vying for local support, new regional polities emerged with political cultures that combined local parochialism and imperial cosmopolitanism.

The Pallava regime at Kanchipuram is a good example. It emerged from under the canopy of empire thrown across the southern peninsula by imperial Guptas, Vakatakas, and Chalukyas. Pallava kings rose from vassal status to become imperial powers in their own right. Kanchipuram had been a centre of Buddhist learning featured in *Manimekalai*, a Buddhist epic composed in the Tamil language in Gupta times, when Pallavas were Vakataka feudatories. Under the Pallavas, Kanchipuram became a Hindu sacred site and a royal capital; its seaport, Mahaballipuram, was adorned with monumental rock sculpture and temple carving to popularize the worship of supreme Hindu gods, Siva and Vishnu. Under the Pallavas, Kanchipuram became a Hindu pilgrimage site and centre for Sanskrit learning, whose temples received endowments from dignitaries and gifts from patrons in localities all across the southern peninsula. On its temple walls, dynastic inscriptions record the Pallava cosmic genealogy and wars of imperial expansion that spawned Pandya and Chola regimes farther south. Thus ancient imperial authority was slowly transformed into numerous independent medieval regimes across the wide frontiers of late antiquity.

TWO

Changing Medieval Territories

A ncient South Asia was very thinly populated. Dense forests covered much of the land. Vast expanses of open scrubland separated countless, tiny, scattered communities of nomads, shifting cultivators, hunters, gatherers, and settled farmers, who multiplied over the centuries but left few records behind. As we have seen, history's first great transformation occurred in the millennium spanning the Maurya and Gupta empires. By Gupta times, the ancient landscape held an array of densely populated, complex societies that thrived in fertile lowlands astride major rivers. Their peoples left us most of our historical records. Their agricultural settlements were still surrounded by dense forest and open scrubland but they were expanding visibly, and they were extensively connected to one another and to many others across Eurasia.

By the middle of the first millennium of the Common Era, a second great transformation was well underway. It spanned eleven centuries from late antiquity to early modern times, from the sixth to the seventeenth century. Its early history took off from ancient trends but also left them behind. Its later history would shape the character of modernity, but its diverse, changing cultural territories came to be seen in modern times as a world of unchanging tradition. This long medieval transformation is first visible for historians in a proliferation of inscriptions carved into stone and etched in metal that document social activity in dynamic regions of dynastic authority that embraced ever more diverse populations. In this chapter, we first consider major innovations that transformed societies and social identities during early medieval centuries, before 1000 CE; then we trace major changes that occurred during a medieval transition running from the later centuries of the first millennium into the early centuries of the second millennium; and finally, we consider the late medieval centuries that shade into early modernity after 1500. In Chapter 3, we survey the regional contours of the eighteenth-century societies that emerged at the threshold of modernity.

A MEDIEVAL EPOCH

Like the Pallavas and Pusyabutis, whom we met in the last chapter, other early medieval dynasties had ancient genealogies. Like the Guptas, most medieval kings had their homelands in fertile places in river basins. But in medieval societies, people built many more of these fertile places by digging wells, by constructing dams, channels, and reservoirs, and by lifting water for crops with devices that were more and more often powered by bulls in harness. Medieval domains of royalty that emerged in these new fertile places were not mere off-shoots of ancient cultures: they were novel organizations of social power that produced new kinds of social identities. Their elites had various origins and spoke many languages. Inscriptions indicate a virtual revolution in the geographical character of social life in early medieval times as they name and locate thousands of peoples and places that seem to come from nowhere as they appear in the historical record for the first time.

Medieval social environments evolved over the centuries in the context of two long-term economic trends: sedentary farmers increased the productivity of land with specialized labour and technology, and mobile groups extended transportation and communication by land and sea from South Asia to Central Asia, China, and the Mediterranean. Already by the seventh century, we can see that long arteries of human mobility running across Eurasia were connected to regional veins in South Asia and to local capillaries running through vibrant areas of agricultural production. Most new dynasties that sprang up in the first millennium developed in places where long trade routes crossed fertile valleys and deltas. In Kashmir, they surrounded Srinagar, and in Nepal the

Kathmandu valley. In Punjab, they dotted the foothills. They multiplied along the rivers Ganga, Narmada, Tapti, Sabarmati, Mahanati, Krishna, Godavari, Pennar, Kaveri, Vaigai, and Tambraparni. In the peninsula, they thrived most of all where rivers met the sea. In the flatlands of northern Sri Lanka, they expanded around irrigation reservoirs that received water running down from mountains in the centre of the island.

Any map that depicts the details of political geography in medieval times looks kaleidoscopic, because the extent of dynastic territories often changed. But the social environments that developed in medieval domains were based in relatively stable economic areas, and major dynasties had an average lifespan of more than three hundred years, compared with 135 and 230 years, respectively, for the Mauryas and Guptas (Table 2). The secret of their success lay in the central role that dynasties played in building social systems to organize physical and spiritual power. Dynasties helped to organize creative interactions among people involved in mobile and sedentary ways of life, in places were local elites dominated villages and towns that also served itinerant merchants, warriors, craftsmen, and pilgrims. As a result, dynasties became cultural symbols of tradition in cultural territories that provided roots for many modern social identities.

New forms and constellations of social identity came into being during three long periods of historical innovation. The early medieval period lasted roughly until the end of the first millennium. Its inventiveness was concentrated in compact domains of dynastic authority where kings allied with local elites to direct the course of social change. From the tenth into the fourteenth century, a medieval transition occurred. Warriors became prominent agents of change in old medieval territories and in new lands outside them where military regimes developed around hill forts on trade routes and projected their power widely with cavalry and military discipline. After this transition, a later medieval period ensued. Its leading political figures were sultans, the greatest of whom created the Mughal empire in the sixteenth century. In two centuries of political dominance, the Mughal empire changed the social landscape substantially. Like the Maurya and Gupta empires, it spans the onset of a new epoch, which we call 'early modern' and will consider in Chapter 3.

TABLE 2. A REGIONAL CHRONOLOGY OF MEDIEVAL DYNASTIES

Location/period	Dynasty	Locations
Andhra Pradesh		
1000s–1300s	Kakatiyas	Warangal–Telengana–coast
1500s–1600s	Qutb Shahis	Golconda–Telengana–coast
Bengal		
750s–1170s	Palas	Gauda–Orissa–Jalandhur
1000s–1200s	Senas	Navadvipa–Vijayapura
1200s–1700s	Ilyas Shahis	Dhaka
1500s	Husain Shahis	Dhaka
1700s	Nawabs	Murshidabad
Ganga river basin		
500s–840s	Pusyaputis	Sthanisvara (near Delhi)–Ujjaini–Orissa
700s–1150s	Gurjara-Pratiharas	Ujjaini–Gujarat–Punjab–Bengal
800s–1300s	Candellas	Khajuraho–Awadh–Gorakpur
1000s–1200s	Gahadavalas	Kasi–Kanyakubja–Awadh
1162–1206	Ghaznavids	Lahore–Ghazni–Persia–Central Asia
996–1118	Ghurids	Afghanistan–Lahore–Sindh–Kasi–northern Bengal
1206–1526	Delhi Sultanate	Delhi–Afghanistan–Sindh–Gujarat–Deccan–Bengal
1540–1555	Sur Shah	Bengal–Punjab
1527–1707	Mughals	Kabul–Kashmir–Delhi–Gujarat–Assam–Mysore
Gujarat		
900s–1200s	Caulukyas	Anahilapataka
1500s	Nizam Shahis	Aurangabad
Karnataka		
500s–750s	Chalukyas	Vatapi–Narmada–Guntur
1000–1340s	Hoysalas	Dvarasamudram (to both coasts)
1336–1672	Vijayanagar	Raichur Mysore north – both coasts
1500s–1600s	Adl Shahis	Bijapur
1500–1831 (1947)	Udaiyars	Mysore region
Kashmir		
620s–850s	Karkotas	Srinagar–Kabul–Vidisa–Bengal
900s–1300s	Loharas	Srinagar–Kashmir

TABLE 2. *CONTINUED*

Location/period	Dynasty	Locations
Kerala		
300s–1100s	Cheras	Kollam–Trivandrum
1700s	Zamorins	Calicut
1700s	Travancore	Trivandrum
Maharashtra		
600s–900s	Rashtrakutas	Vidarbha (Nagpur)–east coast
800s–1300s	Yadavas	Devagiri
1300s–1500s	Bahmanis	Ahmadnagar
1500s–1600s	Nizam Shahis	Daulatabad (Devagiri)
1600s–1818	Marathas	Pune–Malwa–Nagpur
Nepal		
400s–700s	Licchavis	Kathmandu valley
900s–1700s	Mallas	Kathmandu valley
Orissa		
300s–1400s	Gangas	Kataka–Bhuvanesvara
1300s–1500s	Gajapatis	Jajnagar
Rajasthan		
800s–1300s	Paramaras	Ujjaini–Dhara (Malwa)
900s–1100s	Cahamanas	Ajayameru–Sakambhari
1200–1750 (1948)	Rathors	Jodhpur–Mandur
1300s–1700s (1948)	Sisodiyas	Udaipur–Chitor
Sri Lanka		
200s BCE–1200s CE	Lambakannas	Anuradhapura–Polunnaruva
1200–1500	Savulus	Kotte–west coast
1700s	Kandy	Kandy–highlands and coasts
Tamil Nadu		
300s–900s	Pallavas	Vengi–Kanchipuram–Tanjavur
600s–1300s	Pandyas	Madurai–Tanjavur–Kanchipuram
800s–1200s	Cholas	Tanjavur–Kanya Kumari–Sri Lanka
1336–1672	Vijayanagar	Vijayanagar–Karnataka–Andhra–Tamil Nadu
1600s	Nayakas	Madurai–Gingi–Tanjavur

Throughout the medieval millennium, social environments were being slowly but steadily transformed, providing new kinds of social experience, new settings for the socialization of each few generations. Whole new societies emerged in each period. Some ways of life died away as others came into being. Additions of new peoples and new cultural elements also accumulated inside old cultural areas to form more and more complex composites. Overall, people became more identified with villages, towns, and the regions around them. Societies became more complex, differentiated, and intricately stratified.

EARLY MEDIEVALISM

In the early medieval centuries, the places where these changes occurred were not typically big cities like those that hosted ancient imperial societies. Ancient cities were large for their day but surrounded by open land and by communities disconnected from city life. Ancient cities depended on long-distance lines of support that snapped when new dynasties carved out regional domains. Early medieval trade wove dense connections among localities that filled up with farms and markets; and these domains were less dependent on long-distance trade and wide military operations, which carried on nonetheless, with deeper local grounding. Each medieval domain resembled a grove of banyan trees that hosted various travellers who moved among the groves, enriching their growth and depending on their sustenance.

Medieval kingdoms arose from the power of social groups in dynastic core regions. Medieval domains were smaller than ancient empires but in aggregate much richer, more powerful, and more productive; because medieval dynasties were more intricately involved in regional societies, which were increasing their productive capacities at an unprecedented rate. In this context, dynastic elites enriched themselves with tribute and taxes, amply recorded in the inscriptions. They used their wealth on projects of interest to local elites, such as building temples and monasteries, conducting rituals, extending irrigation, supporting learned monks and Brahmans, protecting farms and towns against robbers, defending territory against incursions, and sending armies to bring tribute from other areas. Local elites paid taxes and tribute to sustain their own local powers over land and labour, and they invested jointly with rulers to increase the productivity of land. Local elite involvement in dynastic order deepened a dynasty's local support in its core region and sustained its longevity. All the major medieval dynasties significantly shaped local elite identities, many of which are still visible today.

The organization of political systems differed among regions and changed over time, but documents indicate general patterns. Most records depict transactions among people with titles in dynastic ranks and indicate that sovereignty emerged from these transactions rather than being dictated by legal or constitutional rules. Sovereignty consisted of honour and deference expressed in public interactions by people whose activity inscriptions record. Inscriptional transactions were mostly gifts, contracts, and commitments that individuals engaged in to express respect and support for people they recognized publicly thereby as being superiors or subordinates.

Dynasties grew as rising kings subordinated existing local elites and officially recognized their stature in public ceremonies. Replacing old local rulers in the lower ranks of sovereignty was fraught with risk because it threatened alliances around them. Local alliances gave local strength to rising dynasties and aspiring kings thus strove to strengthen them by bestowing titles and honours on their leadership. Dynastic lineages competed with one another for supremacy over locals who were often pressed and courted by more than one ruler and often recognized more than one sovereign. Multiple sovereignties formed ranked layers as a king (*raja*) became a great king (*maharaja*) or 'king of kings' (*maha-adhi-raja*) by adding the names of more subordinate rulers (*samanta*s) to the list of those who bowed to him. As a result, local people often bowed to a raja who bowed to a bigger raja, and so on, up the ranks. The bigger any raja became, the more he received obeisance from people who also recognized other rajas.

Early medieval rulers, like their later medieval successors, typically increased their power not by deepening their direct control over local resources but rather by extending their domains to cover more localities and by propagating more exalted titles for themselves in ceremonies in more distant places. Royal domains also spread with agricultural colonization. Although each dynasty concentrated attention on its core territory, it could only grow by spreading its canopy. Expansive dynastic development spawned new small centres of royal authority in new localities more than it created big concentrations of population in major urban centres, which was a logical trend in the sparsely populated medieval landscape, where vast expanses of open land allowed for countless new farms and new village settlements. Such expansion also increased the power of local elites who organized and controlled village agriculture. No large state-sponsored schemes of agricultural colonization are recorded anywhere in early medieval South Asia. Local elites controlled the expansion of farming and thus had their hands most immediately on the resources that medieval dynasties needed.

Political geography as depicted in the inscriptions is composed of localities where the inscriptions appear. In these localities, multiple, layered sovereignties overlap spatially as local rulers recognize dynasties whose royal canopies spread in various directions. Large tracts with no inscriptions surround places with many. Dynastic domains thus resemble shifting archipelagos of inscriptional sites rather than fixed state territories with stable boundaries. Archipelagos overlap as islands bowing to one king mix with those bowing to others. This spatial pattern of sovereignty continued until the gradual onset of modern political institutions that begins in the sixteenth century and matures in the nineteenth.

Most medieval dynasties combined elements of imperialism, regionalism, and localism. Many expanded like empires. All formed regions of competition and overlapping sovereignty. Early dynasties thrived on local support from core constituencies. Present-day Tamil Nadu exemplifies the kind of shifting cultural territory they formed. Beginning in the sixth century and running through the seventeenth, overlapping sovereignties among Pallava, Chola, Pandya, Chera, Vijayanagar, and Nayaka dynasties described a broadly shared Tamil language and textual geography of territorial authority that extended into adjacent regions in Karnataka, Kerala, Andhra Pradesh, and northern Sri Lanka. The largest dynasty to embrace Tamil territory arose at Vijayanagar, in Karnataka, in the fourteenth century, and featured rulers who spoke Telugu and Kannada. All the dynasties that ruled Tamil-speaking people were attached primarily to localities in their own home regions. Inscriptions from Pandya country (around Madurai) treat Chola conquest as imperial domination and Chola inscriptions in Tanjavur treat Pandya conquest the same way. In medieval terms, Chola and Pandya kings ruled separate countries that were defined by personal loyalties rather than by territorial boundaries. The most resilient early medieval territory was called a *nadu* and encompassed a small circle of villages. There were thirty *nadu*s south of Madurai in the Pandya country alone. A medieval *nadu* was a local domain around which were woven extensive networks of personal loyalty, alliance, and fealty. Local domains were defined in wider networks of culture, however, as indicated by the fact that the term '*nadu*' appears all across the overlapping domains of sovereignty that encompassed what is now Tamil Nadu.

SPIRITUAL POWERS

Personal relations in medieval domains included gods. The medieval cultural milieu included divinity and humanity, drew no sharp line between them, and contained various kinds of beings that moved back and forth between them and lived ambiguously at their conjuncture. One Gupta inscription records a royal gift to a local *guru* who traced his lineage to a god. Royal genealogies typically had celestial ancestries including the sun and moon. The spirit world was everywhere in everyday life. Celestial beings brought victory in war and commanded human fates. Spirits of nature caused disease, drought, flood, and fertility for animals, crops, and humans. Visible and invisible powers mingled capriciously. Priests, rulers, mystics, and saints evoked divinity and gods lived in society. Medieval domains were institutional environments for organizing, deploying, and controlling powers that circulated among people and gods.

As with politics, also with religion, it is useful to take a bottom-up, locality-first approach to early medieval history, and trends in Tamil *nadu*s provide a useful example. In ancient times, before the Common Era, Tamil verse portrayed localities full of spirits. One of these spirits was called Seyon, and was red like the hills where he lived. Feared and propitiated, Seyon became the subject of stories that dramatized his power. Personified in ancient Tamil verse, he became a living being with a personality, a human divine. He later acquired various names, one being Murugan; and sometime in the middle of the first millennium, Murugan became a son of Siva, identified with Skanda. Thus an ancient local spirit was gradually incorporated into the textual tradition of the Puranas. The *Skanda Purana* was recreated in the Tamil language by translation from Sanskrit. Other Sanskrit texts were similarly adapted to new settings, most famously, the *Ramayana*, whose Tamil version endows Sita's captor, Ravana, with a rather more heroic character than the Sanskrit version. Many *Ramayana*s were composed. Hundreds of local spirits and gods were incorporated into a pantheon in which Siva and Vishnu reigned like two great rajas complete with their own sprawling clans.

A diverse Hindu cultural complex spread across medieval domains, endowing many local traditions with common features but also being defined distinctly in each place as local people continued to embrace local traditions. Learned Brahmans received gifts of support from rulers and local elites to organize temples and to conduct ceremonies that incorporated local deities, sentiments, and practices. At the same time, Brahmans rationalized and ritualized the local status hierarchy by defining local identities in the ritual vocabulary of *varna* and *jati*. Brahmans used high-culture elements from ancient Sanskrit texts to compose locally grounded Hindu ritual domains that multiplied disparately in bits and pieces, in a motley pattern of ad hoc adjustments.

Brahmans spread Hindu cultural forms in much the same way – and at the same time – as other religious specialists were spreading Jainism, Buddhism, Islam, and Christianity. They travelled extensively. They settled in strategic places under dynastic patronage. They worked with local and regional allies to translate and interpret ideas and rituals into local vernaculars. They merged rustic and cosmopolitan elements. They vied for local elite support. Competing royal patrons backed competing religious specialists, often at the same time. In this lively world of cultural politics, Brahmans defined Hindu orthodoxy in local terms. Their success depended on innovative adaptations to evolving social environments. They were active in two distinct arenas: one was inside the state itself; the other, outside the state, in local society, particularly in rural society. Brahman rituals and Sanskrit texts became widely influential in medieval dynasties. The prominence of Sanskrit prose, Puranic deities, and divine genealogy in the inscriptions' *prasasti*s indicates a sweeping royal agreement across South Asia (and in parts of South-East Asia) that Brahmans brought to medieval governance a powerful symbolic technology. Most inscriptions are bilingual documents that symbolize the two-tier cultural space in which medieval dynasties worked. Brahman Sanskrit cosmopolitanism met vernacular languages in the inscriptions. Many early medieval Sanskrit *prasasti*s report the royal conduct of Vedic rituals, and vernacular texts in many inscriptions record a ruler's financial support for Brahman settlements, Vedic learning, temple building, and temple rituals. There were many ways to sponsor Hindu culture and they all centred on temple precincts, where most inscriptions appear and most Hindu identities were initially formed. The spiritual powers of Brahmans mingled with those of gods who became central figures in medieval life.

GEOGRAPHIES OF RELIGION

Brahmans were among many cultural activists who vied with one another to organize the operation of spiritual power, and they all needed mundane local patronage to flourish. Patterns of financial support from ruling dynasties, merchants, and landed elites had a major impact on the changing religious content of cultural regions.

Buddhism and Islam became most prominent along routes of trade and migration that ran from one end of Asia to the other. In the sixth century, Buddhists received most of the patronage available in Afghanistan, the upper Indus basin, and Himalayan regions from Kashmir to Nepal; and moving eastward across Central Asia, Buddhists then established themselves firmly in Tibet, China, and Japan. After the eighth century, however, eastward and southern migrations by Arabs and Turks from West and Central Asia shifted religious patronage to Islam in Afghanistan, along the Indus, in Punjab, and in Kashmir. But Buddhist monks had a permanent political base at the hub of the Indian Ocean trade in Sri Lanka, and from the eighth century onward, they won state support in regions from Burma south into South-East Asia. In Java, early medieval kings patronized Hindus; in the ninth century, Buddhists supplanted Hindus at court, though Hindus remained influential in royal circles in Bali, alongside Buddhists. By the tenth century, Arab traders were expanding their operations in the Indian Ocean. Muslim centres multiplied along the peninsula and on coastal Sri Lanka, and merchant patronage for Islam drew local rulers away from Buddhism around many South-East Asian ports in the later medieval period.

In Bengal, Buddhists were well established at the start of the medieval period and the Pala dynasty patronized Buddhism for four hundred years. In the eleventh century Hemantasena, a Pala tributary, declared his own independent dynasty. His successor, Vijayasena (1095–1158) defeated the Palas, pushed Sena armies west across Bengal and northern Bihar, patronized Vishnu worship, and expelled Buddhists. Vaishnava Hinduism flourished in Sena domains. The last Sena raja, Laksmanasena, patronized the most famous Bengali Vaishnava poet, Jayadeva, who wrote the widely influential devotional poem, *Gitagovinda*. In 1206, Laksmanasena was driven out of Bengal by the Turk conqueror, Bakhtyar Khalji, who shifted state patronage to Islam. After the Khalji conquest, there was a general drift of patronage for Islam to eastern regions of Bengal, where the Senas had not uprooted Buddhists; while Vaishnava Hindus received support from merchants, landowners, and local rulers in the western regions. Brahman influence in Bengali society was enhanced from Sena times onward by a distinctly Bengali system of hypergamy in which high-caste women married Kulin Brahman men who fathered children with multiple wives; this produced a multi-caste elite that included merchants, landowners, and administrators who flourished under later medieval regimes. From Khalji times onward, Muslim converts and migrants populated new agricultural settlements in eastern Bengal, where Vaishnavism in particular but Hindu temples, arts, poetry and music in general also flourished under the patronage of Hindu landlords, merchants, and administrative elites.

Like multiple sovereignties in medieval domains, multi-religious cultures developed where patronage sustained diverse religious institutions. Popular rituals and local sentiments often merged and overlapped, crossing the lines of religious tradition, particularly in the spiritual domain of devotional cults that revolved around charismatic individuals.

The Kathmandu valley was a Buddhist stronghold ruled by Hindu kings. The Buddha had been born in the southern foothills (Terai) of Nepal, where Ashoka inscribed a column. In Gupta times, Licchavis began their long reign, and claiming Kshatriya status, they launched a tradition of sovereignty in which high-caste kings from the Ganga lowlands maintained supremacy over a mostly Buddhist population. Powerful medieval kings in Tibet made Himalayan passes to the north major arteries of culture, commerce, and politics reaching into China, which brought more and more Buddhists and patrons for Buddhism into the valley. Kingdoms around Kathmandu became a mixing ground for Hindus from the south and Buddhists from the north, and like dynasties in Bengal, they made multi-cultural patronage a long-standing religious tradition.

In the western plains – in Gujarat, Rajasthan, Malwa, and Bundelkhand – medieval Hindu dynasties of Kalacuris, Caulukyas, Paramaras, and Candellas also patronized Jains, who were prominent among merchants. One Caulukya king is said to have become Jain. Hindu and Jain cultural features blended into one another. Jain temple worship and Hindu–Jain marriage became common. In Gujarat – Mohandas Gandhi's homeland – it became difficult to say where Jainism ended and Hinduism began. Non-violence, the fundamental Jain virtue, became philosophically prominent among Hindus in this region, where patrons for Jainism included archetypal Kshatriya warriors, the great Rajput lineages. Gujarati Bania (merchant) castes made their version of Vaisya culture very Jain, a cultural phenomenon with its origins in the mixed patronage of medieval dynasties.

In the peninsula, medieval worshippers of Siva and Vishnu displaced Buddhism and Jainism from the cultural prominence they enjoyed in early medieval times, especially in Madurai and Kanchipuram. Pockets of Jainism remained, however, and all along the peninsular coast, most prominently in Kerala, Hindu kings patronized diverse merchant communities that were essential features of life along the Indian Ocean coast, including Jains, Zoroastrians, Muslims, Christians, and Jews. Arab Muslim settlements received patronage from non-Muslim rulers all along the peninsular coast, as they did across the Palk Straits in Sri Lanka.

Inside medieval Hindu cultural environments, trends in popular religion indicate the increasing influence of religious feelings of a distinctly non-Brahman kind that first achieved prominence in temple worship farthest from the original home of classical Brahman orthodoxy. In the far south, from the eighth century onward, non-Brahman cultural activists took the lead in spreading Siva and Vishnu worship in old *Dakshinapatha* by inventing devotional (*bhakti*) worship that valued emotion above knowledge, discipline, and ritual; by composing vernacular verse in Tamil, not Sanskrit; by promoting female saints and mass participation in deity worship; by giving devotees a direct relation to god independent of Brahmanical mediation; by making low-caste status respectable in the eyes of god; by making songfests ad hoc sites of worship; by praising poet saints over Brahman gurus; and by creating pilgrimage places rooted in local traditions. *Bhakti* poets produced a new style of emotive, popular cultural politics. Devotionalism made divine frenzy and passion for god a high virtue, and by the tenth century these energies had been turned against religious competitors. Several texts indicate massacres of Buddhists and Jains. Under Chola kings, worshippers of Siva (Shaivas) prospered at the expense of Vishnu worshippers (Vaishnavas), triggering battles among their respective sectarians.

Bhakti devotionalism and sectarian competition challenged Brahman elite proponents of traditional Sanskrit religion as it attracted more patronage from ruling dynasties. To cultivate a popular following, many rulers in the south supported Vaishnava (Alvar) and Shaiva (Nayanar) *bhakti* poets. The most celebrated Hindu intellectual of the early medieval age, Shankaracharya (788–820), made his name during his short life by developing a Sanskrit high-culture rendition of Tamil devotional poetry, by reconciling Shivism and Vaishnavism through a non-dualist *advaita* philosophy that drew on the Upanishads and incorporated elements from Buddhism, and by travelling from Kerala to Kashmir and back again to establish monastic centres. Shankara helped to absorb and normalize popular devotionalism in elite Brahman high culture. Populist challenges to the spiritual power of Brahmans were mostly of local importance, but one of major

regional stature emerged in the Kannada-speaking interior of the
peninsula, where the *bhakti* saint Basava established a Siva sect
called Virashaivas (also called Lingayats) with a non-Brahman
jangama priesthood. Virashaivism attracted royal patronage and
many adherents from merchant communities and became regionally dominant in northern Karnataka, where Lingayats remain
predominant today.

Popular devotionalism attracted thousands of passionate
believers to temples and pilgrimage sites. This made public
patronage increasingly complex and fraught, because sects could
provide decisive military and financial support for dynastic
contenders. Multiple and layered sovereignties continued among
the gods, nonetheless, in the established medieval manner.
Dynasties gave privileges and funds in various forms – minimally
as tax exemptions – to various religious institutions and their
leaders.

Popular movements made such support contentious. Rulers
had to balance support for their core religious constituency with
support for others, which brought condemnation from allies.
Muslim rulers often faced criticism for patronage they typically
gave Hindu groups, following established precedent. Devotees of
Vishnu and Siva could be equally unforgiving. As *bhakti* travelled
north along Shankara's tracks, competing Hindu sectarians not
only wrote poems like Jayadev's *Gitagovinda*, but also raised
armies to fight for sectarian control of pilgrimage sites and temple
festivals. From at least the fifteenth century, armies of Shivite and
Vaishnava ascetics fought to protect sectarian wealth against raids
from competitors and to capture revenues from popular religious
gatherings like the *kumbh mela* in Hardwar and Prayaga
(Allahabad). In the sixteenth century, the Mughal emperor Akbar
witnessed a pitched battle between two sects of Shivites. Akbar's
own religious eclecticism reflects an effort to reconcile contentious
devotional loyalties through the medium of mystical speculation.

MAKING HINDU SOCIETIES

New kinds of society came into being as medieval agrarian
domains expanded into landscapes inhabited by nomads, hunters,
and forest dwellers. Kings, Brahmans, and local landed elites led

the drive to extend and protect the moral authority of *dharma* (sacred principles of social identity, spiritual discipline, and moral order). For kings, peace and prosperity in their domains were definite signs of righteousness, as in Rama's kingdom in the *Ramayana*. Protecting *dharma* enabled royal families and local elites to form ranks of honour and spiritual merit that also disciplined the labour force, coordinated economic activities, and secured rights over landed property. Medieval texts on *dharma* do not insist that a king be a Kshatriya, and in much of the subcontinent medieval caste (*jati*) ranks developed without the presence of all four *varna*s. Medieval texts, *sastra*s, instead prescribe that the king's sacred duty – *rajadharma* – is to protect local custom. The *Manusmriti* also says that *dharma* includes the sacred right of first possession for people who first cleared the land for cultivation, even if they had taken the land from hunters and pastoralists, which was typically the case. Kings needed to give grants of farm land to temples and Brahmans to express dynastic support for *dharma*, but they also had to protect local rights to land. Kings, Brahmans, and local landed elites had to work together to realize *dharma*.

Political territory became *dharma*'s abode as ritually ranked kin groups became ranked caste groups (*jati*s). Coercion was certainly involved in the creation of caste societies, but the practice of ranking *jati* groups according to *varna* was attractive for many groups, particularly at the higher social ranks. Caste norms stabilized communities, organized production, and sanctified power. Rituals of caste ranking facilitated family alliances by measuring family status. The labour, land, and assets of low-ranking *jati*s came under the control of dominant high caste families who made strategic alliances with Brahmans and kings. Dominant castes came into control of local communities in dynastic territories. The expansion of caste society appears to have been a top-down process that did not typically depend upon everyday coercion. It emerged as an evolving caste hegemony in which the coercive features were hidden by beliefs in *dharma* that became widely accepted as they provided everyone a place in the social ranks.

The spread of *jati* ranking as a feature of social life seems to have been propelled by ritual alliances among upwardly mobile groups. New dynastic realms were places where the building of ranking systems made good sense. Dynastic lineage leaders and Brahmans were critical actors in creating these systems of social difference, status, rank, and power. New Hindu societies came to include new social groups and new institutions that were shaped by the models of behaviour, identity, and aesthetics codified in Sanskrit texts and interpreted by the Brahmans. Rising families hired Brahman genealogists, patronized Brahman temple priests, endowed feeding places for mendicants and pilgrimages, staged festivals, fed saints, and variously joined in activities that brought gods, kings, and farmers into communion.

All this occurred as farmers expanded their control over land and labour and as populations of peasants, nomads, pastoralists, hunters, and forest tribes were slowly finding new social identities. Over many generations, people became high caste landowners, kings, protectors of *dharma*, Kshatriyas, Vaisyas, Superior Sudras, Inferior Sudras, untouchables, and aliens beyond the pale. Dominant agrarian castes came into being in different regions: Jats, Rajputs, Kunbis, Vellalas, Velamas, Reddys, Kapus, Nayars, and many others. In this long process, ancient identities were lost. In ancient times, the Hoysala kings' ancestors were Melapas, hill chiefs in the Soseyur forests. Udaiyar and Yadava dynasties descended from herders. Tevar kings descended from Marava and Kallar hunters. Gurjaras and Rajputs had once been pastoral nomads. Places, too, acquired new identities as they became known by the names of dynasties and of the local groups in control. Land became ethnically marked by traditions of group control. Dominant castes identified with dynastic territories that became their homelands. The only people who could be equally at home in all the lands of *dharma* were Brahmans. Even today, Brahmans have high status in all Hindu societies, but all the other high castes have regional identities according to territories of traditional residence and stature; and these territories are in turn identified with their dominant caste groups.

Activity that dramatized emerging social identities appears in temple inscriptions. Rituals performed by Brahmans using Sanskrit liturgies brought cosmic spiritual powers down to earth to sanctify a caste social order. Temples were divine sites for enacting social rank among worshippers who protected *dharma* and financed rituals; and the rituals brought a variety of local, regional, and imperial gods together. Though medieval societies witnessed many kinds of rituals – by all kinds of spiritualists and officiates, from all kinds of social backgrounds, in all manner of locations – which brought rain, secured crops, drove away disease, delivered healthy babies, and bolstered dynasties, medieval inscriptions treat only rituals conducted by Brahman priests for Siva, Vishnu, and their Puranic relatives. Temples to these great sovereign gods rose on the land as towering sacred landmarks and monuments to political power.

The Hindu temple as a ritual and architectural complex emerged in full form in the later Gupta period. Its elaboration and spread from the sixth to the fourteenth century provide a glorious medieval legacy, from Mahaballipuram to Khajuraho. The absorption of local deities, rituals, symbols, and spiritualism into Puranic literature and related myth, folklore, and artistic representation constituted Hindu worship by enhancing the cultural potency of local deities, their devotees, and their patrons. Local cults were woven into Puranic traditions and temple rituals as local communities came under royal authority. The greatness of the gods enhanced the glamour of royal patrons. Rich centres of temple worship combined many of the technical skills – controlled by Brahmans – that were needed to develop agrarian territories, from architecture and engineering to law and financial management. Building a great temple attracted Brahmans and established a theatre of royal grandeur. Great kings built great temples and supported many learned Brahmans. The distribution and content of temples and inscriptions thus map medieval social geography. Lands rich with inscriptions are concentrated in eastern and central Uttar Pradesh, West Bengal, Gujarat, western Maharashtra, and along the coastal plains. Where we do not find many medieval temple inscriptions – in Punjab, in Jat territories in the western Ganga plains, and in most mountainous regions – we can surmise that Brahman influence was small and cultures less Hinduized.

Social identities emerged around temples as people and gods lived together. Gifts by kings, landed elites, merchants and others to Brahmans and temples increased the spiritual stature of the donor. Inscriptions are contracts and advertisements. The more popular a temple became – the more praised in song and more attractive for pilgrims – the greater became the value of its patronage and the number of people whose identity attached to it. Rising *bhakti* devotionalism enhanced the virtue, volume, and commercial value of pilgrimage, as it increased temple donations and investments. Donations became increasingly popular as a means and marker of social mobility as temples became commercial centres, landowners, employers, and manufacturing centres. Increasing participation in temple rituals made them more effective sites for social ranking, since temple honours were distributed according to rank and all worshippers were positioned in ranked proximity to the deity. Rulers came first. Other donors received honours in proportion to the value of their temple endowments. Popular *bhakti* movements made sovereign gods ever more central in everyday social life, even for the poorest people who did all the hardest manual labour, who were prohibited from ever setting foot in the temple, whose exclusion marked them as the people of the lowest social rank. Some powerful *bhakti* saints came from the lowest of the low, and their devotion was so strong that gods came out of temples to return their love.

People who joined temple society gave gifts to gods and Brahmans that increased the status of donors, executors of the grant, and, by extension, all their kin. Over time, kinship circles formed around lineages and clans that fed gods and Brahmans, and these kin groups formed high-status, non-Brahman elite *jati*s, elevated above others in ritual and society. Brahmans reaped major benefits. In the open spaces of Rashtrakuta power, one inscription records a gift of eight thousand measures of land to one thousand Brahmans, and four thousand measures to a single Brahman. In each specific context, an inscription of this kind appears to mark an effort by a non-Brahman power bloc to enhance its status and that of its local allies.

Such gambits were not without risk. A small but significant set of inscriptions records opposition to Brahman settlements, to their collection of taxes, and to their claims on local resources like pastures. The authority of Hindu kingship spread slowly – often violently – into the vast spaces that lay outside its reach in early medieval centuries. In many instances, land grants appear to mark frontiers of royal power, and here resistance might be expected. Even where local society did accept the ritual and social status of Brahmans, fierce competitive struggles might flare up over land grants. In the ninth century, local conflicts of this kind accompanied new Brahman settlements on the Tamil coast. In the Rashtrakuta realm, inscriptions warn that violence and curses will be heaped upon people who oppose Brahman land grants, and texts proclaim that people who murder Brahmans will be punished harshly, which implies that such murders did occur.

THE RISE OF THE WARRIORS

Many violent conflicts occurred during ancient and early medieval times. One typical ninth-century royal inscription brags that Candellas reduced to submission 'wild tribes of Bhillas, Sabaras and Pulindas'. Conquering enemies and tribes preoccupied most dynastic genealogies. Valorous killing and death pervade literature and folklore. The *Mahabharata* and *Ramayana* popularized epic war in medieval times. In ancient and medieval times, hero stones memorialized local warriors and their widow martyrs, who became eternal *sati* by immolating themselves on their husband's funeral pyre. Ancient Tamil poets praised kings' bloody deeds. Buddhist tales depict the gore of graveyards, cremation grounds, and battlefields to convey life's suffering and impermanence.

The character of organized warfare changed over the centuries. Mauryas and Guptas had made war a civilizing force and medieval kings fought to define the ranks of *raja*s and *samanta*s as they fought to conquer nomads and forest people who became the 'wild tribes' outside the world of *dharma*. Tribal societies outside *dharma* occupied most of the land around villages and towns. Subduing tribes, expelling unruly elements, protecting farms against nomads, and assimilating tribal groups into caste society all required organized violence. The steady absorption of tribal peoples into complex agrarian societies helps to explain the increasing prevalence of animal deities and blood sacrifices in Hindu worship that were missing in Vedic rituals and ancient Brahmanism. Medieval dynasties had a basic commitment to the expansion of permanent field cultivation, which required constant fighting on the frontiers of farming. Violent conflicts among sedentary farmers, pastoral nomads, shifting cultivators, hunters, warriors, and forest dwellers indicate that many groups opposed the rule of *dharma*. But many pastoral and tribal peoples were also assimilated; their proportion of the agrarian population was particularly high in the western plains, central mountains, Punjab, western Gangetic basin, and the interior peninsula. In these regions, tribal groups retained substantial political power. Rajput rulers recognized Bhil chiefs as their allies and Bhils acquired a central role in some Rajput coronation ceremonies.

Farming communities expanded agriculture in medieval domains by pushing pastoral nomads and forest cultivators away; but at the same time, herders, hunters, nomads, and other peoples also entered expanding agrarian societies, becoming labourers, farmers, craft producers, animal breeders and keepers, transporters, dairy producers, soldiers, traders, warriors, sorcerers, and kings. Agricultural territories included more diverse populations, not only different kinds of farmers – including peasants, landlords, and landless workers – but also non-farming groups who were essential for farming: artisans, cattle herders, hunters, transporters, traders, collectors of forest produce, well-diggers, priests, engineers, architects, healers, astrologers, and warriors. Many of these people were newly embraced by the rule of *dharma*. Without them, economies could not expand; their incorporation was an important social project.

In this context, warriors expanded their influence. Various factors promoted the rise of warrior power and one was certainly the increasing number of people with specialized military skills living in agrarian societies. Warriors with nomadic roots often became military specialists, most prominently in Rajasthan and surrounding regions, where warrior dynasties emerged from the Gurjara Pratihara clans that conquered most of the Ganga basin after the eighth century.

By the tenth century, professional military cadres became features of dynastic power generally, and old dynasties used large armies to accumulate wealth outside core territories that could no longer sustain their acquisitive ruling classes. The Cholas exemplify this trend. In the tenth century, the Chola dynasty boasted a vast administrative apparatus and huge temples in the Kaveri delta, and Chola pioneers were moving up the Kaveri to build new domains on the slopes below Mysore. Chola armies then campaigned across the peninsula from Andhra and northern Karnataka to Kanya Kumari and Kerala; they crossed the Palk Straits to fight in Sri Lanka. They conquered the Pandyas, made themselves a new ruling elite, and brought Brahmans and service castes to work for them. Chola expansion spawned new dynasties among competitors. Warriors pushed out of coastal Andhra by the Cholas established a new Kakatiya dynasty at Warangal in the interior uplands. Kakatiyas built irrigation tanks that were marvels of the age. Similar dynastic inventions occurred in the Mysore region, where Chola pressure combined with Chalukya expansion in the Deccan to generate a new Hoysala dynasty, whose temple sculptures record the professional character of the Hoysala armed cavalry.

In Sri Lanka, trends took a different turn. Tamils had migrated and settled on the island since ancient times. Their settlements mingled among those of Sinhalas. Eleventh-century Chola conquests appear to have aggravated local conflicts that already undermined the operation of irrigation systems on which the population depended. Irrigation may also have reached a physical limit; malaria may have become prevalent. Between 1200 and 1500, the ancient irrigation system collapsed, the agrarian economy lost its foundation, the Sinhala population moved south-west to the coast around Colombo, Tamil kingdoms arose in the far north, and malarial lands spread between Tamil and Sinhala regions. This epochal transition occurred when the island was becoming a hub in Indian Ocean trade; and for thirty years after Cheng Ho's fleet landed, in 1430, Chinese emperors collected tribute from rulers in coastal Sri Lanka.

A MEDIEVAL TRANSITION

As the first millennium of the Common Era gave way to the second, the contours of political geography shifted substantially. In Sri Lanka, virtually the whole population shifted to the coast. In the peninsula, after Chola imperial expansion reached its limit, the weight of dynastic power shifted from the coast into the interior uplands, where warrior nomads and pastoralists were transformed over centuries into warrior–peasant alliances on farming frontiers.

New centres of dynastic power arose in Karnataka, Andhra, and Maharashtra, where local warriors faced enemies who galloped along routes across Malwa, Rajasthan, Afghanistan, and Central Asia. Late medieval militarism in the Deccan – based in Khandesh, Berar, Maharashtra, Andhra, and Karnataka – had social origins with ancient histories on the land. Dynasties emerged from the mobilization of warriors inside and around farming communities where peasants struggled with but also came from pastoral, hunting, and mountain societies. Earlier dynasties were more pastoral, and later dynasties more agrarian: standing to fight became part of farming. In the Deccan, where drought was common, running off to war in the hot dry season came naturally. All the dominant agrarian castes that came into being in the medieval Deccan included both soldiers and field cultivators.

By contrast, in Rajasthan, a single dominant warrior group evolved, called Rajput (from *rajaputra* – son of a king), which rarely engaged in farming, even to supervise farm labour, because farming was literally beneath them; farming was for their peasant subjects. In the ninth century, separate clans of Rajput Cahamanas (Chauhans), Paramaras (Pawars), Guhilas (Sisodiyas), and Caulukyas (Solankis) were splitting off from sprawling Gurjara Pratihara clans, whose distant ancestors were pastoralists and who formed an imperial medieval dynasty that spread across Rajasthan, Malwa, and the Ganga basin. In later centuries, separate Rajput lineages spread out across the plains and adjacent mountains, settling in fortresses, and ruling over peasants. Rajput nobles endowed temples and employed Brahmans, but their devotion to war, clan, and supremacy over peasants was the true measure of Rajput *dharma*. They attracted allies and imitators as they made themselves a model of *rajadharma*, ideal Kshatriyas.

Rajput cultural influence spread widely among allies, competitors, and imitators. The genealogies that constituted the valorous record of a Rajput ancestry became coveted assets among the aspiring rulers who multiplied east of Rajasthan until, in the eighteenth century, a cultural Rajputization of tribal kingdoms occurred across the mountains of central and eastern India. Rajput supremacy also stimulated the rise of warrior Jat peasant clans in the western frontiers of old *Bharat* – in Rajasthan, the western Ganga basin, and Punjab – where Rajputs and Jats built fortified villages and hilltop forts, sometime allied with one another, but most often at odds.

The third population of warriors that propelled the medieval transition in South Asia consisted of huge clans of Turk, Afghan, and Mongol horse nomads, who dominated warrior society in the uplands north-west of the Indus, Punjab, and Rajasthan, in Afghanistan, Persia, and Central Asia. They became the dominant military force in the lowlands after the tenth century, when Paramaras held Malwa, Cahamanas fought for northern Rajasthan and routes across the Indo-Gangetic watershed, Hindu Shahis fought Rajputs from their base in Punjab, and Sultan Mahmud assumed power in Ghazni, Afghanistan.

Mahmud of Ghazni's father, Sabuktigin, fought Hindu Shahis in Punjab to acquire tribute to support his wars in Afghanistan and Persia. A deeply clannish Turk leader, he professed Islam – as Timur would do, centuries later – to make strategic alliances. Mahmud succeeded his father in 997 and extended his patrimonial ambition in all directions. He conquered Afghanistan and Persia, he obtained the title *Yamin al-Daula* (Right Hand of the State) from the Caliph, and he took tribute from local rulers in seventeen raids across the Indus basin. Mahmud defeated Hindu Sahis in 1018; then he sacked Mathura and Kanyakubja; and, in 1026, he sacked the pilgrimage centre of Somanatha, on the coast of the Saurashtra peninsula in Gujarat. His deeds became literally legendary. They were memorialized, often fancifully, by genera-tions of admirers and detractors who bestowed upon him everlasting fame for his pillage, plunder, and murder of heretics and infidels, including Muslims and non-Muslims. He became symbolic in cultural politics. In the fourteenth century, two Sunni authors, Barani and Isami – writing in Delhi and in the Deccan Bahmani kingdom, respectively – praised Mahmud as an ideal Muslim ruler because he persecuted rival Muslim sects of Shias and Ismailis, as well as non-believers.

Mahmud of Ghazni also used some of his wealth to support Al-Biruni, the master geographer, who lived in Lahore in the 1040s and compiled a brilliant account of medieval India using material provided by his Ghaznavi patrons. Al-Biruni had come from Persia and travelled trade routes documented for centuries by Arab geographers whose knowledge had guided Mahmud's expansion to the west and his raids to the east and south. Al-Biruni's geography locates places all across the Indo-Ganga basin and Indian Ocean coast, most importantly, Gujarat and Sind, where merchants brought horses from Arabia, and competed with horse traders from Ghazni. It is likely that Mahmud's raids in Gujarat were in part directed at his compatriots' commercial competitors. Rich Indian merchants in Ghazni would have been able to provide Mahmud with intelligence on the most lucrative sites for military assault. By Mahmud's time, the Indus and Ganga river basins were, like Rajasthan and Gujarat, part of the trading world of Central Asia and Mahmud brought them into Central Asian politics as well.

From the twelfth to the fourteenth century, armies from Central Asia engulfed South Asia's northern plains. Between the time of Al-Biruni's geographical tract (1048) and the travels of Marco Polo (1271–95) and Ibn Batuta (1325–54), the inland routes of mobility in southern Eurasia became a continuous terrain of dynastic competition that ran from Qum in Persia, to Samarkand in Central Asia, to Delhi, Surat, and Dhaka. At the same time, the Indian Ocean became an integrated commercial system. South Asia became a land of wealth and trade connecting the Silk Road and the Indian Ocean.

In the thirteenth century, a new kind of dynastic domain emerged in Delhi. The Delhi Sultanate had its origins in victories by Mahmud's rival, Muhammad Ghuri, who sacked Ghazni in 1151, and then expelled Ghaznavids to Punjab, in 1157. Muhammad Ghuri marched into the Indus basin to uproot the Ghaznavids in 1186. On the way, his armies conquered Multan (1175), Sind (1182), and Peshawar and Lahore (1186). In 1190, he occupied Bhatinda, in Rajasthan, which triggered battles with the Rajput Prithviraja Chauhan, whom he finally defeated in 1192. Having broken the Rajput hold on western routes to the Ganga basin, the Ghurid armies marched eastward until Bakhtyar Khalji finally defeated Laksmanasena in Bengal, in 1200. Muhammad Ghuri died in 1206. His trusted Mamluk (ex-slave) general, Qutb-ud-din Aibak, governor of Delhi, then declared an independent dynasty in Delhi. His dynasty was the first in a series that became collectively known as the Delhi Sultanate. Later Ghurid and Ghaznavid efforts to bring Delhi back into their fold were finally repulsed by the Delhi sultan Iltutmish in 1211–36.

The Delhi Sultanate became an epoch-making Indian dynasty by repelling the Mongols, who were unstoppable elsewhere in Asia. Genghis Khan (born 1150s or 1160s, died 1227) unified the Mongol tribes to produce the largest political territory ever known to that time. His grandson, Batu Khan, commanded Mongol armies assigned to conquer Europe in 1237. Batu Khan conquered Bulgaria, Moscow, Kiev, Hungary, and Poland, forcing local rulers to pay tribute to the Golden Horde. Another grandson, Kublai Khan, conquered northern China and became the Yuan emperor in 1271. His armies finally defeated the southern Sung in 1279 and his dynasty ruled until 1368. Across Eurasia, a Mongol postal system and a roadway network extended from China to Turkestan, Persia, and Russia, fostering overland trade that brought gunpowder, the compass, and printing to Europe from China. Along these routes, Marco Polo travelled from Venice to China and back. But the Mongols could not conquer India. Mongol horsemen grazed in Punjab for some years and raided Lahore, Multan, and Sind. One son of the Delhi Sultan Balban, Muhammad, governor of Sind, died fighting the Mongols, in 1285. Having failed time and again to conquer the armies of Delhi Sultans, the Mongols withdrew from the Indus basin to concentrate their powers elsewhere, with spectacular success.

Turk warriors related by marriage to Mongols did, however, succeed in India. Timur was born at Kesh, near Samarkand, in a short-lived Mongol successor state, the Chaghatai Khanate of Trans-Oxiana. The man called Tamerlane by Europeans became the governor of the Chaghatai district and then vizier to its Khan. In 1370, he usurped the Khan's power and made himself Amir. He professed Islam but slaughtered people of all religions in the disciplined manner of a Mongol warrior. By 1387, he had conquered Persia and Afghanistan, and in 1398, he swept into India. He took Multan on the way to Delhi, where he put its sultans to flight and destroyed their citadel. He then conquered the Ganga basin and put the governor of Multan on the Delhi throne on his way back to Afghanistan. His victories had killed the imperial authority of the Delhi Sultanate, which then broke into an array of satellite sultanates and survived as a regional power until its territory was conquered, in 1526, by Babur, the founder of a Mughal dynasty. Babur claimed descent from both Timur and

Genghis Khan. His conquest of Delhi and the Ganga basin was the penultimate step in the rise of warrior power in South Asia. As we will see, his grandson, Akbar, took the final step in the sixteenth century by establishing the Mughal empire.

The medieval transition that began at the end of the first millennium separates early and late medieval history. In early medieval times, internal developments inside core regions of dynastic authority played the leading role in changing local societies. By 1200, this was no longer true. Warriors from distant homelands became prominent in local histories everywhere. The rise of the warriors had begun with Gurjara Pratiharas and imperial Cholas. Warrior ascendancy over agrarian elites had spread far and wide before Mahmud of Ghazni arrived on the scene. Ghaznavids and their successors extended, integrated, and institutionalized professional warrior imperialism; and they also marked a shift in the regional origins and cultural composition of military overlords. Rajputs were Kshatriyas who patronized Brahmans and worshipped Puranic deities, and one of their responses to the new military competition they faced was to seek followers for a new Rama cult to support their cause. Their enemies were Turks, Afghans, and Mongols from Central Asia, some of whom, like Mahmud of Ghazni, praised clan victories in the name of Islam.

Central Asian warriors became supreme during South Asia's medieval transition by deploying swift-horse cavalry skilled in shooting arrows at full gallop, volley after volley; by raising vast armies dedicated to siege and open-field combat, undeterred by local alliance building; and by organizing cavalry that ran rapidly over long distances, staying on the move to subsist on the fruits of conquest, well-supplied with saddles, stirrups, and the latest weapons. Turk and Afghan tribes supplied the best men for this kind of warfare. Their ethnic solidarities instilled discipline and motivation. Their central Asian steppe grasslands and herds provided horses at low prices. Routes across Mongol domains provided them with superior military technology. In 1200, Indian dynasties east and south of the Hindu Kush relied on horses that came through Turk and Afghan lands and from Arabia by sea; they fought as commonly on elephants as on horses; they rarely fought to the death; and they rarely built forts in which to survive onslaughts from cavalry.

Before 1200, India had served Central Asian warriors as a rich place to raid to finance Central Asian wars. Ghaznavids, Ghurids, Mongols and Timur all regarded India in this way. Trade routes across Punjab were easy targets and Multan was a jewel *en route* to Gujarat. The Ganga basin was a huge source of wealth for the taking. The Delhi Sultanate's defeat of the Mongols changed the political environment, however, because it marked a domestication of Central Asian sultans inside India, where they had rich territory to defend and where they became part of a changing political culture.

Mongols thus had many indirect effects in South Asian regions they never saw. Warriors like Qutb-ud-din Aibak were trained in Mongol warrior skills and used them to defend their domains against the Mongols. Turk and Afghan sultans who settled in the Indian lowlands became members of local societies. Turk and Afghan sultans were leaders among diasporic Central Asian migrants resettled in India. The Delhi Sultanate brought Mongol technologies into the project of building dynasties that could thrive under later medieval conditions. Migrant warriors from Central Asia continued to conquer in the Indian lowlands in the wake of the Mongols because they had better access than local rivals to the trade routes in the Central Asian interior that carried the latest military technology. Babur is a dramatic example: in the sixteenth century, he used matchlocks and cannons against the last Delhi Sultans who held fast to honourable but by then archaic methods of steppe warfare.

MOBILITY AND CULTURAL MIXING

Vicious Mongol attacks on cities and towns across southern Eurasia launched centuries of migration into India. Warriors, scholars, mystics, merchants, artists, artisans, peasants, and workers followed ancient trade routes and new opportunities that opened up in the new domains of Indian sultans. Migrants walked and rode down the Hindu Kush; they travelled from town to town, across Punjab, down the Ganga basin, into Bengal, down the Indus into Sind and Gujarat, across the Vindhyas, into the Deccan, and down the coast. From Bengal and other sites along the coast, some continued overseas. They moved and resettled to find work, education, patronage, influence, adventure, and better living. They travelled these routes for five centuries, never in large numbers compared with the resident population; but as time went by, newcomers settled more often where others had settled before; and their accumulation, natural increase, and local influence changed societies all across South Asia forever. This was one of the world's most significant long-term migratory patterns; and it carried not only people and wealth into South Asia but also a complementary flow of commodities in the opposite direction from South Asia to Central and West Asia and Europe.

Regions of southern Asia were lands of wealth and opportunity. Immigrants altered societies most where they settled most commonly, in urban centres along trade routes. Among the overland migrants who came into India primarily from southern regions of Central and West Asia, two social categories can be usefully distinguished. Leading the way, warriors organized fighters, military suppliers, and service providers on ethnic lines in groups defined by tribe, clan, and lineage, mostly Turks and Afghans. Even these groups were multi-ethnic, but groups in the second, non-military category were even more so. Migrants in both categories coming from Persia increased over time, especially after 1556, when Persian literati came into Mughal service and the centre of gravity of Persian culture shifted into South Asia. Most immigrants were Muslim non-combatants. They generated multicultural centres of social change, mostly in and around urban centres. They caused a huge burst of urbanization. Historical documentation also increased with waves of immigration, often as a consequence of patronage by sultans. Most new documentation pertains to the sultans' activities and interests, rather than to those of ordinary immigrants. Al-Biruni's *India* (1048) begins the new documentation and carries a feeling of discovery and exploration. New architectural documentation begins in 1311, when Alauddin Khalji's Alai Darwaza arose in Delhi, a massive gateway that makes a solid Muslim cultural statement. We know much more about sultans, however, than about Al-Biruni's Lahore or about the people who built and passed through the Alai Darwaza.

From the thirteenth to sixteenth century, Turk and Afghan warriors pushed old medieval dynasties into subordinate positions and carved out independent domains for themselves. They formed a new, culturally distinct, ruling class, poised above old dynastic clans and village elites. Thus the new dynasties added new layers to the multiple sovereignties of medieval history. As before, losers in war fled to fight elsewhere. As during Chola expansion, chain reactions ensued. Conquered Rajputs conquered local rulers in the western Himalayas and Punjab hills, who climbed to fight in higher valleys. As they arrived in Nepal, Yaksha Malla (1429–82) divided his kingdom among his three sons, who ruled Kathmandu, Patan, and Bhaktpur (all now inside the city of Kathmandu); and each son had to fight Kshatriyas who had fled defeat on the plains. Fighters from north India also moved south, where in the fourteenth century two brothers Bukka built a new dynasty at Vijayanagar on the southern edge of Turk and Afghan expansion. Telugu and Kannada warriors fled Bahmani sultans in the Deccan to conquer Tamils farther south and form new dynastic enclaves on the south-east coast.

Centuries of competitive interaction imbued military rulers with many common traits. Subordination, alliance building, emulation, and learning brought cultural borrowing, diffusion, and amalgamation. In new dynastic domains, a new kind of cultural complex emerged that gave rulers many options, one of which was to define Hindu and Muslim religious sects in opposition to one another, but they more typically engaged in multi-cultural patronage. In later medieval societies, the spirit and practice of Hindu *bhakti* mingled with those of Muslim *sufi* mysticism around saintly exemplars of spiritual power and in music, poetry, and eclectic expressions of divine experience. Spiritual guides, teachers, mystics, poets, festivities, and sacrificial offerings attracted people who worshipped at temples and mosques. Turkish, Afghan, Persian, and regional Hindu aesthetic and engineering motifs mingled in the arts, fortresses, palaces, and consumer taste. The regalia of royalty formed a symbolic language of honour that was spoken by rulers of all religions, who recognized one another's authority and engaged in common rituals of rank. Rajas and sultans fought, taxed, invested, administered, and transacted with one another using the same lexicon and technologies, learning from one another. Vijayanagar provides one good example of such mingling. Its Rayas faced deadly enemies in the Bijapur sultans, who eventually destroyed

Vijayanagar; but the Rayas themselves became Hindu sultans and their techniques of power closely resembled Bijapur sultans. Nayakas in the south and Rajputs in the north likewise assumed the mixed character of Hindu sultans.

URBAN GROWTH

At the heart of each new dynastic domain, capitals needed serious fortification. Big stone forts arose in rapid succession on major arteries of mobility running east–west in the northern plains and north–south in the peninsula: at Kota (1264), Bijapur (1325), Vijayanagar (1336), Gulbarga (1347), Jaunpur (1359), Hisar (1361), Ahmedabad (1413), Jodhpur (1465), Ludhiana (1481), Ahmadnagar (1494), Udaipur (1500), and Agra (1506). In this context, Delhi began its long career as an imperial capital, strategically astride routes down the Ganga and into Malwa and the Deccan.

The new dynastic capitals were often not located in the most fertile agricultural tracts or in old medieval centres in riverine lowlands, but rather in the uplands, on dry ground in strategic sites along routes of communication, march, and supply. As new dynastic domains grew richer, forts became fortified cities with palaces, large open courtyards, gardens, fountains, garrisons, stables, markets, mosques, temples, shrines, and servant quarters. The architectural elaboration of fortified space became big business; it produced a new kind of urban landscape. Even the elegant Taj Mahal is encased in fortifications. Inside a typical fort, we find palace glamour as well as stables and barracks; we see a self-contained, armed city, most of whose elements came from far away. Permanent armies drawing specialist soldiers and supplies from extensive networks of trade and migration sustained these new urban centres. No new dynasty of any significance rested primarily on resources from its capital's immediate hinterland; and to this extent, they were all imperial, however small.

Political geography no longer focused as much as before on agrarian core regions; rather, it followed the routes of armies. A typical sultan's domain consisted of a series of fortified sites, each with an army that lived on taxes from its surrounding land. Dynasties expanded as local fort commanders submitted to one central command; they fragmented when their commanders declared independence, as they often did. The two great imperial success stories were the Delhi Sultans, whose five dynastic lineages embraced a shifting collection of subordinate rulers for three hundred years, from 1206 to 1526; and the Mughals, whose one lineage controlled a vast military command for about half that long, from the day of Akbar's coronation, in 1556, to the day of Aurangzeb's death, in 1707.

Urbanism reached new heights under military regimes that promoted vast physical and social mobility. Armies protected trade routes and sultans built strategic roads. The army provided the surest route to upward mobility, which always required extensive travel. In 1595, Abu Fazl's treatise on Akbar's reign, *A'in-i Akbari*, suggests that the military may have employed (directly and indirectly) almost a quarter of the imperial population. Many men travelled long distances to fight. It became standard practice for peasants to leave the Bhojpuri region, on the border of Bihar and Uttar Pradesh, after the harvest each year, to fight as far away as the Deccan, to collect wages and booty, and then return home to plant the next crop. Short distance seasonal military migration became an integral feature of peasant subsistence in the Deccan. Dynasties expanded only because warriors migrated to the periphery, where they fought, settled, and attracted new waves of military migration. War pushed peasants away from home by disrupting farm operations, and by forcing villagers to feed armies. Life on the move became a common social experience for many people: seasonal migrants, people fleeing war and drought, army suppliers and camp followers, artisans moving to find work and peasants looking for new land, traders, nomads, shifting cultivators, hunters, herders, and transporters. Altogether, people on the move for at least part of each year may have comprised half the total population of major dynastic domains in the seventeenth and eighteenth centuries.

All this mobility increased commerce in various ways, as we will see. But the specific kind of urbanism that characterized late medieval domains came from concentrations of goods and services and of commercial supply and demand around fortified sites of dynastic military power. Armies at home and on the move needed diverse goods and services, from horses to weapons to cuisine, rugs, jewelry, art, and entertainment. Rulers accumulated cash and credit to pay troops and buy war materials. Getting cash to support war required rulers to supply virtual military cities moving across the land for months at a time, filled with all sorts of army personnel, suppliers, retainers, and allied service groups. To maintain his supremacy, a sultan needed cash to finance his wide-ranging display of military power. Financial support became harder to find in times of dynastic distress; and as a result, bankers and merchants became powerful in politics as they also became influential in urban society and culture.

New taxes supported later medieval dynastic regimes. The Delhi Sultans instituted the first tax system designed to sustain an imperial military by making land grants to its officers, which were called *iqta*, as in the Ottoman empire. The old practice of granting land to Brahmans and temples was now extended to the military by sultans who granted tax territory to commanders, who used the proceeds to support the army and themselves. Taxes paid to local authorities ascended the chain of military command. In practice, most taxes were spent in the regions where they were raised, on things needed to support the military and administration – which in turn fuelled the growth and concentration of wealthy urban centres.

EXPANDING COMMERCIALISM

Ibn Batuta travelled the new Asian world that emerged in the Mongols' wake. Born in Tangier, in Morocco, he embarked in 1325 overland to Mecca, across Persia, and via Samarkand to Delhi. He lived at the sultan's court in Delhi for eight years and served the sultan as an emissary to China, and returned by sea via Sumatra, Sri Lanka, Kerala, Goa, and Gujarat, before heading back to Morocco. His astute observations often concern commercial conditions. In Turkestan, he found that 'horses . . . are very numerous and the price of them is negligible'. He found Bengal to be 'a vast country, abounding in rice and nowhere in the world have I seen any land where prices are lower than there'. On the road from Goa to Quilon, he wrote, 'I have never seen a safer road than this, for they put to death anyone who steals a single nut, and if any fruit falls no one picks it up but the owner.'

Though early medieval inscriptions do indicate substantial commercial activity, including long-distance trade by major merchant communities, late medieval documents indicate that commerce expanded dramatically after 1200. As Ibn Batuta indicates, specialized commodities were produced in abundance in particular regions, and rulers protected traders' activities inside their domains. In addition, his route itself – like that of Marco Polo a century before – indicates that inland transport across Central Asia was part of a wider circuit of mobility that included the Indian Ocean and South China Sea. South Asia was a huge land bridge between Central Asia and the southern seas.

A web of long and short trade routes in the Indian Ocean was attached to the coast from ancient times. Long routes between China and Europe always touched South Asia, where they met coastal routes among localities from Gujarat to Bengal. Fisher folk and coastal traders plied the western seas in Harappan times. Gujarat was already a lively spot in Mauryan times, and eighteenth-century Armenian merchants who brought wool shawls and rugs to Europe from Kashmir and Turkestan travelled through Gujarat and Punjab to meet suppliers. Early medieval Geniza records in Cairo describe voyages to Gujarat and Malabar; and for many merchants from the Mediterranean, Cochin was India's port of entry. Many Christian, Muslim, and Jewish traders from the west settled in early medieval Kerala, where Hindu rulers depended on them to increase dynastic wealth. Ibn Batuta observed that 'most of the merchants from Fars [Persia] and Yemen disembark' at Mangalore, where 'pepper and ginger are exceedingly abundant'. In 1357, John of Marignola, Pope Benedict XII's emissary to China, called Quilon 'the most famous city in the whole of India, where all the pepper in the world grows'. Europeans began building fortified settlements for permanent residence on the west coast after Vasco da Gama arrived in Malabar, in 1498. As we will soon see, the east coast and Sri Lanka were equally active. Ancient Tamil poets depicted the coast as a place of longing where women waited for their men to return from the sea.

After 1200, the coast and its overseas connections became increasingly important for people living in the inland interior. Sri Lanka is an extreme but telling example. After the Sinhala population had moved out of its old northern homeland and resettled on the south-west coast around Colombo and Galle, the main source of dynastic wealth shifted from agriculture to the sea trade. Spices from the mountains were the major exports, above all, cinnamon and pepper. Spices became royal monopolies. Kings contracted with overseas merchants, set prices, and turned profits into royal revenue. Arabs became the major overseas merchant settlers along the coast. Sri Lankan kings – like their contemporaries elsewhere on the coast – encouraged sea traders to settle in their territory; and in this endeavour they competed with other coastal kingdoms. In 1283, King Bhuvanaika Bahu I sent 'an embassy to the Mamluk sultan of Egypt to make a commercial agreement.

Various connected trends made Indian Ocean ports more important for inland societies. Warriors needed horses imported by sea. Exports became more numerous as farmers pushed agriculture into the interior uplands, where more diverse productive localities entered trading systems strung along rivers leading to the sea. Upland foresters sent spices, timber, honey, fruits, elephants, and many other valuable commodities to the coast in return for rice, meat, tools, and other goods that travelled coastal trade routes. In this context, farmers began specializing in growing cotton that thrives in black volcanic soil. By 1500, cotton and silk textile manufacturing, trade, and consumption involved many specialists: growers, spinners, weavers, dyers, transporters, bankers, wholesalers, and retailers. Consumers of cloth were concentrated initially in urban centres, where urban traders, bankers, wholesalers, and weavers became critical links in complex chains of commercial transactions that expanded the scale of manufacturing and stretched along the coast and out to sea.

EMERGING IDENTITIES

Along the coast and in the inland interior regions, new societies were born and old ones changed. The most dramatic events occurred in hundreds of urban sites, large and small, strung along routes between Central Asia and the Indian Ocean. Knowledge about these events comes to us in new kinds of documentation. In late medieval centuries, pen-and-ink manuscripts slowly surpassed carved inscriptions as records of history. Inscriptions and other old sources like architecture and oral texts also reflect a shift in the substance of texts, however, which indicates an important feature of social change. Individuals become more prominent.

Individual identities appear more clearly and elaborately in the records of the second millennium. Famous individuals thus take on a larger role in historical writing. Authors like Ibn Batuta and Abul Fazl left historians rich accounts inscribed with personal experience. Like other authors, they had patrons who wanted to see their name in lights. Rulers commissioned dynastic chronicles, courtiers wrote biographies and hagiographies, and writing history became part of cultural politics. The brightest stars in later medieval history are individuals we can denote with the word 'sultan'. This was an actual title for many rulers, but generically it denotes a kind of personal identity that came to be shared by many people of importance, because the sultan became an ideal type, or cultural model, for patriarchs wielding power in society.

What did it mean to be a sultan? In the Qur'an, this Arabic word connotes a man with spiritual power. Mahmud of Ghazni was the first man to be styled 'sultan' by contemporaries, which indicates his success in cultivating admirers. The title seems to have been popular first among the Turks. Seljuq dynasties ruling Palestine and Persia in Mahmud's day were the first to use it routinely, and later, Ottoman Turks made it famous in Europe. When the Caliph began conferring the title, it spread quickly among Muslim rulers and changed along the way. In a fourteenth-century chronicle of Firuz Shah Tughluq's reign in Delhi, Ziauddin Barani said that 'History is the knowledge of the annals and traditions of prophets, caliphs, sultans, and great men of religion and government.' By this time, sultans had exalted company.

Sultans took various titles that indicate their ethnic origins and cultural affiliations in addition to marking personal status. The greatest sultans in South Asia were the Mughal emperors, who (though part Turk through Babur and Timur) adopted Persian imperial culture and took the Persian title *Padshah* to lift themselves symbolically above Turks, Afghans, and all other sultans. Hindu rajas never used the title but many styled themselves, their court cultures, and their symbols of sovereignty in the manner of sultans.

Whatever his title, a sultan was a man of personal greatness, not only as an army commander but as a spiritual and moral being. A man of civilization, his wars were civilizing, by definition, though what this meant varied and changed. A sultan's grandeur emerged from the work of people around him. Putting halos on Muslim sultans was a job for poets, scholars (*imam*s and *ulema*), architects, chroniclers, biographers, spiritual guides (*sufis*), and Friday prayer leaders at the *jama masjid*, the great congregational mosque. For Hindu sultans, the same job fell to Brahmans, priests, genealogists, myth makers, dramatists, singers, temple builders, and festival organizers. Skilled service providers and cultural activists competed for the honour to glorify sultans, and in doing so advanced their own careers and spiritual stature at the same time.

Public debate, drama, and glamour surrounded sultans and formed their legacy. Mahmud of Ghazni became his own publicist. To impress the Caliph, he probably exaggerated his damage to Somanatha, where local accounts do not indicate the same destruction to temples that he claimed to have wrought. Three hundred years later, chronicles by Barani and Isami depicted Mahmud as an ideal ruler and as the founder of Muslim rule in India, both inaccurate claims; and clearly these two poets were using Mahmud's fictive image for their local political purposes. They were probably engaged in debates about patronage, which were often intense around sultans. Should the sultan support leaders of various religions, promote his sufi guides over others, persecute non-Muslims and 'deviant' Muslims like Ahmadis and Ismailis, patronize Hindu temples, ally with Christians, or tax Muslims and non-Muslims at the same rate? Such questions became matters of recorded public dispute among the intelligentsia who prodded sultans and gave guidance and support for dynastic politics. For Mahmud, looting Hindu pilgrims (which he did) was clearly not as laudable as breaking the Somanatha temple idol (which he probably did not do), so it was the latter deed that preoccupied contemporary and later publicists seeking allies among like-minded militarists. In the sixteenth century, Akbar took the opposite tack. He made a virtue of marriages with Hindu Rajput families and brightened his halo by patronizing leaders of various religious groups. His great-grandson, Aurangzeb, turned in the opposite direction. He imposed the *jizya* tax on non-Muslims. He encouraged anti-Hindu feelings among Muslim allies who fought Marathas who fostered anti-Muslim feelings among their Hindu allies. In all these cases and many more, sultans cultivated appropriate support from religious experts.

The sultan's personality thus emerged in context. Experts and allies around him shaped his opinions, policies, and priorities. He cultivated people to secure his success, and his power depended on their power. Thus the social institution of a sultan's power extended well beyond the throne. Early sultans like Mahmud of Ghazni relied entirely on kin and close ethnic allies. As the political landscape became more complex, more complex personalities developed and under the Mughals assumed epic proportions.

Sufis of the Chisti order were one of the organized groups of cultural activists who enabled sultans to overshadow others. The founder of the order, Khwaja Miun-ud-din Chisti, lived in Ajmer, where he died in 1236. His tomb remains one of the holiest Muslim sites in South Asia. When Akbar built his vast red sandstone fortress-palace-city at Fatehpur Sikri (between 1565 and 1589) – abandoned for lack of water two decades later – he put a lovely marble tomb for Sheikh Salim Chisti in its *jama masjid* mosque. Imperial visits to Ajmer to venerate Khwaja Miun-ud-din Chisti became a Mughal ritual, recorded and illustrated in the *Padshahnama*. Chisti influence was more than spiritual, because Chisti followers had serious clout. For example, in 1400, Chisti leaders (*sheikh*s) in Bengal objected to the local sultan's patronizing of Brahmans and allowing non-Muslims to hold high office, and they appealed to the sultan at Jaunpur to back them in their struggle. Their strategy seems to have worked, because the Bengal sultan increased patronage for the local Chistis, though he also continued to patronize others as well.

The sultan's body, speech, piety, personal habits, hobbies, family, household, ancestors, wives, sons, and in-laws formed the inner core of his public identity; they appeared in public gossip, art, lore, song, and chronicle. A daily dramatization of the sultan's public self occurred in his court, at his public *darbar*, where he received guests, ambassadors, suppliants, allies, and payers of taxes and tribute. The institution of the *darbar* evolved over time. Its early Central Asian home was a regal tent on the battlefield; in later centuries, it acquired architectural grandeur, as at the Mughal fort-cities in Fatehpur Sikri, Agra, and Delhi, whose *darbar* halls are massive stages for the emperor's performance of power. Many *darbar*s incorporated Hindu and Muslim traditions of display and drama. We have a detailed rendering of *darbar* scenes in eighteenth-century paintings that now accompany the seventeenth-century *Padshah-nama*, the chronicle of the third Mughal emperor, Shah Jahan. These illustrations show hanging rugs that recall the *darbar*'s nomadic heritage, and each and every person depicted in the paintings had a specific rank at court and relation to the emperor.

The *darbar* became a place for dramatizing in public all the personal identities that were being defined in relation to sultans. To dramatize all the various personalities of power that comprised his domain, a sultan took his *darbar* wherever he went. A *darbar* spent considerable time on the move, especially in battle. The ruler's travelling court became an enduring cultural phenomenon; and in later centuries, touring administrators, tax collectors, and politicians effectively became the touring sultans of modern times.

A sultan's retinue, regalia, and family symbolized his greatness. Sultans were sticklers for public etiquette and sumptuary protocol, lest subordinates exceed their station. The sultan had to have the biggest, richest, most elaborate, extravagant, valuable things visible on his person, to dramatize his ascendancy constantly. Vijayanagar Rayas styled themselves 'Lords of the Eastern and Western Oceans' by adorning their bodies with precious commodities from overseas trade, specifically, perfumes and precious things like Chinese porcelain. The sultan's home was a larger version of his own body and dramatized his powers to accumulate, command, control, and define wealth, value, and taste. The grandiose habits of consumption of the great potentate became an enduring fact of political life in South Asia.

Significant features of a sultan's persona emerged in publicly visible domestic dramas, above all, marriage. Weddings were great events of political life because marriage was the most secure method of political alliance. In the *Padshahnama*, warfare and weddings are depicted by the artists most elaborately. Even the Mughal empire was at base a family affair. In the inner secret precincts of the palace, family members vied for influence and engaged in the intrigues that often culminated in wars of succession, in which relatives killed one another, as they did in the epic *Mahabharata*. At home, the sultan's honour rested on the stainless virtue of his mother, wives, daughters, and sisters. Sequestered women of the palace lived behind a curtain, *pardah*; and women in seclusion, *pardahnasheen*, became the sultan's own virtue. Practices of female seclusion spread among elites who modelled themselves on sultans, Hindus and Muslims alike, at all levels of society. In this and many other respects, Rajput rajas became model Kshatriyas who were also model sultans.

MEDIEVAL EMPIRE, MODERN THRESHOLD

In the sixteenth century, the rise of the Mughal empire marks an epochal change comparable to the rise of Mauryas and Guptas. Its dynastic founder, Babur, bears comparison to the two ancient Chandraguptas. His empire arose, like theirs, from the work of previous empire builders, in his case the Delhi Sultans, specifically, the last Lodi dynasty. Like them, he had more famous successors and made his mark as a military commander. His imperial legacy is equally impressive and hard to explain. Like the ancient imperialists, the Mughals did more than conquer and dominate: they invented an imperial society that took its strength from many sources and continued to expand its influence long after emperors were unable to compel submission. All these empires open new epochs. The greatest medieval empire spans the wide threshold of early modern times.

Babur was a Chagatai Turk who fled patrimonial lands near Samarkand to escape Uzbek armies. He followed opportunity into the Ganga basin, where he used Uzbek-style fast-horse phalanx cavalry equipped with muskets and cannons to sweep away the opposition. In 1526, he had conquered sultans from Punjab to Bengal. But opposition survived. Thirteen years later, an Afghan soldier who had fought for the Lodis and for Babur, and who styled himself Sur Shah to demonstrate his Persian education (at Jaunpur), declared a new dynasty in Bengal and Bihar. Sur Shah's armies then beat Babur's son, Humayun, back to Afghanistan, where Humayan raised his own son, Akbar, in exile. The Sur dynasty did not survive the Shah's death, though its lasting accomplishments included administrative innovations and a trunk road from Bengal to Punjab. Soon after Sur Shah died, Humayun conquered Delhi, in 1555. He died there by accident. His twelve year old son, Akbar, then ascended his throne under his regent, Bairam Khan. Akbar was crowned in 1556, as Bairam Khan conquered strategic fortress cities at Lahore, Delhi, Agra, and Jaunpur. Bairam Khan also conquered Malwa and Rajasthan before he was ousted as regent and assassinated.

Akbar ruled for fifty years (1556–1605). He continued to conquer to the end. His armies surpassed all before in their size, funding, leadership, technology, and success. At his death, his domains stretched from Kabul, Kashmir, and Punjab to Gujarat, Bengal, and Assam; and they were still increasing in the south and up into mountains on all sides. His mantle was passed in wars of succession to his victorious son, Jahangir (1605–27), then to his grandson, Shah Jahan (1627–58), and to his great-grandson, Aurangzeb (1658–1707), whose death was followed by imperial fragmentation, though the dynasty survived until 1858, when the last Emperor was dethroned by the British, as we will see in Chapter 4.

The secret of Mughal success was that each emperor deployed many armies under his own supreme authority. Mughal armies fought in many places simultaneously and kept winning against the opposition that rose constantly against them. Previous imperial sultans had used commanders like Sur Shah to win victories, only to lose their loyalty when commanders were strong enough to strike out on their own to declare a new dynasty. Mughal commanders had to be individually strong, mobile, well equipped, and decisive, but they also had to remain loyal for the empire to survive. Centralizing power over commanders might keep them loyal for a time, but it would also weaken their ability to respond quickly and decisively to local challenges and opportunities, because transportation and communication were slow and expensive. Too much central control would spark disloyalty among the most ambitious and powerful commanders. Mughal emperors succeeded because and for as long as they sustained the personal loyalty of nobles who controlled decisive military force. To maintain the precarious balance between noble autonomy and loyalty, imperial wealth had to increase.

The empire needed to expand to survive. Expansion provided opportunities for individually powerful military commanders to enrich themselves, kin, clients, retainers, and heirs. The inheritability of a commander's imperial assets posed the single biggest organizational problem for Akbar. If imperial assets became a commander's private patrimony, his dependence on the emperor declined, and if loyalty to the emperor prevented passing one's patrimony to one's sons, rebellion would be the only way to ensure patrimonial inheritance. An expanding empire produced new opportunities for ambitious sons, who would thus not need to rely for their fortune on their inherited patrimony. A commander thus had incentives to remain loyal to an emperor who could allocate appointments and resources among his warrior nobles. Expanding imperial resources provided incentives for loyalty and penalties for disloyalty were effective only when loyalty could pay secure dividends. As soon as the emperor could not guarantee a noble's sons a share in the imperial wealth, the sons had incentives to strike out on their own with their own loyal followers.

In the context of vast military expansion, Akbar built the centralized Mughal system of rules and regulations that made his empire more bureaucratic than any before. Using the methods of the Lodis and Sur Shah, Akbar divided his territories into administrative units independently of existing local usage. Groups of villages formed *pargana*s, then *sarkar*s, and finally *subah*s; which correspond roughly in size to townships, districts, and provinces. The *subah* of Bengal, for instance, contained nineteen *sarkar*s containing over six hundred *pargana*s. This naming of territories in standard imperial terms had important symbolic as well as practical effects. Standardizing territorial nomenclature identified all people, however important they were locally, with imperial places; and it located all places inside the ranks of imperial sites whose individual stature was equated with the rank of the imperial elites who controlled them. People and places thus acquired stature within a unified imperial status hierarchy. Empire imposed an ideology of imperial ranks on social identities in all regions of the empire. Imperial standardization progressed further into regional and local societies with the dispersion of Mughal titles, coinage, weights, measures, road names, town names, property rights, taxes, government functions like post and police, and criminal and civil law. Terminologies of governance formed a vocabulary of political order that crossed boundaries among languages and regions. Akbar introduced silver currency that set the standard for all imperial payments and receipts. Coins from Mughal mints made the emperor's face a monetary symbol.

Mughal receipts came primarily from taxes on cultivated land, which was duly measured in standard units, its output ascertained in cadastral surveys. Tax liabilities marked the relations between officials and subjects. A person responsible for paying land tax was called a *zamindar*, literally, 'one who has land'. The *zamindars* were actually revenue intermediaries who stood between Mughal officials and local communities, where local elites allocated local tax obligations among themselves. Beneath the ranks of *zamindars*, localism reigned. Imperial standardization began above the *zamindar* in his *pargana*. In 1596, a record of assets and assignments in Mughal territory compiled by Abu Fazl in his empirical paean to Akbar, the *Ain-i-Akbari*, became the first ever standardization of data on administrative and economic conditions to cover land spanning Punjab, Malwa, Gujarat, Bengal, and all the Gangetic lands in between.

Imperial wealth increased with the value of land, and expanding cultivation became an imperial project. The total area under cultivation in the Ganga basin and Bengal increased by sixty per cent from Akbar's coronation to Aurangzeb's death. The most dramatic change occurred in eastern Bengal, where Mughal troops cut down jungles to promote farming, and where in 1666 one grant (*sanad*) gave 166 acres of jungle to support a single mosque. Nobles made 288 grants of tax-free land in the Chittagong region to support mosques and shrines, in the style of temple grants in medieval inscriptions, and with much the same effect: Islam suffused the foundation of new agrarian societies in the cleared jungles of eastern Bengal. The men given grants were local leaders who became land clearance entrepreneurs. They contracted with *zamindars* to finance cultivation; *zamindars* advanced funds to peasant farmers and received crops and labour in return.

INDO-PERSIAN IMPERIAL SOCIETY

Many elements that would constitute modern social environments began to appear in the sixteenth century, and for this reason we can aptly use the phrase 'early modern' to refer to the period *circa*

1550–1850. In expanding agrarian regions, urbanism increased dramatically. In 1595, Abu-l Fazl's *Ain-i-Akbari* mentions 180 large cities and 2837 towns. Hierarchies of rank that distinguish central places in regional systems of authority also emerge more clearly in Mughal times. Large cities held the highest officers of state, smaller cities lesser officers, and so on down the line. Bureaucracy and geography shaped the identities of places and thus people inside them. The highest elites were urban elites in the biggest cities, surrounded by provincial elites and local elites.

The bureaucracy that the *Ain-i-Akbari* records rested on personal loyalty to the emperor among nobles who held all the places in the empire together. The nobility was the backbone of imperial society, commanding armies financed with taxes from imperial territories. The emperor had the biggest army under his private command, but he could not defeat a substantial alliance of great nobles. Warriors with independent means initially became nobles (*amir*s) by being assigned a rank or dignity (*mansab*) with assignments of salary or income from lands. In 1590, Akbar revised the system to remunerate nobles in proportion to the number of men and horses under their command. This linked imperial rank explicitly to noble military assets. The plan was to create an elite corps of military commanders who maintained the dignity of their aristocratic warrior status through service and loyalty to the emperor.

Assignments of all *mansab*s to *mansabdar*s officially came at the emperor's discretion, as did appointments of provincial governors, *subahdar*s. Such officers were meant to (and routinely did) circulate bureaucratically among provinces; this in theory prevented them from establishing independent regional bases of political support. In practice, however, all assignments and appointments were political decisions that took into account a noble's independent power. The risk of collusion against the emperor always remained, because a noble's troops were loyal to him personally. Troops came from their commander's ethnic group and formed kinship and patronage ties with him. Provincial *zamindar*s, bankers, and other resourceful people could also be expected to side with *amir*s or *subahdar*s, who were both typically *mansabdar*s with their own armies. Keeping the empire together required a Mughal emperor to use his own personal power to engage in the politics of alliance-building and opposition-breaking to keep his own nobility under his supreme authority. Each Mughal war of succession ended with wars that demonstrated which one of Akbar's aspiring descendants had bested his rivals in attracting allies among the nobility.

Akbar's strategically fundamental alliance was with Rajput rajas whom he invited to join his nobility and with whom he cemented alliances, in the normal fashion, by marrying their daughters. We will consider the importance of such family systems of patriarchal alliance in more detail below; and we will also see that Akbar spent considerable energy trying to balance the influence of the various ethnic groups who comprised the imperial officer corps, Rajputs among them. Eventually, all but one major Rajput clan married into the Mughal dynasty. Family disputes inside the dynasty generated wars of succession that hinged on the shifting loyalties of the nobility. Prince Salim, whose mother was a Rajput, rebelled against his father, gathered nobles around him, and had his name read as emperor at Friday prayers in the Allahabad *jama masjid*, in 1602, three years before his father's death. His rebellion failed, but he nonetheless succeeded Akbar to become Emperor Jahangir, after he defeated his own rebel son, Khusrau, whom he blinded and committed to life in prison. When Khusrau died, in 1622, Jahangir's other son, Khurram, also rebelled unsuccessfully. He was not killed or imprisoned, but rather exiled to fight in the Deccan. He returned to Agra triumphantly, surrounded by great nobles, five years later, after his father's death, to become Shah Jahan, the great Mughal patron of the arts. Shah Jahan commissioned the *Padshahnama*, in 1647, and built the jewel-bedecked Peacock Throne, the Taj Mahal, and a new capital city in Delhi, named for himself as Shahjahanabad. When Shah Jahan fell ill, in 1639, his eldest son, Dara Shukoh, and his youngest son, Aurangzeb, began fighting for the throne. Twenty years later, Aurangzeb finally won and began his long reign as the last great Mughal.

Aurangzeb died, in 1707, at eighty-nine, still at war with Maratha rebels in the Deccan whom we will meet shortly. Within a few years of Aurangzeb's death, the power balance between emperor and nobles had shifted noticeably. Nobles gained the upper hand. Rebellions in the provinces could not be quelled. By

1725, Bengal *subah* was effectively independent, and others followed. Yet regions of the empire remained imperial provinces under Mughal authority long after the emperor's power to enforce subordination had disappeared.

Regions of Mughal authority lasted longer than the empire itself. Even the British used Mughal titles and engaged in rituals of respect for the Mughal emperor until 1802. This resilient authority came from the fact that regions had changed fundamentally as political territories under Mughal supremacy. The process of change combined elements drawn from many sources. Most importantly, however, an elite imperial society imbued with Indo-Persian culture had emerged in all the Mughal regions. This imperial society not only survived but continued to flourish and spread after Aurangzeb's death left the later Mughals without a single supreme commander for all their armies.

Mughal imperial society combined personnel as well as material and cultural elements drawn widely from circuits of mobility in southern Asia. Its military features included Mongol and Turk techniques and technologies that were already widespread when Babur began his career. Babur added Uzbek cavalry and artillery, muskets, and infantry that circulated around the regions of Ottoman expansion. New fighting skills, strategies, and equipment arrived with each wave of migrants from Central Asia, and also from Europe after Vasco da Gama arrived in 1498. Military innovations from all over Eurasia arrived in Delhi and in regions along the coast with increasing regularity. Turkish influence was also important in revenue administration, beginning with Timur's adaptation of *iqta* assignments of land to support military commanders, which Ottoman and Delhi Sultans adapted. Under the Mughals, Persian influence became predominant as Akbar recruited Persian administrators, judges, sufis, artists, and others to expand, stabilize, and refine the empire. Even so, Mughal administration was eclectic. The *mansabdari* system was a combination of Mongol ideas about warrior dignity, Turkish techniques for allocating taxes to military commanders, Persian bureaucratic formalities that separated military, tax, and legal authority, and regional traditions of elite control in local communities.

Multiple, layered sovereignties continued to thrive under the Mughals' bureaucratic standardization. Elaborate Persian imperial institutions unified a Mughal polity that also danced to the tune of personal loyalties embedded in regions of cultural mixing. Imperial elites broadly organized by Indo-Persian institutions that spread under Mughal authority became leading figures in these regions. Their identities developed in mixtures of ethnic and religious loyalties inside their regions; but their influence and livelihoods were organized under the umbrella of Mughal supremacy.

Imperial society long outlasted the great emperors because Mughal power strengthened regional elites who were also imperial subordinates, so that when they became independent, in the eighteenth century, many retained their imperial identities, and all drew upon the strength that was a legacy of Mughal power. We consider regional histories in the next chapter. In all the Mughal regions, the imperial system absorbed not only great warriors, rajas, and landlords, but also locally dominant caste groups. Royal endowments to temples and Brahmans continued, mostly in the form of tax-free grants of land carried over from earlier dynasties. Brahmans continued to be prominent landowners and state officials. Mughals thus applied old medieval principles by strengthening subordinate rulers (*samanta*s), and Indo-Persian imperial culture gave multiple, layered sovereignties a new legitimacy derived from a supreme emperor. Aurangzeb revitalized a legal proclamation of the *Manusmriti* in his famous 1665 *farman*, declaring that 'whoever turns [wasteland] into cultivable land should be recognised as the [owner] *malik* and should not be deprived [of land]'. Local landed elites obtained entitlements to village sovereignty from the highest authority.

Among regional elites, the Persian language provided a common lexicon for politics, administration, and law. Persian literati received vast patronage under the Mughals. Persian immigrants became a privileged elite in Mughal ethnic politics; they formed a cultural elite in and around the courts of the emperor and his nobles. Persian poetry and prose filled the Mughal court, petitions, tax accounts, and writing by and for the nobility. A Persian cultural elite developed first in imperial cities – Lahore, Delhi, Agra, Allahabad, and Jaunpore – and then in regional capitals like Lucknow, Dhaka, and Hyderabad. In the northern Mughal domains – from Afghanistan to Bengal – emerging urban vernaculars and literary languages, Urdu and Hindustani, combined elements from Sanskrit, Arabic, Persian, and local dialects. Upward mobility in imperial society came with admixtures of Persian. In urbane Indo-Persian cultural settings, the more Persian one's language, the more elite; the less Persian, the more lower class. Though the Mughal emperors most elaborately patronized Indo-Persian culture, it acquired an independent life.

Indo-Persian cultural forms and vocabularies imbued with Mughal authority spread well beyond the imperial reach in many vernacular forms. One example is the word '*sarkar*', which came to mean 'government' in vernacular speech, and hence became a title, honorific, a place name, and a respectful greeting. As people attached the honorific, '*sarkar*' to personal names and used it to give respect, it came to be part of family identities and hence a family name. Many other official titles also became personal names. Mughal terms thus travelled through imperial society and spread from city to city with Mughal expansion; and then they spread out into society at large with the deepening penetration of military, administrative, and judicial power exerted by local officers whose local status rose when they became imperial appointees.

By 1700, the ideas, rituals, lexicon, and routines for ordering interactions among the leaders of society who sustained Mughal power had informed the creation of new cultural territories. As we see in Chapter 3, regions had different histories, but in all regions touched in any way by Mughal authority – which excludes only Sri Lanka – regional versions of Indo-Persian political culture informed elite activity. The idea that a supreme emperor was an all-powerful authority became very widespread. This idea drew strength from ancient and early medieval ideas about imperial supremacy. The authority of the emperor was therefore not merely coercive; it was moral, aesthetic, legal, and spiritual; so it did not depend on the everyday exertion of physical force. The idea that there exists an all-powerful emperor who validates all the ranks of all the officials who work in his name, and of all the people who receive entitlements from those officials, down to the smallest village, became a pervasive feature of everyday life. Like the Persian language, Indo-Persian political culture was most elaborately developed in the Mughal heartland, in the Indus and Ganga basins.

But it also spread in many vernaculars to the far corners of Mughal expansion and beyond; even eventually to the southernmost tip of the Indian peninsula, where no Mughal emperor ever set foot, and where Mughal authority arrived only in the 1750s with armies dispatched by a governor (Nawab) at Arcot (near Madras) who had never obeyed the dictates of any Mughal emperor.

Indo-Persian political culture underlay the imperial standardization of political order in regions of layered sovereignty. It subordinated all sultans, rajas, communities, and institutions under one supreme *sarkar*, government. This political order made room for everyone; in fact, it demanded that everyone pay something to a *sarkar* official to receive a definite rank. Local tax and tribute payments went up the ranks of imperial society; they constituted the ritual enactment of respect for authority by each individual, who thereby obtained a position of respect. Tax payers paid officials in return for entitlements to land and other assets, including rights to receive payments from others below them in rank. Local communities paid taxes through headmen who obtained official recognition as community leaders by conveying taxes up the ranks. Imperial supremacy thus reinscribed layered sovereignty as every member of imperial society enjoyed a specific rank by paying respect to superiors. Official ranks – each with their own duties, symbols, powers, and responsibilities – collectively defined a normative structure for *sarkar* authority. Everyone in society had a rank, from top to bottom. Payments went up the ranks; entitlements came down. Everyone's official entitlement to land, office, or social status carried the symbolic authority of the emperor. At the apex of authority, the emperor was symbolically responsible for everything and officially authorized all the ranks of those who received payments of respect from inferiors.

The public display of subservience dramatized one's personal rank *below* one's superiors, which in turn gave all the ranks under the emperor superiority over others below them. In this cultural context, the institution of the public *darbar* spread among people of rank at every level. Thus the cultural model of the sultan spread among people at all levels as they aspired to demonstrate the superiority of their personal position in society. Ritualized subordination defined the ranks of authority in layered systems of sovereignty and entitlement. Thus *darbari* culture spread far and wide as every man endowed with a piece of sovereignty held his own *darbar* to receive those below him who came to pay respect and tribute. Elaborate public dramas and literary productions of praise, flattery, and devotion became media for elevating men whose glory secured the authority of subordinates. Conversely, conferring honours on underlings defined sovereignty at every level. Subordinates retained their power by recognizing a superior who conferred honour on those below, in return for ritual recognition and political support. Layers of sovereignty became elaborately graded with Persian bureaucratic formality. Gradations in the imperial ranks became units of measure for social mobility in everyday life. Where a person or group stood in imperial society was marked precisely with symbols and rituals of ranks that became coveted social assets.

FORMING ETHNICITY

Social groups were officially named as collective entities whose representatives received honours, ranks, and entitlements in imperial society. These groups were thus officially inscribed with collective social identities, which attached to all the people in them. Akbar perhaps deserves credit for inventing imperial strategies of ethnic balancing. His minions kept accounts of which groups received which honours and ranks. He was particularly concerned to counter-balance the Turks and Afghans who initially dominated his imperial service, whose ethnic loyalties made them suspect; to off-set their power, he recruited Rajputs, Persians, and Indian Muslims into the nobility. Strategies were also devised for dividing ethnic groups by pitting leaders against one another in competitions for rank, thus to reduce their ability to mobilize warrior clans against imperial armies, as for instance among the armed Paxtun tribes that controlled regions around the Hindu Kush.

The *Padshahnama* shows that among the 443 'intermediate *mansabdars*' – a rank that swelled to include more nobles as the empire expanded – Iranis (Persians) comprised twenty-eight per cent, Turanis (Turks) twenty-three per cent, Rajputs sixteen per cent, Indian Muslims fifteen per cent, Afghans six per cent, and Marathas two per cent. This suggests that about seventy-two per cent were Muslims, strategically divided by ethnicity. At lower imperial ranks, locally dominant caste groups were counter-balanced by foreigners and immigrants when possible; and this was most critical in the Mughal heartland. The *Ain-i-Akbari* shows that ten *pargana*s of *sarkar* Delhi were held respectively by *zamindar*s of different ethnic groups of Muslims and Hindus: Tonwars, Shaiksadahs, Rajputs, Gujars, Jats, Brahmans, Ahirs, and Afghans. Afghans received the greatest proportion of tax-free support for mosques and shrines, indicating their recruitment into the area by Mughal authorities; but locally powerful Rajputs and Jats clearly had the stronger military position, and Rajputs were left in command of two major hill forts, reflecting their independence and loyalty to the emperor.

In local societies, imperial ranks entered older systems of social ranking and inflected their historical development. As we have seen, Hindu societies evolved as upwardly mobile groups used *dharma* to sanctify a ritual ranking of castes (*jati*s) in the *varna* idiom, which put priests and warriors on top and merchants and peasants below. Many different local Hindu ranking systems evolved in dynastic realms where rulers defined *jati* ranks, top down; and expanding agrarian societies filled out the *jati* ranks, bottom up. In Mughal times, social change outstripped the regulatory capacity of Hindu ranking institutions. Various sultans, rajas, and state officials had conferred honours that redefined social ranks outside the ritual complex of Hindu temple life. The *darbar*s of great men competed with temples as ritual sites for acquiring the honours that marked social mobility.

Several long-term trends in effect secularized the ranks of Hindu societies. Social differentiation and assimilation had produced too many roles and ranks for *dharma* to manage. Elite and ordinary weavers, for example, occupied various *varna* ranks. Kayasthas, an elite non-Brahman clerical *jati*, had no clear *varna* status. A huge population of poor, landless workers had fallen out of the bottom of *varna* ranks into a catch-all category of 'outcaste' or 'untouchable'. Many *jati*s – like the large *jati* of palmyra palm tree cultivators called Shanars in the southern Tamil country, whom we will meet again later – lived on the margins of Hindu communities and were not allowed into sacred temple precincts, but they were also essential in everyday economic activity, where they maintained an ambiguous *varna* standing. The majority of

Hindus lived in a world of human interactions that included and surpassed *dharma*. Urbanization and migration allowed new arrivals in many places to claim higher caste rank than they enjoyed at birth. For example, when Saurashtra weavers migrated from Gujarat to Madurai, in the seventeenth century, they claimed to be Brahmans and their claim received support from local rajas. Many revisionist *dharmasastras* rationalized countless post hoc adjustments of caste standing.

Hindu societies also included important non-Hindus, and in the widening expanse of Mughal domains, *varna* became a kind of rule-of-thumb guide to social standing. All the later medieval political regimes were in effect multi-cultural. Rajputs raised their rank by marrying the Mughal nobility and by forming Hindu–Muslim family ties. Shivaji Bhonsle, the founder of a staunchly Hindu Maratha empire – to which we return shortly – launched his career by serving Deccan sultans whose honours enabled him to rise in the ranks. Eighteenth-century Tamil Hindu Nayakas married Sinhala Buddhist kings at Kandy to create a Hindu–Buddhist regime. All the armies in Mughal and post-Mughal times included various cultural groups. Business families engaged in financial dealings across cultural lines that by 1650 delineated many religions and sects of Jains, Bohras, Sunnis, Ahmadiyas, Banias, Khatris, Arabs, Chettiyars, Armenians, Jews, Dutch, English, and others. People shifted among sub-cultural sites with increasing regularity, blurring their boundaries. Christian and Muslim converts typically kept their old *jati* identities. Buddhists in Sri Lanka maintained caste ranks. Tribal groups who became Hindus kept many elements of tribal culture, including marriage practices and rituals.

All the cultural mixing of later medieval centuries made social ranking on strictly Hindu lines part of a larger multi-cultural scene where people attained rank in various ways and *sarkar* became a powerful arbiter of status. At the top and bottom and in the vast middle ranks of Hindu societies, activities that determined social rank crossed cultural boundaries defined by religion; strictly Hindu ranking systems became inadequate to the task of establishing social status even among the most observant Hindus.

In all the regions and vernaculars of Indo-Persian culture, however, wealthy warriors, priests, merchants, and *zamindars* occupied the upper social ranks, regardless of religion. And equally regardless of religion, poor people of all occupations – who numerically were mostly manual workers, nomads, forest dwellers, fisher folk, and such – lived at the bottom ranks. Aspiring peasants, artisans, shopkeepers, and countless others struggled for ranks in between. Individuals acquired social standing by obtaining honours in public rituals. The number of institutions that distributed honours grew, and in regional societies, groups focused their attention on those institutions most important to them locally. Rajas, sultans, priests, gurus, sufis, and monasteries conferred honours. Businesses, farming communities, urban centres, and dynasties offered opportunities for honour. Social groups formed around institutions that defined their internal ranks and connected them to the wider world of ranks.

With increasing commercialism in societies pervaded by warrior power, markets and war were lively sites for upward mobility, and became more so in the eighteenth century, as we shall see shortly. But strategic marriage alliances remained a basic technique for raising one's social standing. Marriages among families involved in the political project of maintaining and improving their social rank created new social groups, which combined attributes of social class and ethnicity. Rajputs provide good examples. When Rajput families allied with Mughals, they entered into an imperial ruling class and also increased their status as leaders of Rajputs. Their Kshatriya aura never lost its *varna* glow, but its social influence increased in proportion to Rajput success in a politics of social mobility that escaped the confines of *varna*. The status of Rajput became that of a regional ruler under Mughal authority and the conduct of *jati* marriages took on implications outside that of *jati* rank in the *varna* scheme.

In regional societies, many *jati* groups blurred into collections of status-marked ethnic groups in Indo-Persian cultural ranks that crossed religious lines. This process marks another feature of the early modernity that emerges under the Mughals. A modern style of government standardization begins with Akbar. The imperial monetary system made Mughal India into a new kind of economic region. The spread of Mughal authority gave India its political identity for the Europeans who operated in world markets for Indian products that integrated India into a global economy that spanned the Atlantic and Pacific. In this perspective, the centuries of Indo-Persian cultural prominence contain both medieval and modern aspects. Textual evidence also indicates a transition to modern forms of social description and social order. Both the *Ain-i-Akbari* and early nineteenth-century English census enumerations list caste (*jati*) groups alongside other groups that are not defined not by *varna* but rather by language, religion, occupation, and native place.

The term '*jati*' came to connote a specifically South Asian style of multi-cultural ethnic identity. The term could denote virtually any type, category, or group of people with similar characteristics who tended to inter-marry, live together, engage in similar customs, worship alike, dress alike, eat similar food, speak alike, and be represented by group leaders. Thus diverse kinds of groups like Iranians, Brahmans, Christians, Armenians, Biharis, and Firangis (Europeans) became *jati*s. The term 'caste' came to mean an ethnic group with a ranked position in social relations. 'Caste' comes from the Portuguese *casta*, which takes no account of *varna* but does encode ranks among status groups. When Akbar engaged in ethnic politics, he explicitly balanced Afghans, Persians, Turks, Rajputs, Indian Muslims, Jats, and other *jati*s, because in his cultural scene any honour bestowed on any individual always carried implications for the entire ethnic group to which that person belonged. In cultural regions of ethnic ranking that emerged from the Mughal empire, regional and local rulers played ethnic politics among 'castes' that included Buddhists, Muslims, Jains, Christians, and other non-Hindus, who did not use *varna* categories, but engaged in similar strategies of social ranking. The similarity of cultural strategies employed by various groups eased social mobility and communication across cultural boundaries inscribed by religion and language. Where Muslims were poor, as were Muslim peasants in rural east Bengal or Muslim workers in Gangetic cities, Muslims ranked low among the local Hindus. Where Muslims were rich and powerful, as were nobles and *zamindar*s in the Mughal heartland, Muslim leaders ranked high in society and received due respect from Hindu elites. As a result of this cultural mixing and diversity, 'caste' became a flexible term with distinct connotations in each of the regions of early modernity.

THREE

Early Modern Regions

The eighteenth century is a bridge to modern times. Some elements that characterize modern social environments appear in Akbar's day, but they multiply and become prominent after Aurangzeb. By 1700, everyday social life had settled into geographical patterns of ethnic association and regional culture that even today influence people's sense of who they are, where they come from, and where they belong. But the regional forms of social identity that typify modern history emerged in the eighteenth century. By 1700, Indo-Persian elites resembled modern officials. The Mughal imperial system of rules, roles, and ranks made government (*sarkar*) more bureaucratic. And yet, in a world of layered sovereignties and shifting alliances, Mughal officials, like their contemporaries and successors, kept personal powers that made government work. They often had their own armies. Personal honour defined their identity. Their s*arkar* retained the ambiance of a sultan's *darbar*, complete with supplicants bowing down. The combination of bureaucracy and *darbar* became part of modern institutional life, and many officials today still live like little sultans.

Sharp discontinuities also separate the eighteenth century from Mughal times, however. Old identities perished to make new ones. The old Indo-Persian elites had come into being inside an ever-expanding empire, and the force behind their imperial identity died with Aurangzeb. Maratha armies reversed Mughal expansion. The loyalty of the nobility wasted away. Rulers in the provinces became independent. Rebels multiplied among *zamin-*

*dar*s and rajas. Layers of empire came unglued. Regional regimes emerged. In the regions, administrative centralization defined the outlines of modern state territories. Indo-Persian imperial identities lingered in memory and longing among ruling elites in regional capitals. By the end of the eighteenth century, the rising power of the British in Calcutta gave the old elites of that city new imperial opportunities.

Geographies of belonging kept changing with the times. In the century after Aurangzeb's death, in 1707, new regional identities came into being. New maps of social experience informed peoples' attachments to cultural territories and ethnic landscapes. At the end of the century, another new empire expanding up the Ganga from Calcutta invented a new spatial orientation for ruling elites in old Mughal domains. In the 1760s, the British East India Company ruled Bengal and Bihar from its capital in Calcutta, under the authority of the Mughal emperor. By 1802 they had conquered Delhi and taken the emperor under their protection.

The British succeeded, where the Mongols had failed, to incorporate South Asia into a world empire. But the British empire in South Asia was also typically South Asian. Like earlier imperial conquerors, the British built on the work of others. They expanded from core regions of economic development. Their military conquered trade routes that fed imperial expansion. Like most old dynasties, they relied on ethnic solidarity in core institutions like the army. They first came to power in regions on peripheries of old empires. They made strategic alliances in areas of contested authority to sustain their expansion. Like older empires, theirs gave rise to an imperial society whose influence became much greater than the empire itself. The British empire also occupied a familiar time span, a bit less than two centuries.

We still live in the wake of British imperial history. Many scholars see it as the prime mover of modernity in South Asia. Like the Maurya, Gupta, and Mughal empires, however, the British empire might also be considered as a part of larger historical transformations, rather than their cause. Establishing a perspective to make that consideration possible is one goal of this chapter. Early modern regional histories indicate that in the eighteenth century, changes that would accumulate to form modern social environments were emerging in South Asia quite independently of

British imperialism. The British in fact depended on regional developments for success in their imperial venture. In this chapter, we begin by exploring some of the ways that history in the eighteenth and early nineteenth century carried the influence of medievalism into modernity; then we trace the process of British imperial expansion, which forced all the regions into a distinctively modern imperial geography.

ETHNIC TERRITORY

By the eighteenth century, social identities that were expressed in overlapping ethnic idioms of religion, language, caste, class, and occupation were typically attached to geographical places – villages, towns, and regions – that were separated from one another and ranked in relation to one another. Residential segregation was the norm for ethnic groups. Within regions, groups that made competing claims to the same social rank typically occupied different places; they separated territories from one another in the manner of dynastic lineages. Competing business groups concentrated in their own market towns and bazaars; European merchants did this in the same way as Arab, Bohra, Balija, and Chettiyar merchants. Dominant landed castes controlled distinctive territories: Jat, Rajput, Bhumihar, Kunbi, Vellala, Velama, Reddy, Kapu, Kamma, Nayar, Marava, and countless others. Sectarian religious groups were often concentrated in particular territories.

Inside territories, ranked divisions among segregated groups held each in a proper place. The *darbar* was a dramatic site for ranking people-in-place, because all individuals in the *darbar* occupied their proper places in rituals that marked their respective rank. In towns and villages, groups of different rank typically lived in separate quarters. This segregation encouraged group solidarity and reinforced group identity. It gave new migrants to any place a clear sense of where they belonged and provided immediate access to social support networks. It also discouraged mingling, inter-marriage, and inter-dining with people deemed unsuitable. It facilitated policing of group divisions. It gave each group their own ritual space, unpolluted by others; and it made the exclusion of low ranking people from the otherwise open public places that belonged to elites – most critically, temples – a natural feature of social environments.

As places were identified with groups that occupied and controlled them, and as groups were represented to *sarkar* (government authority) by group leaders in the ranks of layered sovereignty, geographical areas assumed the character of ethnic territories, large and small. Territory became ethnically identified through traditions of group rank, power, and ritual activity as people identified increasingly with territories that became literally their 'home' lands.

Regions with distinct territorial traditions of group identity also had their own languages, literatures, popular cultures, and pilgrimage sites, as well as histories of dynastic authority, like Tamil Nadu, which we considered briefly above. Many cultural regions evolved in later medieval centuries around urban centres and networks. In the fourteenth century, Warangal, Golkonda, and Vijayanagar defined an 'Andhra *desa*' that included both the coast and interior, an emerging 'Telugu country'. In the west, it bordered an evolving Marathi linguistic and cultural area, which was centred first at Devagiri and then at Ahmadnagar, Aurangabad, Junnar, and Pune. Telugu, Marathi, and Tamil regions all bordered a Kannada region that began to emerge when Hoysalas built their capital at Dvarasamudra, named for its irrigation tank (*samudra* in Sanskrit) and poised above the Mysore plateau in the upper Kaveri basin. In Mughal times, Dhaka and Chittagong became urban centres on the eastern frontiers of an expanding Bengali language region.

Bundelkhand is a good example of a region defined by constituent ethnicities. It stretched from Malwa and the eastern edge of Rajasthan across the hilly uplands south of the Ganga plains. Senior Rajput lineages had begun conquering these parts by the tenth century; they became regional rajas who flourished under the Mughals; and they were still expanding eastward in the early nineteenth century, driven in part by Marathas in Malwa, as we will see. Beneath senior Rajput ranks, lesser lineage brethren called *thakur*s formed ranks of *zamindar*s. Each lineage ruled over a specific local community composed of major subordinate farming castes: Lodis, Kurmis, Kachhis, Ahirs, and Gujars. Among these farming castes, Kurmis rose up in the political ranks, but Ahir families also formed family ties with Rajputs and enjoyed special patronage as a result. Individual villages were composed of several settlement clusters that were linked to one another across Bundelk-hand by inter-marriage, by land ownership, and by labour migration. Under the Mughals, Bundelkhand became a region that was named after and identified politically with the dominance of its ruling Bundela Rajputs. As senior lineages and larger, wealthier Rajput clans settled on the eastern frontier, the independence of subordinate thakurs increased in older western regions of Rajput colonization. Thus, though Bundelkhand was unified by Rajputs under Mughal authority, it was also partitioned horizontally among competing Rajput clans and vertically among groups inside localities. After Aurangzeb's death, in 1707, Bundela Rajputs renounced the Mughals and fought against subordination by Maratha armies marching north from Maharashtra and by British armies marching west from Bengal. In 1857, many Bundelas rebelled against the British, but Rajputs in the east had little influence on the loyalties of Rajputs in western districts near Malwa.

In many regions, ethnic territories formed in Mughal times became politically prominent when the Mughal imperial umbrella collapsed. We will look at the political histories involved in more detail below. In some regions, like Bundelkhand, a single dominant ethnic group spread across diverse localities and became supreme. In the Ganga lowlands, from Awadh to Bihar, combinations of Muslims, Brahmans, Bhumihars, Rajputs, Kayasthas, and Banias comprised a multi-caste *zamindar* ruling class under which farming castes – mostly Ahirs, Kurmis, and Koeris – ruled over landless workers like Chamars and Bhuinyas. Many dominant castes formed regional ethnic mini-polities, as in the central mountains, where the emulation of Rajputs by tribal warrior chiefs produced many ethnic kingdoms. In the Tamil country also, Kallars, Nayakas and Maravars formed compact caste polities, each with their own king. Mughals and their successors typically confirmed and enhanced these ethnic polities by endowing their rulers with authority. As it had been for Akbar, the ethnicity of territory remained a basic feature of politics as the Mughal empire crumbled.

At the low end of the social ranks, exclusion, marginality, and poverty attached to people and places that were identified with one another. Excluding outsiders and low people from sacred precincts maintained ritual purity. As we have seen earlier, aspiring *bhakti* poets had often struggled against exclusion to reach god. Low status, poor people worshipped at their own separate temples, while exalted gods in beautiful temples received lavish presents from the rich and powerful. For example, Shanars who tapped palmyra palms near the tip of the peninsula were excluded from high caste villages, so they settled outside on poor land to grow palmyras and millet, the poor people's grain, in dry, sandy soil. Ahirs were excluded from Rajput villages in Bundelkhand and lived in their own villages along rivers and in ravines, where forests gave them access to land for farming and grazing. Meanwhile, the dominance of the dominant caste was expressed in the richness of their farms. The lowliest landless workers were untouchable low castes who worked for landed families but moved to and from their fields and their separate, defined settlements at a respectful distance, lest they pollute their betters by their physical proximity.

FAMILY AND PATRIARCHY

Families created ethnic territory in its most intimate personal form. Families built dynasties and empires. Families made sultans great. Families passed rights and entitlements down the genera- tions. Kin groups joined together to clear land, build fields, dig wells, cultivate, and make war. Settlements and communities formed around collections of kin. Marriage networks connected villages, towns, and regions. In villages and empires alike, family suffused all the institutions of entitlement. On the Tamil coast, for instance, the word *pangu*, meaning 'share', came to refer both to an individual's share in family property and to a family's share of village assets, so that *pangali* referred to relatives and also to share- holding landed gentry families in a farming community. The term *kulam* likewise referred to a household, lineage, clan, and local caste group (*jati*); and *nadu* meant an agrarian space (as opposed to *kadu*, forest) defined by its prominent leaders (*nattar*).

Patriarchs became lynchpins of group identity who mediated transactions among identity groups of all kinds. Clan heads among tribal groups, merchant guild leaders, caste headmen, nomadic chiefs, and warriors from virtually any background could ally with one another through the mutual recognition of their respective patriarchal powers. Heads of households and heads of state could negotiate as patriarchs because they could rely on one another to command labour and allegiance, assets and loyalty from their kinfolk. Patriarchy sustained trust, confidence, and stability in transactions that relied upon personal promises and pledges, whether for loans, contracts, or taxes paid in return for entitlements to land. Patrimonial entitlements defined property rights. Rulers and financiers took payments of taxes and tribute that constituted ranks of patriarchal entitlement. Family heads thus held property under state protection. Rituals of taxation, *dharma*, *darbar*, markets, and conquest all established patriarchal patrimony. Genealogies that began with founding patriarchs produced legitimate authority for the headmen of prominent families, community leaders, village elders, and family heads.

The rise of the warriors accentuated the power of patriarchs. Ghaznavids, Ghurids, Khaljis, Tughluqs, Yadavas, Calukyas, Paramaras, Sisodiyas, and many other warrior groups had much in common in this respect. They rallied around family and made alliances by marriage. They conquered farming groups to rule and protect them. They lived in fortress towns and formed an elite strata ranked above farmers. They formed alliances among families, lineages, and clans. Their families followed strategies of political hypergamy in which daughters married up and sons married down the ranks. Subalterns among warrior clans were junior patriarchs in the ranks of lineages and dynasties. A son born to a lineage inherited a family position that provided a specific set of options for the ranking of his own family. Alliances gave subaltern families leverage in struggles to maintain and to improve their position. Becoming a subordinate ruler raised a subordinate family's rank in relation to peers and competitors. Accumulating subordinate patriarchs under one's own authority defined a king and an emperor.

Among the great warrior clans, families married their daughters up the ranks to express the father's subordination and pursuit of upward mobility; and they married their sons down the ranks to express the father's superiority and acquisition of subordinate allies. Polygamy further expanded the possibilities of subordinate alliance building, as women became hostages to fortune and some became the mothers of kings. In these settings, *pardah* and *sati* became auspicious expressions of female purity, piety, devotion, and heroism. Strength and sacrifice sustained one another. In the political institutions formed by competitive alliances among warrior patriarchs, subordination was a moment of power in which all alliances were built upon measurable inequalities of rank. Dominance rested upon extensive alliances with subalterns whose movement up the ranks often meant challenging superiors in war. War and marriage, militarism and family ties, rank and alliance, negotiation and resistance – all together formed patriarchal power in the warrior clans.

When Rajputs and Mughals married, they wedded two traditions of patriarchal power with commonalities that formed a coherent logic of ranking, competition, and alliance. Mughals became apical agents and icons of ranking for all patriarchs below. In Indo-Persian culture, mosque, temple, or church could mark communities of sentiment; sacred genealogies could be reckoned from Rome, Palestine, Arabia, or Aryavarta; because Mughal institutions of patriarchal power – within which patriarchs ranked one another and held patrimonial entitlements – superseded and encompassed the ideology of *dharma*. No religion constrained a sultan's power to confer rank on subordinates. A sultan's status arose from rituals of conquest and entitlement whose authority went back to the days of the Gurjara-Pratiharas; and eventually, as we shall soon see, officers of the British East India Company became imperial Christian sultans.

Thus the increasing number of Muslims in positions of dynastic power in South Asia should never be conflated historically with the expansion of Islam, for at its culmination the Indo-Persian imperial system set itself apart from all its predecessors by making rituals and conditions of patriarchal entitlement more agnostic than ever before. Imperial entitlements and modes of patriarchal ranking entered family strategies of marriage alliance and influenced kin-group formation at many levels of society. Patrimonial entitlements came to rest on personal recognition by a superior patriarch under the authority of the emperor. In families, occupational groups, sectarian organizations, and caste and tribal societies, an officially recognized headman had to attain his status – at a price – in rituals of state. The courtly *darbar* became the stage for dramas that defined the ranks of all the patriarchs. Superiors granted honours, titles, and entitlements to those below. Inferiors paid tribute, taxes, service, and allegiance to those above. At the lowest echelons, peasant patriarchs paid for titles to land and for authority over landless workers.

Thanks in part to Akbar's political strategies, great patriarchs among ethnic groups achieved more political prominence. As we will see in more detail below, rustic patriarchs rose to become dynastic contenders. Emerging group identities based on language, religion, and region informed new dynastic projects among Rajputs, Marathas, Jats, Rohillas, Durranis, Paxtuns, Baluchis, Sikhs, and, at lower registers, among Maravas and Kallars. Shivaji was the most successful upstart warrior of the seventeenth century. A tenacious Mughal adversary, he built a kingdom, spawned an empire, and became a legendary icon for regional ethnic solidarity in the modern state of Maharashtra. In the 1670s, he founded a Maratha kingdom along the base of the Western Ghats, beginning with a small revenue territory, a *jagir*, inherited from his father, who obtained it by serving the Ahmadnagar sultan. Shivaji continued his father's project of constructing a multi-caste Maratha fighting force of warriors and farmers. His military victories enabled him to acquire official honours, titles, and assignments of tax revenue from other Deccan sultans. His armies fought Mughals with swift cavalry attacks and when pursued, fled to home villages in the mountains. Thus a patriotic guerrilla ethos suffused early Maratha struggles that at the same time defined a distinctly Maratha ethnic territory. Over generations, during a long process of competitive alliance building, conquest, and institution building, warrior Maratha patriarchs became deeply involved in the enforcement of Maratha *dharma*, including codes of family rank and female behaviour. Marathas built their territorial identity in alliance with Brahman traditionalists who became increasingly powerful in Maratha domains, and by the eighteenth century, as Maratha power expanded after Aurangzeb's death, Maratha mythology made Shivaji the perfect Hindu ruler. In retrospect, however, we can see that Muslim sultans and Mughal ranks nurtured Maratha leadership; and that Shivaji became a semi-deified patriarchal icon around which a new Maratha collective identity was formed that combined ethnicity, language, and religion.

By the eighteenth century, regional differences had evolved in the family systems within which patriarchy operated in everyday life. These regional patterns are still visible today. In regions where societies were not as significantly shaped by great warrior lineages – that is, on the margins of Mughal power, in the north-east mountains, southern peninsula, Sri Lanka, and Nepal – marriage customs tend to elaborate local family ties, enhancing local ethnic identities. Women typically marry inside or near their natal village. Marriage to kin is preferred. Female seclusion (*pardah*) is not common, and as a result, rates of female participation in higher education and the workforce today are relatively high. Women commonly work in public, in fields, in shops, and in offices; and unmarried women often walk the streets and use public transportation alone or with friends, both male and female. By contrast, in regions ruled by the great warrior clans – that is, in the heartlands of Mughal power across Afghanistan, Pakistan, Punjab, Rajasthan, Uttar Pradesh, Bihar, and east to Bangladesh – extensive marriage practices prevail. The regional rank of families is critical. Marriage is normally forbidden within villages and to close kin. Families prefer women to marry at some distance from the natal village, particularly into high status families. *Pardah* is widely practised, and as a result women's participation in education and the labour force is low. A woman's place is definitely at home, where her virtue is family honour. It is less common to see women working in public or travelling without male kin. In between these extremes, societies in the central mountain regions, Maharashtra, and in West Bengal mix village endogamy, close-kin marriage, and *pardah* to varying degrees.

INVERTING THE MAP

Home may be the centre of the world for families everywhere, but only families in the Ganga basin imagine themselves in the centre of South Asia. Like the power of patriarchs, the idea that South Asia has a cultural heartland needs to be unpacked historically. In Chapters 1 and 2, we saw that *Aryavarta* and *Bharat* were homelands for elites who broadcast their ideas in Puranas; and that the Ganga basin was actually only one of four ancient imperial regions, the others lying in present-day Central Asia,

Rajasthan, and Maharashtra. We saw that the Turks and Afghans followed the tracks of ancient Kushanas when they conquered three ancient imperial regions during the medieval transition; and that conquests of one region by people from another provoked literary images of *Kali Yuga* and Islamic victory. Now we can better appreciate that when Aurangzeb died, the Deccan remained an unconquerable frontier for Gangetic imperialists, though many cultural elements, like literature and marriage customs, moved easily across borders that warriors could not erase. Maurya, Gupta, and Mughal imperial societies all spread from north to south, from lowlands into mountains, and from the Ganga plains into Bengal and Assam. Indo-Persian elites composed imperial cultures in Sanskrit and Persian. This mixture of languages spread among diverse dialects across northern river basins, across Punjab, south into Rajput territory, east wherever Rajputs conquered, and up into the mountains all around; its vernaculars became Hindi and Urdu. The literary cultures of all the imperial societies saw their own heartland as the centre of civilization and history. External regions are, for imperial elites, peripheries.

The repeated overlapping of imperial capitals on land between Delhi and Patna produced a strong sense of geographical identity among pre-modern elites writing in Sanskrit and Persian. In Chapter 4, we will see how this same geographical identity became modern as nineteenth-century intellectuals defined what it meant to be Indian. The ocean marked the outer limits of this identity. Thus Europeans' overseas origins particularly marked them as aliens, even more clearly than their Christianity, which was variously relevant for Hindus and Muslims. For Sanskrit and Persian elite cultures alike, the sea was foreign territory. Elite Hindus avoided pollution that came with sailing 'dark waters' (*kala pani*) of the sea (a phrase that resonates with ancient Greek). Sultans never had navies. Ocean crossing was for merchants who lived under Indo-Persian imperial authority and for pious Muslims on pilgrimage to Mecca.

In a landlocked Indo-Persian view of the world, the fact that British power began on the coast and travelled inland from Calcutta, Bombay, Madras, and Colombo represents the essentially alien character of British rule in South Asia. But historical geography reveals another reality. Maurya imperialism expanded from a core region in the eastern Ganga basin; the Guptas expanded their core to include regions further west; and expansive early medieval dynasties inside the Indo-Gangetic basin expanded from regions still further west. This indicates that long before 1000 CE imperial aspirations projected themselves outward from various places that were united by empire. In ancient and medieval times, empires that began in other imperial regions re-united the Ganga basin and redefined it as an imperial heartland. The British did the same in the nineteenth century, and in a great symbolic act of imperial continuity, moved their capital to New Delhi in 1911. So once again, a South Asian empire reinscribed the Indo-Persian heartland with imperial supremacy, more indeed than any previous empire; and in this respect – among others, as we will see – British India was a most Indian empire.

In the eighteenth century, this modern outcome was anything but inevitable. Regional rulers established strong independent positions for themselves in the wake of Mughal decline. Imperial Maharashtra was more powerful than ever under Maratha commanders who conquered north into Punjab, south into Tamil Nadu, and east into Orissa and Bengal. As in medieval centuries, new ruling powers emerged in strategic places where their military force drew upon and often reinforced economic expansion. Eighteenth-century regional economies revolved around urban centres that flourished under the Mughals, where Indo-Persian elites were often prominent: Dhaka, Calcutta, Lucknow, Delhi, Agra, Lahore, Multan, Surat, Ahmedabad, Bombay, Pune, Bangalore, Hyderabad, Madras, Cochin, and Trivandrum. The most expansive regional economies generated wealth at the intersection of inland and overseas trade. Strategic access to the sea became a predominant source of political strength.

The eighteenth century inverted the Indo-Persian map of cultural order. New empires attacked Delhi from Afghanistan, Iran, Maharashtra, and Bengal. Regional kings in Punjab and tribal chiefs in the hills expanded into old imperial territories and expelled the nobility. Foreigners were everywhere. This explains why the time between end of Mughal supremacy and the rise of British imperial society was understood by historians until quite recently as a time of chaos and decline. Because for the Indo-Persian elites whose ideas informed modern historical writing, cultural degradation, economic upheaval, and political turmoil were rampant. This was another *Kali Yuga*, an age of chaos.

Inside new regimes that arose in the eighteenth century, this same time looked quite different. It was an age of florescence for innovative elites in Punjab, Afghanistan, Nepal, Maharashtra, Assam, Andhra Pradesh, Karnataka, Kerala, Bengal, Gujarat, Tamil Nadu, and elsewhere. Coastal regions achieved unprecedented political importance. Societies along the coast had always embraced the sea and now they included more overseas migrants and more mixed populations than ever. The market value of coastal trade, overseas trade, agricultural output, and manufactures increased dramatically. By 1750, most cotton cloth in world markets came from ports in Gujarat, Maharashtra, Bengal, and the Carnatic (the south-east peninsula). Merchants, weavers, and rulers who depended upon and fostered the wealth of coastal regions became politically powerful. It was an age of creative regionalism within a new world economy that formed the first phase of modern globalization.

EIGHTEENTH-CENTURY TERRITORIALISM

Aurangzeb died fighting Marathas, and after his death his empire weakened with every year. One by one, Mughal subahs became independent and regional elites built new states using technologies, ideas, and personnel that were circulating in the eighteenth-century world economy. In their growing capital cities, regional rulers increased taxation, government wealth, and thus incentives for political activism. Authors wrote more literature in regional languages. Cults, sects, pilgrimage centres, and cultural activism bolstered assertive regional identities. Most new state elites pursued aggressive policies of administrative centralization. Political transactions became more intensely embroiled in commodity and financial markets. In Bengal, Gujarat, Punjab, the Carnatic, Sri Lanka, Maharashtra, and the Ganga basin, businessmen invested in trade and politics simultaneously. Politics merged with business. Warriors sold services to rulers who fought for taxes transmitted to treasuries by financial speculators who commanded armies of their own. Official profiteering became customary. The century after Aurangzeb's death was the heyday of entrepreneurial warriors and

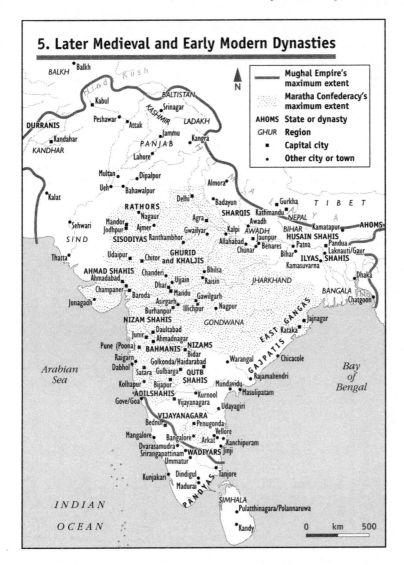

5. Later Medieval and Early Modern Dynasties

———	Mughal Empire's maximum extent
(dotted)	Maratha Confederacy's maximum extent
AHOMS	State or dynasty
GHUR	Region
■	Capital city
•	Other city or town

BALKH • Balkh

Hindu Küsh

Kabul •

BALTISTAN

Peshawar • Srinagar
KASHMIR
DURRANIS   Attak •   LADAKH
• Kandahar   Jammu •   Kangra •
KANDHAR   PANJAB
Lahore •

Multan ■   • Dipalpur   Almora •
Ueh •   Bahawalpur •   Delhi ■   • Badayun   • Gurkha   TIBET
• Kalat   RATHORS   SHARQIS   Kathmandu ■   NEPAL   Y   A
• Nagaur   Agra ■   Awadh   BIHAR   Kamatapur   AHOMS
• Sehwari   Mandor   Ajmer •   Gwaliyar ■   • Kalpi   AWADH   HUSAIN SHAHIS
SIND   Jodhpur ■   SISODIYAS   Ranthambhor   Allahabad ■ • Jaunpur   Bihar ■ • Patna   • Pandua
ILYAS SHAHIS
Udaipur •   • Chitor   GHURID   Chunar ■   • Benares   Bihar ■   Laknauti/Gaur
Thatta •   and KHALJIS   Kamasuvarna
AHMAD SHAHIS   Chanderi •   • Bhilsa   JHARKHAND   Dhaka •
Ahmadabad ■   Dhar •   Ujjain   • Raisin
Champaner ■   Baroda •   Mandu ■   Gawilgarh •   BANGALA   • Chatgoon
Junagadh •   Asirgarh •   Illichpur •   Nagpur •
Burhanpur •   GONDWANA   EAST GANGAS   • Jajnagar
NIZAM SHAHIS
Junir ■   Daultabad ■   Kataka ■
Pune (Poona) ■   Ahmadnagar ■   NIZAMS
Raigarh •   BAHMANIS ■   Bidar ■   GAJPATIS   Chicacole •
Dabhol •   Golkonda/Haidarabad ■   Warangal •
Satara •   Gulbarga ■   QUTB   Rajamahendri •
Kolhapur •   Bijapur ■   SHAHIS   Mundavidu •   • Masulipatam
ADILSHAHIS   • Kurnool
Gove/Goa •   • Vijayanagara   Udayagiri •
VIJAYANAGARA
Bednur •   • Penugonda
Mangalore •   Bangalore •   • Vellore
Dvarasamudra •   Arkat •   • Kanchipuram
Srirangapattinam •   WADIYARS   Jinji •
Ummatur •
Kunjakari •   Dindigul •   Tanjore •
Madurai •
PANDYAS
SIMHALA
• Pulatthinagara/Polannaruwa
• Kandy

Arabian Sea

Bay of Bengal

INDIAN OCEAN

0   km   500

adventurer financiers. Armies were rampant. Military employment boomed. Social mobility accelerated for people who could grab land and new opportunities. Struggles for territory settled into civil routines for a few decades, here and there, but rampant armed conflict signalled countless challenges to any status quo.

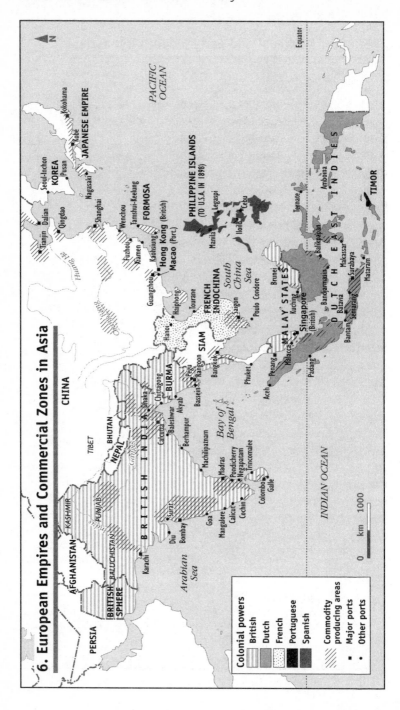

6. Europe an Empires and Commercial Zones in Asia

TABLE 3. A CHRONOLOGICAL FRAMEWORK FOR THE EIGHTEENTH CENTURY

I. Mughal disintegration and regional dynasties

1704	Bengal	Murshid Quli Khan Nawab, 1704–1725. Murshidabad, 1706.
1707	Mughals	Aurangzeb dies in the Deccan.
1708	Rajputs	Independent of Mughals.
1709	Afghanistan	Nadir Shah and Ahmad Khan Abdali conquer Herat, Kabul, Punjab.
1713	Hyderabad	Nizam Asaf Jah independent of Mughals.
1714	Agra	Jats begin building state.
1720	Assam	Ahoms expand along Brahmaputra and into the southern mountains.
1724	Hyderabad	Asaf Jah conquers Khandesh and Berar.
1725	Marathas	Mughals concede right to taxes in Gujarat.
1730	Bhutan	Vassal of Tibet and China; becomes independent.
1733	Bengal	Independent from Mughals.

II. Maratha and Durrani expansion

1740	Tamil Nadu	Arcot Nawab under Nizam. Maratha invasions.
1740	Travancore	Martanda Varma begins unification.
1742	Marathas	Bhonsles control Nagpur and Chhattisgarh.
1745	Marathas	Raid Bengal 1742–51.
1746	Marathas	Malwa ceded by Mughals in 1738; confirmed 1746.
1747	Afghanistan	United by Ahmad Khan Abdali under Durrani dynasty.
1747	Mughals	Durranis conquer Delhi. Mughals under Awadh protectorship.
1752	Marathas	Conquer Orissa.
1752	Punjab	Afghan province.
1757	Marathas	Occupy Ahmadabad; end Mughal rule in Gujarat.
1761	Marathas	Defeated at Panipat by Durranis. End of imperial phase.

III. Regional reorientations

1744	Tamil Nadu	War of Austrian Succession brings battles between French and British.
1753	Andhra	Coastal region ceded to French, then to British in 1766.

TABLE 3. *CONTINUED*

III. *Regional reorientations* continued

1757	Bengal	Company becomes *zamindar* of 24 *parganas* after victory at Plassey.
1763	Agra	Jats fall to Marathas and then British.
1763	Mysore	Haider Ali coup. Expansion under his son, Tipu Sultan.
1765	Bengal	British Nawabi of Bengal and Bihar.
1765	Nepal	Company force expelled from Terai by Gurkhas.
1766	Sri Lanka	Dutch wars with Kandy from 1736 extend territory all around the coast.
1766	Hyderabad	Coast ceded to British as Northern Circars, Madras Presidency.
1768	Nepal	Gurkhas conquer Kathmandu valley under Prithvi Naryan Shah.
1770	Bengal	Famine kills huge population under East India Company rule.

IV. *British expansion*

1772	Rohillas	Independent until 1792, then protectorate of Awadh.
1773	Awadh	Native state under British.
1773	Cooch Behar	Native state under British.
1790	Nepal	Gurkhas conquer Garhwal and Kumaun; ceded to British in 1815.
1791	Cochin	Native state under British.
1792	Nepal	Commercial treaty with British.
1792	Malabar	Ceded with Kanara to British by Tipu Sultan.
1793	Bengal	Permanent settlement, Lord Cornwallis.
1793	Laccadives	Conquered by British.
1794	Benares	Conquered by British.
1795	Travancore	Native state under British.
1796	Sri Lanka	British conquer Dutch.
1798	Hyderabad	Native state under British.
1798	Orissa	Native state of Jeypore under British.
1798	Punjab	Ranjit Singh appointed Afghan governor; forges Sikh kingdom.
1799	Mysore	British conquer Tipu Sultan. Make Udaiyars native state rulers.
1799	Mysore	Substantial territory ceded to Madras Presidency.

Marathas

The Mughals had conquered three of the four old regions of imperial expansion: Afghanistan, Rajasthan, and the Ganga plains. The Deccan eluded them, as it had the Guptas, Gurjara-Pratiharas, and Delhi Sultans. The Marathas did not join Mughal imperial society in the manner of the Rajputs, Turks, Afghans, and Persians, although Mughal institutions spread across the Deccan. Maratha warriors simultaneously participated in and rejected the Mughal imperial system. They came from peasant stock and from pastoral clans recruited by Deccan sultans to balance the influence of Muslim ethnic groups. Marathas came from a Marathi-speaking countryside where Vaishnava peasants and *bhakti* poet saints alike resented the fact that Mughal nobles patronized non-Marathi Muslim urban elite allies more than temples, Brahmans, and pilgrimage centres.

Under the Mughal imperial umbrella, however, Maharashtra's agrarian economy was expanding along trade running north, south, and overseas. Village farming elites prospered as cotton that thrived in black volcanic soil flowed into weaving centres that fed textile markets inland and overseas. Commercial agriculture sustained Maratha warrior-peasant chiefs, *deshmukh*s, who expanded their local power by capturing groups of villages that numbered between a few dozen and one hundred or so. On this agrarian political base, they raised funds and arms for war.

Shivaji and his successors developed a distinctive style of Maratha warfare using small bands of swift horsemen. Their armies resembled those of the Afghan warriors who also often defeated Mughal armies that lumbered across the countryside like cities on the move from one fort to another. Shahuji, the grandson of Shambuji, Shivaji's successor, led Maratha armies in all directions during his forty-year reign, from 1708 to 1749; he supervised the invention of Maratha imperial society.

The Maratha polity had six features that epitomize trends in other-eighteenth century regimes.

1. Maratha military force emerged from an armed peasantry whose local power resisted centralized authority. *Deshmukh*s often changed sides in battles between Mughals and Marathas

to seek their own advantage, showing the primacy of local loyalties.

2. Maratha expansion provided many routes of social mobility, not only for fighting peasants. Brahmans filled Maratha posts, led armies, and became politically powerful, especially one Brahman lineage that formed an ethnic elite, the Chitpavans. During Shahuji's reign, the post of Peshwa inside the fiscal administration became a Chitpavan monopoly and became all-powerful. After Shahu's death, the Peshwa Balaji Bajirao formed his own Maratha dynasty.

3. Brahman power increased with the size of Maratha armies, the scale of Maratha dominion, the value of Maratha revenues, and the reach of Maratha administration. Carefully graded ranks of accountants, financiers, and record keepers, almost all Brahmans, composed a vast archive of manuscript correspondence penned on paper in a cursive scribal script called Modi, which circulated among officers in villages, towns, and the capital, Pune. These documents record an intricate system of local controls and regional finance, monitored by Peshwas.

4. Peshwa administration came much closer to being a bureaucracy than did the Mughals'. Many of its technical innovations were later adapted by the British, including methods of tax assessment, accounting, census taking, and legal regulation.

5. Maratha administration also included social controls at the village level, where state officials who served as local judges enforced caste hierarchies and patriarchal authority. Elite local Brahmans and high caste landowners sustained a state that punished challenges to their authority.

6. The Maratha empire spread across Rajasthan, central India, and beyond, but it always remained firmly rooted in its Maratha homeland. Maratha ethnic patriotism made Maratha imperialism culturally parochial.

Maratha political culture stood in sharp opposition to the Rajputs, which helps to explain its rejection of Mughal supremacy. Like Rajputs, Shivaji and his father had served Muslim sultans. Like Rajputs, Marathas were staunchly Hindu and could raise Hindu animosities against Muslim enemies. But territorial ambitions among Rajputs and Marathas always opposed one another on the southern frontier of Rajput and Mughal expansion. Maratha *dharma* resisted Rajput *dharma*. Rajput clans thrived by conquering farming communities; they looked down on farmers, as did their peers among the Mughal nobility. Their extravagant consumption, urbane living, rituals of rank, and patriarchal grandeur formed a cultural model for eighteenth-century rulers that Marathas rejected. Marathas came from lower echelons of imperial society, from dominant farming and agro-pastoral communities that sustained rustic Deccan warrior lineages from ancient times.

In this respect, Marathas resemble Jats, who also formed military units under the Mughals, conquered widely in the wake of Aurangzeb's death, ousted noble overlords (often Rajputs), and formed a new ruling class in a new homeland that they invented in the process of their political ascendancy. Like Marathas, Jats combined expansive regional state-building with deepening ethnic dominance in farming communities, and with expanding local control among dominant agrarian patriarchs over farm land, forests, and landless workers.

Jats

Jats are a huge, diverse ethnic group spread all across the western plains and Punjab. Today, Jats are about twenty per cent of the population in Punjab; about ten per cent in Baluchistan, Rajasthan, and around Delhi; and about three per cent in Sind and Uttar Pradesh. In Mughal times, most Jats in the Indus basin became Muslims. To the east, in Punjab, a new devotional sect (*panth*) developed, led by Guru Nanak (1469–1538), who preached a new path to enlightenment for people he called Sikhs, 'learners'. Guru Nanak said, 'There is no Hindu and no Muslim.' By this he meant that neither designation pertained among true learners of the path to god, Sikhs. With this in view, scholars often say that Sikhism combined Hindu *bhakti* and Muslim *sufi* traditions, for, like these, it elevated sacred individuals whose divine words comprise sacred texts. But Guru Nanak's vision was also unique. It was firmly attached to the language and culture of agrarian Punjab.

Nine Gurus succeeded Guru Nanak before conflict with Mughals led to the execution of two Gurus. In the wake of their deaths, in 1699, as Aurangzeb fought Marathas, Gobind Rai founded the *khalsa*, an armed community whose men took the surname Singh ('lion') and women took the surname Kaur ('lioness'). Gobind Singh declared himself the last Guru and made the *khalsa* a leading Sikh institution. His armies were chased out of Punjab, but after he died in exile in Maharashtra, in 1708, his successor, Banda Singh, led the *khalsa* into full-scale military competition with all his rivals for control of Punjab.

In the decades that followed, Punjab became a battlefield for armies from the west, south, and east. In Afghanistan, Ahmad Shah Durrani, born in Multan, in 1722, built a new Afghan dynasty on the rubble of Mughal power. His armies conquered from the Amu Darya to the Indian Ocean and from Khorasan across Kashmir, Punjab, and Sind. In 1757, he plundered Delhi, Agra, and Mathura, and married a daughter of the Mughal Muhammad Shah. His son, Timur, became Viceroy in Punjab and married the daughter of the Mughal Alamgir II. Timur was driven out of Punjab in the next year by Sikhs, Mughals, and Marathas. But in 1759 and 1761, Ahmad Shah expelled the Marathas from Punjab and demolished a Maratha army at Panipat, near Delhi. Sikh armies organized as clan sectarian groups, called *misl*s, collected protection money and taxes to fight Afghan rule; they took Punjab from Ahmad Shah in the 1760s.

The future founder of a Sikh kingdom, Ranjit Singh, was born in 1780, in a Punjab where Afghans again held sway against competitive Sikh *misl*s. He became chief of the Sukerchakia clan; inherited control of Gujranwala; made two strategic marriage alliances; became the leader of a Sikh clan confederacy; and finally seized Lahore, the old Mughal capital, in 1799. He did all this before he was twenty! The Afghan Shah Zaman appointed him governor of Lahore and, in 1801, Ranjit Singh proclaimed himself *maharaja* of the Punjab. He minted coins bearing the image of Sikh Gurus and captured Amritsar, a major commercial centre and sacred Sikh city. To build his kingdom, he dispatched armies that included Sikhs, Muslims, and Hindus, mostly Jats, to subdue Sikh *misl*s and Paxtun warrior clans across Punjab and to conquer adjacent mountain regions, including Kashmir.

South of Punjab, Hindu Jats around Agra and Mathura carved out new territories for themselves around village strongholds. Their eighteenth-century regime expanded well beyond what became the Jat princely state of Bharatpur under British rule. Rajput clans had long controlled this region. Jat armies ousted the Mughals in 1722, when Bharatpur became independent; its most ambitious ruler, Suraj Mal, plundered Delhi in 1753 and seized Agra in 1761. Jat power in this and surrounding regions remained ensconced in fortified village settlements where warrior peasants defended their independence well into the nineteenth century.

Rajputs

Marathas, Afghans, Sikhs, and Jats pushed the great Rajput clans back into Rajasthan, where they consolidated their power around their respective fortified capital cities. A Maratha Scindia dynasty conquered the old Rajput region of Malwa. Here and elsewhere in regions of Rajput warrior settlement – in Bundelkhand, Himalayan valleys, and localities across the Ganga basin – Rajputs remained local lords ruling domains varying in size from one to several hundred farming villages.

Bengal

From Delhi east across the densely populated regions of the Ganga and Brahmaputra lowlands, there were no rustic clans of warriors to dismantle Mughal imperial society, as they did in dry lands west, north-west, and south of the Mughal heartland. Rather, as Mughal power declined, old nobles and aspiring Indo-Persian elites used their attachments to Mughal authority to build new regional states. In the process, *mansabdars*, *zamindars*, and *rajas* as well as many upstarts engaged in shifting alliances and competitions. Lucknow, Benares, and Murshidabad became the major capitals for new political systems that emerged, after Aurangzeb's death, in the Awadh region of the Ganga-Yamuna Doab, in the eastern Ganga valley, and in Bengal, respectively.

Bengal indicates a general pattern among Mughal successor states. When Murshid Quli Khan became the head Mughal revenue officer (*Diwan*), in 1704, he moved his capital from Dhaka west to a new city named for himself, Murshidabad, on the banks of the Hughli, north of Calcutta, where he had better access to trade moving up and down the Ganga between Delhi and the Bay of Bengal. Major merchants and bankers plying this route transmitted Mughal revenues to Delhi; the Diwan invited them to his capital, which became a showpiece of art and architecture. He retained more of the Mughal revenue as Mughal power weakened, when it became easier to prevaricate, avoid sending taxes to Delhi, and also maintain the ritual appearance of loyalty. Investing in his own regime and making alliances with elites in Bengal took precedence over sending taxes to distant emperors. Wealth increased among Bengal's landed elites and merchants, whose donations to temples increased. Increasing temple construction and state wealth increased employment for elite Brahmans and Kayastha literati and administrators. Bankers, merchants, *zamindar*s, and armed land revenue collectors and financial speculators became more politically prominent. In this context, the British East India Company played the politics of competitive military alliance and captured the office of Diwan with a tricky military victory at Plassey, in 1757, to which we will return. In 1761, the East India Company became the Mughal governor (Nawab).

Gangetic uplands

Weakening Mughal power was not displaced by strong and stable regional regimes everywhere in the Ganga basin, as it was in Bengal, Awadh, and Benares. In the uplands, away from big cities on the river banks, many local chiefs became independent. Old *zamindar*s and local chiefs and *raja*s became rulers from Punjab and Rohilkhand in the west to Gorakhpur, Assam, Sylhet, and Chittagong in the east. In all the mountainous regions, forest was thick on the land. Agricultural expansion was being driven by forceful frontier warriors and financiers who acquired *zamindar* titles by paying taxes that seemed more and more like periodic tribute. Their payments were grudging. Independence gave frontier *zamindar*s new opportunities for expansion that triggered conflict among neighbouring *zamindar*s. In these militarized agrarian societies, armed struggles for land went hand in hand with tax payments to secure titles to land against claims by competitors. Land tax revenues from groups struggling for rights to land fed the treasuries of the regional states that wielded the biggest armies.

In the west, Rohilla Afghan horse traders who had settled on routes in the uplands north of Awadh created their own kingdom. When Rohilkhand was attacked by Marathas, its sultan went to the Awadh Nawab (the Mughal governor, now independent) for protection; he relinquished autonomy to keep his Rohilla ethnic territory intact. Similarly, in localities around Ayodhya, Gorakhpur, Gaya, and across the northern and southern uplands of eastern Uttar Pradesh and Bihar, high caste *zamindar*s, mostly Rajputs and Bhumihar Brahmans, extended their sway as autonomous rulers and frontier subordinates of the raja of Benares and his competitors.

Frontier expansion by *zamindar*s threatened tribal groups who farmed forests at higher altitudes. In response, many tribal groups produced new political territories. One of the oldest and best known is Cooch Behar, which lies below Bhutan. Today it is part of West Bengal and its forests still host rhinos and tigers. It was once an outpost of medieval Kamarupa kings in Assam, and it is populated primarily by the Koch group of Bodo people, who are spread across Assam and Bengal and speak a Tibeto-Burman vernacular. Cooch Behar was conquered by a Koch warrior in the sixteenth century. His son paid tribute to the Mughals and extended his territory east into Assam and south into Rangpur (in Bengal). As the Mughals declined, regional competitors expanded, including Ahom rulers in Assam, up the Brahmaputra valley. In 1772, Bhutan invaded Cooch Behar. The Raja sought help from the British. East India Company soldiers forced out the Bhutanese and the Company's Governor-General, Warren Hastings, negotiated a truce with Bhutan mediated by the Tashi Lama in Tibet. The raja of Cooch Behar then became a vassal of the British, paying them half his annual revenue. Royal titles retained and embellished since Mughal times enabled the ruling family, all their kin, and eventually the entire population of Cooch Behar to take the name Rajbansi (meaning, 'of royal blood'); thus they claimed the *varna* status of *Kshatriya*.

The north-east

Meanwhile, Ahom rulers who were expanding their territory down the Brahmaputra valley were caught between the armies of kings in Burma and of the British Company in Bengal. They sought Company support against the Burmese. Thus they fell under Company control as the Company's wars with Burma gave the British control of Assam, in 1826.

All the territories east and north-east of Bengal were contested between the British and rulers in Burma. All these territories had local rulers who like the Ahom and Koch represented ethnically coherent, though often very small, populations of people who worked in forests and on farm lands on upland and high mountain fringes of medieval dynasties, the Mughal regime, and its successors in Bengal.

Other mountain regions

Many tribal groups in the mountains of central India and in the high valleys from Baluchistan to the Hindu Kush and across the Himalayas to Sikkim, Nagaland, and Burma formed new political territories as they confronted expanding lowland states and frontier *zamindar*s. In central India, Maratha conquests accelerated a counter 'Rajputization' of tribal ruling groups who crowned *raja*s and *maharaja*s with Rajput lineages.

Bhutan and Sikkim

In the Himalayas, Bhutan became a new political territory in the eighteenth century, when a Tibetan Buddhist monk, Sheptoon La-Pha, crowned himself Dharma Raja and his successors consolidated their power over the peoples living in the steep slopes around their forts. Their Drukpa sect of Tibetan Buddhism became a ruling monastic order.

Sikkim was established in 1642, when Phuntsog Namgyal became *chogyal*, a ruler who like the Dharma Raja combined administrative and religious power. The new state rested on the strength of the Bhutias, who began to come from Tibet in the fourteenth century and settled among the Lepchas, who had previously assimilated Naong, Chang, Mon, and other tribes. Armies from Sikkim fought for land all across the mountains, down to the low-lying Terai slopes, and in the process lost land to an expansive Nepal, which sent many migrants into Sikkim, further complicating ethnic political relations.

Nepal

Nepal became an imperial dynastic realm under Prithvi Narayan Shah, who brought many small mountain ethnic territories under a centralized military administration based in the Kathmandu valley. Prithvi Narayan was born in the 1720s into the Shah ruling family of the Gurkha kingdom. At twenty-two, he was crowned king of Gurkha. At forty-nine, he led his armies east across the mountains to conquer the three Malla kingdoms of Kathmandu, Patan, and Bhadgaon. Then, from his capital at Kathmandu, he sent his armies out to annex the Terai, Kumaun, Garhwal, Simla, Sikkim, and parts of Tibet. He died at fifty-two, in 1772, but by then Nepal extended from the Punjab to Sikkim. His regime resembled a Rajput domain ruled by a Kshatriya ruling class, and in the nineteenth century Nepal officially became a Hindu state, when the Rana made the caste system law.

Some general patterns

South Asia's eighteenth-century turbulence produced many disparate regional trajectories but also followed several broad trends. Inside, on the frontiers, and outside Mughal territory, horizontal competition among new regimes fostered battles over assets that they all needed in order to survive and expand. Rising elites sought to establish order in their new domains by various means. Solid state regimes emerged when new regimes could subordinate local warriors, defend their borders, and enforce laws to strengthen their social foundations. They often used religious elites, sanctions, and institutions to consolidate power, as did the Rajputs, Marathas, Sikhs, Ranas, and kings in Bhutan and Sikkim.

Many eighteenth-century political innovations were financed by expanding commercial production in urban centres and in the countryside that fed state treasuries and private accounts at the same time, and which supported new states and rebels alike. Private capital and royal authority needed and used one another in a host of ways, most basically because war depended on revenues drawn from taxes and tribute. Virtually all new royal personalities modelled themselves on great sultans and they thus demanded a steady flow of elite commodities into capital cities to display their grandeur on their bodies, in their homes, in their *darbars*, and in their forts. Markets in arms and official entitlements thrived alongside markets in cloth, jewelry, ornaments, and architectural finery. Militarism and commercialism expanded together.

The peninsula

All these trends appear south and east of Maharashtra, where three new states fought the Marathas. These three new southern states consolidated political power in Telugu-, Kannada- and Malayalam-speaking regions, respectively.

At Hyderabad, a Mughal governor, Nizam-ul-Mulk, established himself in territory previously taken by the Mughals from the sultan of Golkonda. The Nizam's military fended off Marathas along the border between Telugu- and Marathi-speaking regions. In Telugu country, elite cadres of warrior *zamindars* took firm control of the countryside, where villages were dominated by warrior-peasant elites whose genealogies ran back to the Kakatiya kings.

Based in Mysore, the Udaiyar dynasty fought along southern Maratha frontiers to capture territory acquired by Aurangzeb when he conquered Bijapur. The Udaiyars built a powerful military force commanded by Deccani Muslim generals, whose leader, Haidar Ali, usurped the throne in 1763. Haidar Ali and his son, Tipu Sultan, built a military regime that stretched from sea to sea across the peninsula, fulfilling the dream of Vijayanagar Rayas to command ports on both coasts. Tipu Sutan subdued the warrior-peasants and his revenue bureaucracy reached a level of centralized sophistication that rivalled that of the Marathas.

In Kerala, the Travancore Raja Martanda Varma ruled for three decades (1729–58) with a large standing army, subordinated the old Nayar landed elite that had dominated earlier regimes, and fortified his northern borders. His financial fortunes rested on

Syrian Christians, whose landed and commercial interests became politically dominant; and on revenues from licences for trade in pepper and other valuable commodities under his royal monopoly. His successor, Rama Varma, ruled for another forty years (1758–98) and further strengthened Travancore along the same lines against Haidar Ali and Tipu Sultan.

On the east coast, the Tamil-speaking region was parcelled among many mini-kingdoms. Some were held by dynasties of Nayakas whose ancestors had been Vijayanagar deputies. Some *rajas* and *palaiyakkar* (Poligar) chiefs held ethnic domains dominated by caste fellows, mostly Maravas, Kallars, and Nayakas. In the old Chola heartland of Tanjavur in the Kaveri river delta, a Maratha dynasty was founded in the seventeenth century by Shivaji's cousin Serfoji and ruled there until the end of the eighteenth century. Its elite culture combined Maratha, Telugu, and Tamil Brahman influence, and following the Maratha tendency to use royal authority to regulate local social heirarchy, the Tanjavur *raja* commissioned the first ever compilation of Sanskrit texts dedicated solely to the codification of *dharma* for women, the *Stridharmapadati*.

In Arcot, near Madras, a dynasty of Nawabs descended from Mughal governors used an army composed primarily of migrant mercenaries to collect tribute and revenues far and wide under a putative mantle of Mughal authority. The Nawab dispatched armies commanded by profiteering revenue-collectors that comprised the first system of revenue collection that ever stretched from the far north to the far south of Tamil country. But the Nawab's ambition surpassed his assets. By 1770, he depended militarily and financially on loans from local financiers and British East India Company merchants. To repay the Company, he granted the British a revenue territory, a *jagir*, in the Chinglepet district around Madras. The Nawab became a shaky but useful Company ally, whose personal status became increasingly dependent on British finance and military force.

Sri Lanka

In Sri Lanka, a Sinhalese kingdom was established in 1592 at Kandy in the central highlands, and struggled for survival against twin threats from Europeans and the independent Sinhalese landed nobility. After 1658, the Dutch controlled Colombo and other coastal districts and Kandy retained only contested access to the sea. To maintain themselves, Kandyan kings sought allies among the armed coastal merchants who bought spices from the highlands to ship overseas, and they sought protection from both the Dutch and the British, whom they played against one another as best they could. Kandyan elites enhanced their cultural authority by lavishly patronizing Buddhist monks and monasteries with land grants and official status. To raise their status above their aristocracy, Kandyan kings sought marriage alliances with Tamil Nayakas on the mainland. The major ruling Nayaka lineages did not oblige, but other Nayaka families sent daughters along with their brothers and cousins to Kandy to bolster the Kandyan lineage and strengthen its military. In 1707, Tamil Nayakas inherited the throne in a matrilineal succession and they continued to recruit Nayaka families from the mainland to bolster their own position. Fierce Nayaka efforts to centralize administration turned monks and landed aristocrats into rebels who dethroned the Nayakas in 1760, after which the Dutch took the Kandyan kings under their protection.

EUROPEANS ON THE COAST

Sri Lanka was the first region substantially controlled by Europeans and it became a microcosm of European imperial history in South Asia. After 1498, Portuguese soldiers conquered a dozen major port cities on the Indian peninsula and Sri Lanka to build coastal fortress enclaves. Portugal remained the dominant European power in the Indian Ocean during the sixteenth century, when Portuguese captains controlled the western Sri Lanka coast. They lost their position to the Dutch in 1707, and by 1818 Portugal retained only a few settlements in South Asia, including Goa, south of Bombay, which was by then surrounded by British India. Goa has thrived ever since as a coastal society mixing Iberian and Konkani cultures. Portuguese legacies in Sri Lanka survive today in family names and in the prevalence of Catholicism.

Spanish monarchs who ruled Portugal from 1580 to 1640 fought to exclude the Dutch from trade in the East. Dutch merchants fought back and combined to form the United East India Company, in 1602. More commercially oriented than the Portuguese, the Dutch Company concentrated on monopolizing Asian spice supplies for world markets. Under Governor-Generals Anthony van Diemen (1636–45) and Joan Maetsuyker (1653–78), the Dutch took Malacca (1641) and coastal Sri Lankan ports (1658) from the Portuguese, and they used troops, finance, and command of the sea to dominate rulers in surrounding regions. In Sri Lanka, they assisted Kandyan kings against the Portuguese to gain bases for expansion. By 1707, they controlled Sri Lanka's spice exports. In Java, they assisted contenders for the throne in Mataram, in 1674 and 1704, receiving territory in return. By 1755, they controlled most of Java; Mataram was, by then, a small dependency, weaker even than Kandy. These same Dutch policies had less success in Sumatra, which The Netherlands finally conquered in the nineteenth century along with other territories that became modern Indonesia.

In its Asian territories, the Dutch Company initially used existing structures of tax authority to collect tax revenues to finance trade in Asia and exports to Europe. The Dutch used monopolies, sea power, loans, and military attacks to pressure local rulers into using their royal monopolies to supply only Dutch ships with cloves, nutmeg, and mace. Coercive power thus fed Dutch exports. Tribute and taxation, paid in kind, forced native growers to sell to the Dutch Company at set prices. After 1800, the Culture System of forced cultivation through taxation in kind gave the Dutch in Indonesia a powerful position in world sugar markets.

The Dutch loomed over Kandy until 1796, as Dutch administration covered much of the lowlands. The Company divided its territories around Colombo, Galle, and Jaffna into provinces (*dissavani*) and districts (*korales*) in the manner of Kandyan administration. Each *dissavani* was ruled by a *dissava*, who was a Dutch officer, with loyal Sinhalese or Tamil officers under him. The landlocked Kandyan kingdom remained under its own kings. In Dutch territories, Dutch judges brought Sinhala and Tamil elites to assist in determining local customs and they began to codify customary law. In 1707, the *Thesawalamai* codified customs among Jaffna Hindus. Muslim law was applied with the help of

Muslim leaders. Dutch law was applied in the cities and along the sea coast, particularly among Christians. The Dutch thus followed a traditionalist trend that characterized many eighteenth-century states and made religion officially prominent in regional regimes from Sri Lanka to Nepal.

Eighteenth-century British and French merchant companies competed with the Dutch in Asian waters. The British finally uprooted the Dutch from Sri Lanka during the wars that followed the French revolution, when European armies and navies fought overseas as well as in Europe. These wars became a watershed in the history of South Asia.

We have already seen that by 1792 the British East India Company controlled the collection of state revenue in territories around forts in Madras and Calcutta, most expansively in Bengal and Bihar. From the start of the Napoleonic wars, however, the Company pursued an aggressive imperial policy to enhance British fortunes. At the same time, Britain's military became a leading sector in national finance. Annual British state expenditures doubled and tripled in times of war in the 1740s, 1750s, 1770s, and 1792–1815. Between 1781 and 1815, sixty per cent of the state budget sustained the military. British public debt rose to finance military expansion and taxes raised to repay the public debt also provided finance capital for industrial investment. Debt payments rose from thirty-six per cent of public expenditure in 1781–1815 to fifty-three per cent in 1816–50. In 1750, fewer than 75,000 men had typically fought battles in Europe. Napoleon wielded armies of a quarter to a half million men. The British military overseas surpassed all its European rivals. When the British Company became Diwan of Bengal, in 1761, British troops in India numbered 18,000. By 1793, they numbered 90,000. By 1800, they topped 102,000. By 1820, they were nearly 230,000.

Eighteenth-century European wars became world wars as European imperialism changed the political map in South Asia. One indicative personality in the British imperial transition was Lord Cornwallis, whose armies lost to allied French and American troops in Yorktown, Virginia, in 1781; who became Governor-General of British India, in Calcutta, in 1786; and who then led East India Company troops to victory against Tipu Sultan, at Seringapatam, in Mysore, in 1792. Europe's national struggles quickly affected South Asia. In 1795, when France seized Amsterdam, the Rhine valley, and the Pyrenees, the British responded by taking Sri Lanka from the Dutch.

Initially, the British government did not plan to keep the island they called Ceylon. But reports from the field soon convinced parliament of Ceylon's commercial value and it became a Crown colony in 1802. Its administration then moved from Madras to Colombo, out of the hands of the East India Company, and a treaty with Kandy made Britain the king's protector. But British merchants complained that Kandy impeded their commerce and they demanded roads from the west to the east coast across the highlands, so the British used internal dissent in Kandy as a reason to conquer Kandy, in 1815, with help from rebel nobility. Britain promised to maintain rights and privileges enjoyed by landed nobles and Buddhist monks, but soon reversed this policy, which triggered rebellion in 1818. Crushing that rebellion enabled the British Crown to bring Kandy under a central Ceylon administration. In 1833, government codes were formalized and English became Sri Lanka's official language of government and education.

BRITISH IMPERIALISM

British power followed a trajectory similar to the Dutch, and the British used Dutch techniques, later in time, with more spectacular results. British ascendancy falls into five phases that begin roughly in 1600, 1740, 1792, 1820, and 1848. In each phase, the shape and substance of 'British India' changed dramatically.

Phase 1 (1600–1740)

In 1600, knights and merchants of the City of London formed the East India Company, and Queen Elizabeth I granted its royal monopoly charter. The new Company failed to weaken Dutch control of spice supplies but succeeded in establishing fortified trading centres, called 'factories', along the Indian coast; these flourished in the same up-and-down manner as other commercial operations, like those of the French, Dutch, and older merchant communities who worked under the authority of the Mughals and their contemporaries. Leading English factories were in Calcutta,

Madras, and Bombay, strategic sites along the coast in regions undergoing turbulent political change in Aurangzeb's day, when Elihu Yale went to India. Yale (1649–1721) was a man of his day. He was born in Boston, Massachusetts, and raised in England. He joined the East India Company in 1670, rose quickly in the ranks, and became governor at Fort St George in Madras, in 1687. There he made a fortune by dubious means that violated Company rules, which led to his dismissal, in 1692; but he returned to London, seven years later, a very rich man. In 1718, Cotton Mather convinced him to endow Saybrook College, in Connecticut, which took his name to become Yale University.

After Aurangzeb's death, the British Company's operations in India, like those of other Europeans, became more military. But dramatic change occurred only in 1744, during the War of Austrian Succession (1740–48), when British and French ships arrived in India with military officers and troops, announcing that the British and French were at war.

The French had been active in India since 1664, when Jean-Baptiste Colbert, under Louis XIV, formed the French Company of the East Indies with his personal wealth to reduce French payments to the Dutch for Asian commodities. His main concern was for national finance, but French wealth by this time also required colonial markets protected by a strong navy, not only in the Atlantic and the Americas, where France struggled with Spain and Britain, but also in Asia. The French wanted Madagascar but acquired Mauritius instead as a base in the Indian Ocean. Their leading settlement in India was at Pondichery, south of Madras. By 1800, it too was surrounded by British India, and remains today a distinctive coastal society, mixing French and Tamil culture.

Phase 2 (1740–92)

In 1744, François Dupleix was governor at Pondichery. In his war with the British at Madras, he took what he had no way to know would be a revolutionary step by forming a military alliance against them with Chanda Sahib, a rival of the Arcot Nawab. Chanda Sahib agreed to pay the French handsomely with a share of his spoils, if he became Nawab, but as it happened, the British candidate, Mohammad Ali, won the contest instead. He then favoured his British backers with a share of his tax revenues. This episode launched a scramble for native allies by the British and French that heated up again during the Seven Years' War (1756–63), as it also did in the Americas. A long series of multi-sided struggles ensued, pitting French and British in shifting alliances with native contenders, rulers, and financiers. Dupleix secured an alliance with the Hyderabad Nizam and gained influence in Mysore that made the French more powerful than the British in the peninsula for the next several decades.

But the British had their eyes on Bengal. Their big break came in 1756, when the Mughal governor, Nawab Siraj-ud-daula, sought to limit British fortifications in Calcutta. The British refusal to slow down the Anglo-French arms race in Bengal brought the Nawab's armies down from Murshidabad, and during this conflict, British prisoners suffocated in what became known in Europe as the 'Black Hole of Calcutta'. War in the East now appeared in the British press to be a struggle for British survival not only against the French but also against barbarous Indian tyrants.

The British war against France now included Indian enemies. In Britain's military operations in India, however, the Company was in charge, not parliament or king. The British government supplied troops, diplomatic authority, and military funding, but could not control Company decisions in Indian theatres of war six months by sea from London. The British war machine in India was effectively controlled by adventurous Company entrepreneurs, men much like Elihu Yale, who had multiplied in number since Yale bilked the Company in seventeenth-century Madras. Unlike the French and Dutch Companies, which were managed closely by their governments, the British Company depended for its financial strength on private London investors whose sons and representatives sailed in Company ships and worked under Company authority but made deals and fortunes for themselves inside and outside the loose strictures of Company discipline. In the 1750s, such men obtained armies.

One of these men, Colonel Robert Clive, sailed from Madras to Calcutta with a shipload of troops in 1757. In Calcutta, he formed an alliance with two bankers, Jagat Seth and Omichand, who arranged for one of the Nawab's ambitious generals, Mir Jaffar, to withdraw from the field when Clive's troops faced Siraj-ud-Daula's army at the battle of Plassey. The trick worked. The Company won. Mir Jaffar became Nawab and Clive received three million pounds sterling in the Company's name, half paid in cash by Jagat Seth and half pledged by the new Nawab in revenue assignments around Calcutta.

A few years later, another Bengal Nawab, Mir Kassim, strove again to restrain the British military build-up; and this time he enlisted support from the Mughal emperor and the Awadh Nawab. In 1765, Company troops prevailed at Buxar and the Company became Nawab of Bengal. By 1770, as famine ravaged Bengal while Company's revenue collectors reaped huge profits, the Company territorial domains had begun to take a more definite shape. By this time, the Marathas' northern imperial expansion had been checked by Afghan armies at Panipat; regional rulers in the peninsula had to treat the British and French as imperial contenders; and the British Company substantially controlled the revenues of the Arcot Nawab. A Company empire was growing. This provoked hot debates in the British Parliament, where fabled British nabobs were excoriated as men who made private fortunes with British public funds. Adam Smith's *The Wealth of Nations* appeared in 1776, and launched searing critique of government monopolies granted to chartered companies.

But Adam Smith also established that commercial expansion was the secret of national wealth. To finance expanding circuits of trade in Asia, the British like the French and Dutch Companies used taxes paid to Asian rulers, which financed Asian exports to Europe carried in European ships to profit European investors and benefit European consumers. Using local taxes to finance the Asian trade solved a problem that all European merchants faced: Asian goods had insatiable markets in the West, but Asian consumers had little need for anything Europeans had to sell. Sending silver from Europe to pay for Asian goods was unpalatable in Europe and other solutions to shortages of working capital among Europeans in Asia emerged early on. European merchants learned to buy cheap and sell dear in Asian markets to increase their working capital for financing shiploads heading back to Europe. As in many other areas of overseas enterprise, the Dutch pioneered this strategy. But British merchants used their greater freedom to manoeuvre outside Company controls to generate much more local finance from Indian bankers and revenue collectors. Loans given and received by individual Company merchants became the Company's financial backbone.

Europeans also used military power to force local exports onto European ships by forcing local merchants and rulers to sell export commodities to Europeans. This lowered purchase prices and increased supplies. Again, the Dutch were pioneers. The British could not dislodge the Dutch from their domineering position in Asian spice markets, so the British moved into Indian textile exports. Cloth added much more value to merchant capital than spices and European ships soon carried almost all Indian textile exports into the world economy. By 1750, factories in India were fortified warehouses for storing, sorting, ordering, and shipping cloth produced in the coastal interior, where cotton became thread and thread became cloth in native networks of finance and brokerage.

European wars in Asia added still more ways to accumulate merchant capital. Europeans financed political competition in the interior to garner revenues raised by regional rulers. The British rented out Company troops, called Sepoys, who came from local military labour markets and were trained and armed in European style. The Company also rented out British troops, and sold arms, technical advice, and training. Where they or their subordinate allies conquered, they acquired taxes to invest in export trades.

Creative businessmen used militarism to finance the flow of Asian commodities into world trade without relying on commodity sales in Asia or financial outflows from Europe. Military solutions to financial problems became ever more attractive and lucrative as the size and reputation of European armies in Asia increased. Sea power became a military as well as a commercial asset, because Europeans could choke any sea trade that financed enemy rulers, whereas no native ruler could cut European military supply lines at sea. With bases on the coast in India, opportunities opened wide in the Indian interior, where rivalry with the Dutch and French initially drove British expansion. Once the British Company began to acquire territory, its adventurous merchants provoked further expansion by extending their financial operations and using military power to increase their control over commercial assets in the interior. By 1780, the Nawab of Arcot, for example, was so deeply indebted to Englishmen that his land revenues effectively belonged to Company merchants. Native cloth merchants and weavers near the coast soon came under pressure to move their operations into British territory (to lower supply costs for the British) and to deal only with the British, on British terms. The Company's everyday commercial operations became more coercive as its territory increased. In Bengal, land revenue contractors, called 'farmers', used force to collect taxes during a famine in the 1770s that may have killed half the population.

Phase 3 (1792–1820)

In 1792, the French declared war against enemies of their revolution. British operations in South Asia became truly imperial. By that time, Company armies composed of native Sepoys and British troops, and based in Bombay, Madras, and Bengal, were fighting Marathas, Hyderabad, Mysore, Awadh, and local rulers up and down the Carnatic coast. By then, the Company held revenue territories not only in Bengal and Bihar, but also in the Carnatic, ceded by the Nizam, Peshwas, Tanjavur, and Tipu Sultan. In the 1780s, Governor-General Warren Hastings defended the Company's wars against critics at home who complained about the cost and misuse of government troops. He was the last protector of the British nabobs in India, for his parliamentary opponents prevailed. He was forced to resign and to face corruption charges and parliamentary impeachment. In 1784, William Pitt's India Act brought Company adventurers to heel. It gave supreme control of Company affairs to a Board of Control run by cabinet ministers, making the Company a semi-autonomous government institution. The Act decried territorial expansion but the Board of Control quickly appointed a military man, Lord Cornwallis, as Governor-General; Cornwallis arrived in Bengal as commander-in-chief with conquest on his mind.

In 1792, Cornwallis led troops against Tipu Sultan, who was then the Company's single most powerful opponent, vilified in London as a barbarous tyrant. Tipu fell at Seringapatam and was finally killed in 1799. Imperial expansion accelerated. Richard Wellesley became Governor-General in 1798, and Britain's military aristocracy effectively took charge of Company armies in India, which quadrupled in size from the 1770s to the 1790s and then doubled again before 1820. Company armies with larger contingents of British troops and more advanced British technology conquered Delhi (1803), Nepali forces (1816), Maratha Gaekwads, Scindias, Peshwas, and Bhonsles (1818), and Kandy (1818). Nepal retained its independence within reduced borders that still pertain today. In the Company's Indian empire, similar treaties with 'native states' (also called 'princely states') established friendly monarchies in Cooch Behar (1773), Cochin (1791), Jaipur (1794), Travancore (1795), Hyderabad (1798), Mysore (1799), Rampur (1801), Orissa and Cuttack (1804), Pudukkottai (1806), Kohlapur (1812), Cis-Sutlej Hill States (1815), Bastar (1818), Southern Maratha Jagirs (1819), Central India Agency (1819), Kutch and Gujarat Gaikwad territories (1807–20), and Rajasthan (1818), where only Ajmer and Mewar became directly administered British territory.

In 1813, parliament renewed the Company's charter but ended its trading monopoly and opened British India to private merchants and missionaries. As British power increased in India, so did direct control over Indian affairs by Crown and Parliament. Pressure on parliament by powerful citizen lobbies demanded access to British territory everywhere. By 1820, conquest had secured large territories India for the expansion of British national activity. British citizens could now operate in India under Crown protection in Company territories called 'Presidencies', with their capitals at Bombay, Calcutta, and Madras.

Phase 4 (1820–48)

This opening of British India to British national enterprise opened a new phase of British expansion, which entailed deeper British penetration into layers of sovereignty and business activity. British merchants pushed Indian business families out of the export trades. Profiting from sales, supplies, and transport of South Asian export commodities in world markets became British imperial business. Protective tariffs in England kept out Indian textiles and protected British textile manufacturers from Indian competition. The British economy engaged in a long process of import substitution by substituting British-made cloth for Indian cloth imports. Indian exports shifted to primary products like the raw cotton that fed British textile mills and lowered costs for British consumers. British exporters of British cloth now had open markets in India, into which British cloth flowed at low tariffs subsidized by Indian tax payers.

The business of empire extended more and more deeply. The Company's silver rupee became imperial currency and state policy increased its value in relation to Indian commodities so as to increase the value of remittances from India to London. Land taxation was increased and more strictly enforced than ever before. In 1820, commodity prices in British India began to fall steadily and kept falling for thirty years, cheapening Indian exports for merchants who sold them in Europe and increasing the real burden of cash taxes paid by landowners in India. As commodity prices fell, tax payers had to sell more commodities to raise cash for taxes. Coercion by tax collectors and complaints against the Company increased. Meanwhile, forced cultivation of opium for sale in China and of indigo for export to Britain expanded in British Bengal. When indigo prices crashed in London, Bengal and Bihar peasants lost cash for rent and as a result, lost their land. Many peasant tax payers had their land sold at government auctions for failure to pay taxes. The government meanwhile assigned forest land to British investors, who built coffee and tea plantations in the hills of Sri Lanka, southern India, Bengal, and Assam.

In 1833, parliament ended the Company's trading licence altogether, which made the Company strictly an arm of British administration, though administration in British India remained in the hands of Company officers. English became the official language of law and administration, displacing Persian. English education became a key to social mobility in imperial society and India became part of a larger British imperial order. When Britain abolished slavery, in 1833, petitions from British Caribbean planters came to London demanding that the government send indentured workers from Calcutta to keep sugar plantations running in the West Indies. In the 1840s, plans for Indian railways dovetailed with the needs of English textile mills for more raw cotton than could be secured from their major suppliers in the southern United States.

Expanding commercial networks and world trade entailed deeper control of Indian resources, and in this respect, native state rulers remained a source of imperial irritation, as Kandy had been before 1818. Thus British efforts accelerated to bring native rulers under stricter British authority. In 1831, for example, the Madras government took control of the *vdaiyar raja* of Mysore's territory, which it did not return to the *vdaiyar* successor for fifty years. Other native rulers, such as those at Kandy and Awadh were less fortunate. Also in the 1830s, a drive began to bring hill peoples under British control, most strikingly in the north-east, where Naga, Lushan, Garo, Shan, Khasi, Chakma, and Mizo chiefs were all attacked.

Phase 5 (1848–1914)

In the hills and elsewhere, however, the last phase of British conquest began in 1848, when Lord Dalhousie conquered the Sikh kingdom in Punjab, opening the door to the Great Game of imperial competition with Russia in Central Asia, where Bukhara and Samarkand fell to Russian troops in 1863 and 1868. When Dalhousie arrived in Calcutta, Britain was also on the offensive in China. British fleets launched the first Opium War (1839–42) when the Ch'ing emperor tried to stop British opium exports from India coming into China. Impediments to 'free trade' caused by native rulers in Asia became a legitimate basis in Western policy circles for direct military intervention. In 1839, when the governor of Canton seized British opium and drunken British sailors killed a Chinese villager, the British refused to hand over the accused, launched a war, and soon prevailed, forcing the first of a long series of unequal treaties at Nanking, in 1842, which gave Britain a huge indemnity, five ports for British trade, and rights of extra-territoriality whereby British citizens would be tried by British courts in China. Other Western countries quickly obtained the same privileges, and in the second Opium War (1856–60) the French joined the British to force Beijing to open more ports and allow Westerners free travel in the interior.

Under Dalhousie, more native state treaties were abrogated in India on the grounds that rulers obstructed British activity, failed to meet financial obligations, or upset law and order. British intentions to abrogate the property rights of *zamindar*s in Awadh stoked a vast rebellion that began with a mutiny among Sepoys around Delhi, in 1857. The rebellion spread among old warrior regions from Haryana across Bundelkhand into central India. Some rebels fled to the Red Fort in Delhi and secured support from the last Mughal ruler. Others held Lucknow against repeated assaults. Warriors in the uplands south of the Ganga basin carved out rebel states. It took two years for British troops to crush rebels on all fronts. Conquest and punishments were extreme. In the aftermath, the Crown dethroned the Mughal dynasty and replaced the Company Raj with direct Crown rule. Queen Victoria then officially ruled British India through her Viceroy.

The age of High Imperialism thus began in Asia long before European governments convened in Berlin to launch the scramble for Africa in the 1880s, by which time British India was the keystone of global British empire. British wars for Burma began in 1852. Rangoon fell in 1862; upper Burma in 1886. Battles for Kachin territories on the Burma border lasted from 1884 into the 1930s. India's north-eastern hill states were conquered between 1859 and 1893; and Bhutan and Sikkim in 1865 and 1890, respectively. British troops conquered Baluchistan in 1877, 1889, and 1896; invaded Tibet in 1903; and invaded Afghanistan from 1878 until 1891 to establish the political basis of a protectorate legalized in treaties between 1907 and 1919. The mountains north of Assam (now in the Indian state of Arunachal Pradesh) came under British control in 1914, though they do not appear in the 1931 census and, like other high hill areas, were more pacified and occupied by the military than ruled by British civil administration. As the First World War commenced, British India was still expanding into the mountains bordering China, Russia, and Iran. In 1918, conquest in South Asia ended as the modern British empire reached its maximum extent with the acquisition of territories from Germany and the Ottoman empire.

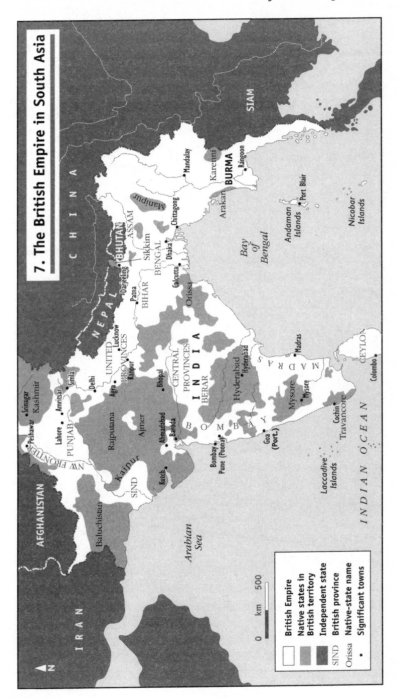

7. The British Empire in South Asia

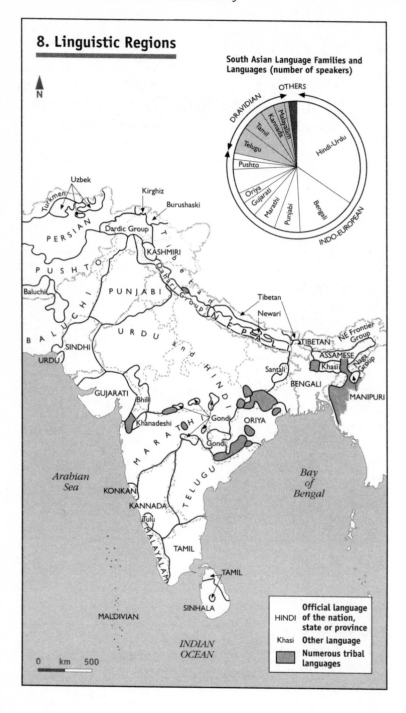

8. Linguistic Regions

South Asian Language Families and Languages (number of speakers)

OTHERS

DRAVIDIAN
Malayalam
Kannada
Tamil
Telugu
Pushto
Oriya
Gujarati
Marathi
Punjabi
Bengali
Hindi-Urdu
INDO-EUROPEAN

Uzbek
Turkmen
Kirghiz
Burushaski
PERSIAN
Dardic Group
KASHMIRI
PUSHTO
Baluchi
PUNJABI
Tibetan Group
Tibetan
Newari
NE Frontier Group
BALUCHI
URDU
TIBETAN
ASSAMESE
SINDHI
HINDI
Khasi
Naga Group
URDU
Santali
BENGALI
MANIPURI
GUJARATI
Bhili
MARATHI
Khanadeshi
Gondi
ORIYA
Gondi

Arabian Sea

Bay of Bengal

KONKAN
TELUGU
KANNADA
Tulu
MALAYALAM
TAMIL
TAMIL
SINHALA
MALDIVIAN

INDIAN OCEAN

0 km 500

HINDI	Official language of the nation, state or province
Khasi	Other language
	Numerous tribal languages

FOUR

Making Modern Societies

B ritish conquest opened the age of modern imperialism. In 1798, the British Company had ruled Bengal and Bihar for three decades, but elsewhere it held small bits of territory at best, and in many regions the British were of little or no importance. Twenty years later – after British victories over Tipu Sultan, the Dutch, Gurkhas, Napoleon, Kandy, and the Marathas – Britain held predominant military power in South Asia, in Europe, and across the Atlantic and Indian Oceans. In the 1820s, the Company tightened its grip on the Ganga basin and on Bengal, Madras, and Bombay Presidencies. In 1833, English became the imperial language. In 1848, conquering Punjab solidified imperial territory. In 1858, conquering rebels secured imperial authority. Queen Victoria became empress of India in 1876. British imperial expansion then continued for another half-century into Burma, Afghanistan, Persia, China, Africa, and the Middle East.

Foundations for a new imperial order were laid in each region as conquest led to administrative incorporation. Imperial authority absorbed many old features of politics, law, and social order in each region. Though British imperialism unified South Asia as never before, pre-modern regional trends continued to play major roles in shaping modern empire. But even as old regional identities entered into modern imperial society, no facet of social life was left unchanged by transformations that occurred in the nineteenth and twentieth centuries. Modernity changed everything, including empire. Not least, it changed the content of old social identities and produced the new ones that would dominate modern history.

The context of everyday social experience changed so dramatically in all the regions that by the twentieth century medieval environments had disappeared virtually beyond memory. South Asia became densely populated for the first time. Its wide open spaces were gone; its open frontiers and free movements of peoples and cultures were forgotten. Its new modern landscape filled up with farming communities, towns, and cities inside territorial boundaries that were fixed in place by the modern state. Urban populations grew more rapidly and with them the need to control resources in the countryside. Regional economies became more complex, productive, and disciplined. Long-term trends from previous centuries accelerated and their effects accumulated to change the face of the land. Farmers extended cultivation to the limits of ecology and beyond, forests diminished rapidly, and nomads and forest cultivators were pushed aside, their land taken away and their peoples incorporated into farming societies, often forcefully. Nomadic ways of life and the social habits of hunters and forest dwellers came to be seen as primitive and even criminal. Sedentary social identities became the norm. South Asia was reinvented as an enclosed collection of officially bounded territories that were called traditional and identified with the land of ancient civilizations.

Modern living conditions evolved inside a new political order that was initially imposed by military conquest, as others had been before. The makers of modern empire pursued the logic of conquest and military command to organize their administration, following a Mughal pattern that continued under eighteenth-century regional regimes. The British empire became distinctively modern, however, by eliminating all its military underlings and potential competitors. Societies were disarmed. The realm of civilian life, shorn of military force, expanded. Civil administration, legislation, and law enforcement were always backed by coercive power, but they did not rely on armed force for everyday operations. This civil dimension of empire was not in itself new, but it grew beyond all precedent because the imperial military more completely eliminated the autonomous powers of armed peasants, warriors, rajas, and sultans to challenge imperial order. In everyday social settings, therefore, a new kind of civil society developed, unarmed but not un-political, where people participated in politics with the venerable skills of literacy and cultural activism.

In this civil realm, literate urban cultural activists produced national identities that by the end of the nineteenth century mobilized public support to challenge British supremacy in the name of nationalism. Political conflict between imperialism and nationalism first exploded in 1905 and reached a turning point in 1920, when nationalists mobilized the first massive public campaign for national autonomy. In 1920, the British empire had also reached the end of expansion with the acquisition of territories from the Ottomans and Germans after World War One: it then embraced a quarter of the world's population – in Canada, Australia, South and South-East Asia, the Middle East, Africa, and elsewhere. In 1920 the British empire came to be called the British Commonwealth of Nations. This re-naming reflects a shift in the vocabulary of imperial governance that turned *colonies* into *nations* inside a new *international* order that was organized in the 1920s around the League of Nations. From 1920 onward, national identities and national politics in South Asia evolved in a world of national societies and international order.

The new world order of the 1920s, like the world war that inspired it, was substantially the work of a handful of globally powerful national governments whose competition and collaboration defined the contours of modern world politics. In the 1920s, a global inter-*imperial* order – produced during the previous seven decades by armies from Europe, Russia, and the United States – became a global inter-*national* order in which Britain's power steadily diminished compared with its rivals. After 1945, *colonies* in Africa and Asia began to acquire *national* independence following a second world war among the great imperial nations, which by 1930 included Japan.

Modern societies around the world took shape inside global imperialism during the century before 1920. Britain had no military rival in South Asia until Japan conquered Singapore and Burma in 1942. In 1876, when Victoria became empress, British imperialism entered its heyday. By this time, truly global kinds of imperial identity had come into existence in South Asia, not only for individuals, but also for regions, which acquired new identities inside a modern world economy. The last decades of Victoria's reign witnessed the most dramatic expansion of global economic integration to that time; and in fact, world trade increased as a proportion of world economic activity faster between 1870 and 1914 than it did any time later until the 1990s. The British imperial heyday was an age of rapid globalization, and territories in Victoria's empire played a leading role. But Britain's glory days were over by 1920, when empire had acquired a musty odour. In 1918, Joseph Schumpeter (a leading economist who became Austria's finance minister) called imperialism an 'heirloom of the absolute monarchical state', an 'atavism' created by rude capitalists and archaic nobility. After 1920, the power and cultural status of imperial elites disintegrated under international criticism and assaults from nationalism, though even in the 1940s diehards remained, like Winston Churchill, who vowed never to give up British India on the eve of national independence.

This chapter explores the making of modern societies in South Asia before 1920. It does not venture out into the global history of British imperial influence, but British India and Ceylon contained seventy-two per cent of the population of the British empire in 1947, a very sizable proportion. Our goal here is to explore the ways that empire and social change in South Asia generated new collective identities, among which national identities became most politically prominent after 1920, when they most forcefully shaped all others.

ORGANIZING EMPIRE

British imperial power, like its predecessors, initially depended on local alliances with rajas, sultans, business families, landowners, mercenaries, and administrative and other elites. The Nizam of Hyderabad, for example, was pivotal in Company wars against Marathas; likewise, loyal troops from Punjab were essential for crushing the 1857 rebellion. British power ascended to new heights with resources provided by the British Crown and by imperial capitalists whose ambition spanned the globe. Britain's bankers and industrialists provided finance for imperial adventures. A twin foundation thus supported The Raj: it had roots in South Asia and also had global reach. These two bases of support reinforced one another until the 1920s, when they unravelled together.

The project of building the empire was a multi-cultural affair that involved various kinds of people in disparate locations, who participated for many different reasons both inside and outside South Asia. Its participants were most often in very poor communication with one another, if they communicated at all; and they often came into conflict, as the East India Company routinely did with parliament and Crown. After 1820, when British victories over Napoleon and Marathas built a doubly firm imperial base, an elite corps of British imperialists gained increasingly autonomous power over their former allies in South Asia, who became more definitively subordinates. British elites then more aggressively forced the formation, shaped the contours, and dictated the terms of an expansive imperial society whose modernity appears most obviously in the comprehensive strictures of bureaucratic hierarchy. As long as the Company remained in power, bureaucratic centralization faced obstacles in South Asia posed by the entrenched interests of Company officials and their local allies. But even under the Company and before 1858, strenuous efforts were made to subordinate all the people in the old layers of sovereignty in regions under direct British adminis-tration. After 1820, governance in British provinces became visibly more bureaucratic and its administration more centralized. This trend accelerated rapidly after 1858, under Crown rule, when the heyday of bureaucratic institution building coincided with the heyday of British imperialism, from 1870 to 1920. In these decades, printed records supplanted penned foolscap manuscripts in the imperial archives. Administrative and legal tomes compiled all the imperial rules and regulations. Surveyors mapped all the British dominions. Comprehensive census operations counted and sorted the population by ethnic group, sect, gender, age, and location. Statistical data on all aspects of economic and political activity were published in annual reports. By 1880, a reader in London could sit in the British Library and read everything that any British official ever needed to know about Britain's empire in Asia.

During the nineteenth century, a more elaborate, comprehen-sive hierarchy of central places, regions, and officials also developed; and, again, its regulation accelerated when Victoria became empress. But modern empire still had its organizational cores and peripheries; and its institutions developed first and most completely in its core regions. Frontiers remained less securely regimented to the end of The Raj and beyond.

London was the metropolitan core of the global empire, and around it, the highest imperial echelons worked in major economic centres like Manchester, and in centres for educating the imperial intelligentsia – Oxford and Cambridge. In the early imperial years, the imperial elite was led by aristocrats like Lord Cornwallis, who suffered the loss of American colonies and tilted East India Company policy to favour India's own conservative elites during the decades of war against France. By 1820, however, middle class men with small-business ties, Utilitarian ideas, and Protestant enthusiasm had risen to the top of the imperial ranks; men like Thomas Munro, who became governor of Madras in 1820, and joined an official generation that launched policy reforms to open India more widely to British national interests, with middle class businessmen and missionaries foremost in mind. After 1858, British politicians, bureaucrats, diplomats, and industrialists presided over High Imperialism; men like Lord Curzon, who was Viceroy to the Crown from 1896 to 1910 and treated India as a national state under the Crown in an age when the Union Jack flew on every continent. By Curzon's day, however, the empire had global competitors: France, Germany, Russia, America, and Japan. Also in his day, critics of empire had arisen in India and in Britain; so that Curzon, the great imperial bureaucrat, was also the first in a long line of defensive British imperial administrators fighting opponents on all sides. By the 1920s, London's position as the metropolitan core of imperial modernity was in visible decline along with its power in South Asia, which made Curzon's successors weaker and weaker.

Cosmopolitan South Asian cities formed second and third tiers of imperial authority. In the nineteenth century, the leading second-tier cities were Calcutta and Colombo, but in 1911 Delhi supplanted Calcutta as the capital of British India. As British power expanded up the Ganga basin, South Asia's old imperial heartland regained its pre-eminence, lost in the eighteenth century. In the Indian peninsula, Bombay and Madras formed a third tier of imperial cities, as capitals of the provinces of Bombay and Madras, respectively. Calcutta dropped into the third tier in 1911 as capital of Bengal Province. Lahore, Karachi, and Rangoon joined the ranks of provincial capitals during the nineteenth century. The second and third tiers of imperial cities housed English-literate elites who articulated imperial modernity in its regions. All the large regional cities were focal points for social change that followed from earlier times and also from British imperial innovations. In these cities, cosmopolitan groups drawing from old and new cultural resources led the regional political systems that would most visibly shape national identities and nationalist politics.

As the empire expanded to incorporate more diverse regions, it also defined a fourth tier of provincial centres and a fifth tier of local centres. These were focal points for most everyday social, political, economic, and cultural activity; and they were with few exceptions centres of regional and local authority in earlier times. At these lower levels, the leaders of the new imperial system forced themselves into environments where their authority took hold among existing social institutions and power relations. As they were integrated into the modern political system, people in these lower-tier centres of power acquired more influence over the course of imperial and national history.

One simple way to indicate the cultural content of the new social identities that attached to residence inside this imperial urban hierarchy is to note that going down the urban ranks, the prevalence of English and the number of British nationals in residence declines dramatically. Urban ranks thus correspond to cultural ranks in the imperial order. The character of empire looks very different at each level. At the top rank, it is all British, but at the bottom a British accent or a British face rarely appears. The most intense cultural mixing of British and South Asian groups occurred in South Asia's high-ranking urban centres, which housed its most influential elites.

At the pinnacle of empire, in London, the Board of Control and parliament supervised Company Raj until 1857, after which elected British governments ruled British India under the Crown. The Colonial Office managed the rest of the empire, including Ceylon. In India, the head of state was the Governor-General in Calcutta (before 1858) and then the Viceroy in Calcutta and Delhi. Though Ceylon was managed as a single colonial territory under

the governor in Colombo, India was divided into many administrative territories with varying degrees of subordinate autonomy.
Though London designed British India's government, regional
governors and rulers in native states retained substantial independent authority. British provinces and presidencies controlled
critical areas of policy and budget allocation like education,
agriculture, and public works.

The imperial bureaucracy in British India was organized
around the Indian Civil Service (ICS), which was centrally trained
and dispatched to high posts in the central government and in the
provinces. The ICS became the 'iron frame' of British rule, an elite
administrative corps for conducting the imperial state's everyday
business down to the local (district) level. Law courts and legal
administration developed separately in each province and were
brought under a centralized framework of legal procedure. In each
province and at the capital in Calcutta (later Delhi) British heads
of state wrote the laws of empire under London's authority; and
each also had an official council to advise them. These advisory
councils had considerable influence as legislative bodies in the
provinces. Their autonomy declined as Company Raj gave way to
Crown rule, but their role and visibility then expanded because
state administration and activists in civil society developed a
common interest in bringing people with social influence into the
official process of law making.

The imperial military mentality remained prominent in the
administration of British territories from beginning to end.
Strictures on activity in civil society enforced early on inside British
settlements were expanded to cover all territories under British rule.
Police searched out dissidents and repressed perceived threats to law
and order. The native press was monitored; censorship ensued when
sedition was suspected. Even popular plays lampooning the British
were banned, though enforcement was difficult outside the major
urban centres. At the same time, however, the administration sought
to expand the scope of local elite representation in government, and
local elites demanded representation. Despite official resistance,
legal petitioners and popular protestors made their impact on
provincial law making from the beginning.

Nationalists sought to expand civil representation. As we will
see, a major agitation in 1905 led to the formation of legislative

councils in 1911, and their powers and electoral base were expanded dramatically in 1920, and 1935, again in response to popular agitation and legal petitioning. This series of constitutional reforms gave increasing powers to regional Legislative Assemblies but left the Imperial Council mostly ceremonial. The division of authority between London's appointees and elected legislators and ministries became the central issue for political activists; and eliminating London's control altogether became a nationalist demand in 1920.

In the lowest tiers of government, in district headquarter towns, District Collectors were ICS men who led local administration; they were the most senior officers most people ever saw. In 1881, local self-government acts established district and local boards of local dignitaries in cities, towns, and district subdivisions to advise Collectors and raise funds to undertake projects like road building, sanitation construction, and education. Increasing authority over the everyday work of government thus devolved onto elective institutions in regional capitals and in local administration, but authority over the imperial system and direct control of the military, external affairs, monetary policy, and civil service remained in the hands of Crown appointees in London, Calcutta, and after 1911, New Delhi.

IMPERIAL CAPITALISM

We have already seen that everyday life in South Asia included substantial commercial activity when Europeans arrived; later economic trends under imperialism reshaped empire and everyday life at the same time. Way back in the fourteenth century, Ibn Batuta had recorded commerce on routes he travelled, and at the end of the sixteenth century, the *Ain-i-Akbari* made special mention of the host of commercial activities that sustained imperial taxation. In the eighteenth century, the revenues of the East India Company in Bengal came from agrarian economies where countless farmers sold rice in local markets. In 1806, when Thomas Munro (a Scotsman) went to collect revenues in Rayalaseema, a dry region in the interior peninsula, he reported that the locals were as much a 'nation of shopkeepers' as the Scots. One of his reports is most instructive:

TABLE 4. A CHRONOLOGY OF THE BRITISH EMPIRE

---

1. Early Company expansion beyond Bengal

1801	Carnatic	Poligars conquered. Madras Presidency formed.
1801	Rampur	Native state established in former Rohilkhand.
1802	Marathas	Peshwas cede first territory to British; other Marathas, 1802–5.
1803	Mughals	British conquer and make Delhi a dependency.
1804	Orissa	Mountain native states established: Cuttack Mehals, etc.
1804	Rohillas	Absorbed by Awadh.
1806	Pudukkottai	Native state in Madras Presidency.
1812	Kolhapur	Native state in Bombay Presidency

2. Imperial expansion after Waterloo

1815	Nepal	Garhwal and Kumaun ceded to British.
1815	Sri Lanka	Kandy last addition to Ceylon as British Crown Colony.
1816	Punjab	Cis-Sutlej and Sikh become states under the Company.
1817	Marathas	Gaikwads cede Cutch Kathiawar as native states to British.
1818	Marathas	Conquered by British to form bulk of Bombay Presidency.
1818	Marathas	Bhonsle Nagpur and Bastar native states (resumed in 1840s).
1818	Marathas	Holkar territories become native states Central Indian Agency.
1818	Marathas	Scindia territory in Malwa becomes native states.
1818	Rajputs	Native states: Mewar, Jodhpur, Jaisalmere, Bikaner, Jaipur.
1820	Madras	Ryotwari system established. Thomas Munro governor of Madras to 1824.

3. Consolidation and further expansion

1833 Charter Act. Company's trade abolished. Abolition of slavery.

1835 Macaulay's Minute on Education. English becomes official language.

1838 British invade Afghanistan. Great Game begins. First Afghan War to 1842.

1846 Kashmir made native state.

1848 Annexation of the Punjab. Lord Dalhousie Governor-General to 1856.

1853 Dalhousie's railway plan. First railway opened. Telegraph from Calcutta to Agra.

1857 The Great Rebellion. Foundation of Calcutta, Bombay, and Madras Universities.

TABLE 4. CONTINUED

4. The first decades of Crown rule

1858 India under the Crown: Queen's proclamation.

1861 Indian Councils Act. High Courts Act. Indian Penal Code introduced.

1867 Deoband school founded by Muhammad 'Abid Husayn.

1868 Punjab and Oudh Tenancy Acts.

1869 Opening of the Suez Canal. Lord Mayo Viceroy to 1872. Jotirao Phule publishes attack on Brahmanism, *Priestcraft Exposed.*

1871 First Indian census. Lord Mayo commissions W.W. Hunter's *The Indian Musalmans: Are They Bound in Conscience to Rebel against the Queen?* (London, 1871).

1875 Arya Samaj founded by Swami Dayananda. Muhammadan Anglo-Oriental College at Aligarh founded by Syed Ahmed Khan.

1876 Queen Victoria becomes empress of India.

1877 Deccan Famine.

5. Imperial heyday and early nationalism

1879 Dadabhai Naoroji publishes *The Poverty of India.*

1880 Famine Commission Report. Famine Codes. Lord Ripon Viceroy to 1884.

1881 First Factory Act.

1882 *Ananda Math* by Bankim Chandra Chatterjee. Swami Dayananda founds first Cow Protection Society.

1883 Singh Sabha opens the Khalsa Press in Lahore. Ilbert Bill controversy.

1884 Local Government Acts.

1885 Indian National Congress founded. Bengal Tenancy Act.

1886 The Sikh reformist *Khalsa Akhbar* begins publication under Ditt Singh.

1887 Tata's Empress cotton mill at Nagpur.

1893 Vivekananda at Parliament of Religions at Chicago. B.G. Tilak popularizes Ganesh festival. Cow protection riots in Uttar Pradesh.

1895 B.G. Tilak revives Shivaji festival.

1896 Plague and famine in India, to 1900.

1897 Khan Singh Nabha publishes *Ham Hindu Nahin.*

1899 Lord Curzon Viceroy to 1905.

1900 North-West Frontier Province created. Punjab Land Alienation Act. Urdu Protection Society founded in Uttar Pradesh.

1904 Universities Act. Co-operative Societies Act. Archaeological Department.

> Almost every ryot [tax-paying peasant] has an account with a bazaar-man and a balance against himself. This account often runs through 2 or 3 generations and is rarely paid off entirely. It usually originates in small advances by the bazaar-man who probably gives seventy or eighty rupees and takes a bond for a hundred with interest at 2.5% monthly (or 30% annually). The ryot in return makes payment in grain, cotton and other articles, which are usually valued against him and he receives occasionally from the bazaar-man small sums for the discharge of his Kists [installments] . . . [In case of default] the creditor has only to produce [before the local court] a bond; an order for distraint usually follows and the ryot is at once stripped of his cattle, grain and implements of husbandry and will most likely never again rise above the rank of common labourer.

Though comprehensive statistics on rural commerce and debt are not available in Munro's day, British tax collectors clearly relied on the commercial proceeds of local trades to satisfy their tax demands. Many rural areas contained complex economies; and they were certainly not, as later conventional wisdom would have it, environments of simple subsistence. In Munro's Rayalaseema, landowning farming families (21%) were well outnumbered by the combined total of craft workers (19%), merchants (12%), and soldiers (10%); and this region had no major cities and lay far from the more commercialized, urbanized coastal areas of southern India.

Local commercialism supported British East India Company operations, first along the coast of the Indian Ocean. Their own personal resources made British merchants more independent than European rivals; they identified less than French or Dutch merchants with their home government and relied heavily on local collaborators. By the mid eighteenth century, financing for Company operations came mostly from Indian family firms that like the Company did business across cultures and made money inside markets that included goods, services, and taxes. Eighteenth-century taxes fed trade and banking, which in turn provided state revenues; and locally, in agrarian societies, people who controlled land, labour, and capital faced mounting tax pressure from eighteenth-century rulers in the context of expanding markets for agricultural commodities. Some proportion of debt incurred by Munro's Rayalaseema peasants would have gone to pay taxes to secure land rights. No tax payments, no land rights; no commercial finance, no taxes. In eighteenth-century South Asia, circular connections among military power, local entitlements, and commercial activity were ubiquitous.

As the British Company began to build an empire by using military force to raise finance capital to buy goods to ship overseas, it turned the existing circular connections among political power, local entitlements, finance, and trade into an imperial bonanza. The Company's military force became the ultimate guarantor of land rights in conquered regions, and in return for granting land rights, it took more taxation than any previous regime. By enriching the treasury, Company and government could use taxes to raise funding from bankers and investors who speculated on future cash returns from further conquest. The British government also incurred public debt from bankers who simultaneously financed British industry and war. Industry produced superior weapons for further conquest. A new circularity was born: war–taxation–entitlements–trade–industrialization. This new circuit of capital accumulation became a bedrock of imperial capitalism.

During the wars with Napoleon, British public debt swelled and public scrutiny of state budgets increased. In 1823, the budget became public record. Cutting the cost of government and raising new revenue to pay state creditors became the order of the day. Political pressure in London forced higher tax collections in South Asia to pay not only Company investors but also the British treasury and private bankers. At the same time, British business sought profits in territories of British expansion, backed by British supremacy at sea. Reflecting public concern in Britain, parliament sought ways to pursue *national* profits in the empire. Political support in London for old monopoly companies had declined steadily since the publication of Adam Smith's *The Wealth of Nations* (1776). Pitt's India Act, in 1784, marked the first step in the replacement of Company privilege by imperial nationalism. In each subsequent Company charter renewal, the autonomy of the Company declined: in 1793, it came under strict state supervision; in 1805, it lost Ceylon; in 1813, it lost its monopoly; in 1833, it lost its business; and in 1858, it died.

Already by 1793, British national interests had been expressed in public debates about the best way to manage Britain's 'Asiatic possessions'. Since the early *eighteenth* century, prohibitions against selling Indian cloth in Britain had protected Lancashire against Indian weavers who made better cloth more cheaply; but after 1815, tariffs also killed re-exports from London of Indian cloth. Imperial tariff policies enabled Lancashire exporters to sell British textiles to India virtually duty-free; and British exporters began to undersell Indian-made cloth inside India. At the same time, India and Ceylon were then targeted to supply British industry and British as well as American consumers. Opium grown by peasants to pay their tax bills in Bengal and Bihar supplied British merchants who sold opium in China and bought Chinese tea and porcelain to sell in Western markets. At home in London, tea from China was sweetened with sugar from Caribbean slave plantations.

After 1820, the tax bureaucracy steadily increased the centralized accumulation of tax revenues. To this end, layers of sovereignty needed to be eliminated, because at each level in the old tax system, people in authority who passed tax payments up the ranks kept a portion for themselves, as a financial benefit and symbol of their personal power. Thus in tax systems that the British inherited, each individual of rank and each headman of a community kept a portion of the tax proceeds that British administrators strove to acquire. The old system gave all the intermediaries in the tax system a personal interest in increasing total tax collections, but also left them with independent discretionary powers and room to negotiate with superiors for tax relief and leniency in tax collections. Eliminating their leverage became the battle cry for obedient British bureaucrats and politically ambitious administrators, like Thomas Munro, who sought to transmit more tax revenues to the central treasury and who also claimed (falsely, as it turned out) that eliminating tax middlemen would lower the tax burden for ordinary peasants.

Under orders from London, the Company tried to turn all tax collectors into salaried bureaucrats and to make tax payers fear the state's power to seize land for failure to pay taxes. This imperial project paid for military expansion and repaid British financiers handsomely. Because the monies involved in British national empire had to move across vast distances separating very different monetary systems, considerable attention had to be paid to monetary policies that kept the relative value of currency in Britain and in South Asia favourable to investors in Britain. The same policies also tried to keep the value of the Indian rupee and the British pound favourable for British importers, exporters, and investors in South Asia, a complicated and ultimately impossible agenda.

Opening South Asia to British investment proved difficult. 1813 marked a beginning, when the Company's monopoly was broken, but the project proceeded slowly because of the cost and risk of ventures so far from home. By the 1820s, British nationals had succeeded, however, in cutting Indian businessmen out of the old multi-cultural commercial partnerships, as British exporters based in India gathered in national prerogatives and took control of the overseas trade. As we have seen, the reduction of Kandy followed cries for a more integrated transportation system in British Ceylon, but British plantation investments remained low for another twenty years. Empire was initially more successful in helping to integrate British business operations globally. When the 1833 abolition of slavery in British territories produced a crying need among West Indian planters for cheap labour to replace freed slaves, imperial officers arranged to send annual shiploads of indentured Bihari workers from Calcutta to work on British Caribbean plantations.

More ambitious imperial plans began in the 1840s, when policy makers in London launched ideas for developing new ports and a railway system in South Asia to lower the cost of overseas exports, quicken military operations, increase revenue, and subsidize British investments. Also in the 1840s, Arthur Cotton argued successfully that crop production could be advanced by state irrigation investments that would pay for themselves with higher taxes on more productive land. Modern state-led economic development was born.

British textile barons led the way. In the 1840s, parliament met to consider ways to improve supplies of raw cotton to Lancashire mills. The Maratha interior districts of Bombay Presidency attracted special attention, along with Egypt. Measures were sought to expand cotton exports from these regions to counter-balance Britain's dependence on the American South. The railway would help to solve the problem, but even before it was built, the US Civil War broke out and Egypt and India filled a void in cotton supplies created by the Union blockade of Confederate ports.

The imperial transition to industrial capitalism consumed the decades 1840–80. In 1853, Governor-General Dalhousie announced the plan to build an Indian railway with state contracts that guaranteed private companies a minimum five per cent return, based on tax revenues; and to secure that return, government kept control of railway construction and management. In the 1870s, the government of India obtained authority to raise loans for productive purposes, and large irrigation projects began, following earlier success raising revenues from smaller projects. These projects were all government endeavours using private contractors and their benefits also accrued to owners of irrigated land. Huge projects opened up arid land formerly used by pastoral nomads in Punjab to vast farming operations in which land allocations by government went primarily to Sikh and Hindu Jat communities that provided steady supplies of recruits for the military. State support for private capital accumulation became a mainstay of The Raj: it benefited British capitalists, Indian landed interests, financiers at all levels, and merchants in commodity markets in South Asia and overseas, all at once.

By 1880, regions of specialized production for world markets had emerged in South Asia. Ceylon was plantation country. Coffee plantations expanded from fifty to eighty thousand acres between 1847 and 1857, and peasants devoted another forty-eight thousand acres to coffee exports. Despite difficulties raising capital in the 1860s, coffee acreage expanded another thirty-five thousand acres before 1871. But in the 1880s, leaf disease killed coffee, which was rapidly replaced by tea, rubber, coconuts, and cinchona. Ceylon and India replaced China as the major suppliers of British tea. A supreme plantation crop, tea required heavy investments in cultivation and machinery, which drove out peasant producers and favoured British capital that also controlled the export markets and consumer access in Europe.

Labour supplies posed the major production constraint for Ceylon tea planters, and the solution was found in the institution of (eventually permanent) labour migration from southern Tamil districts in British India. British plantations in the Malay peninsula also depended on Tamil workers, who settled there in large numbers. British Burma and East Africa also developed within circuits of capital accumulation anchored in India. In Burma, Tamil Chettiyar bankers became the prime financiers for agricultural development in the Irrawaddy river delta, which generated huge exports of rice for world markets, including India, where urban growth rapidly expanded demands for imported rice. In East and South Africa, merchants from Gujarat and emigrant workers from Bombay, Calcutta, and Madras provided both labour and capital for railway construction and urban nuclei for the colonial economy. Between 1896 and 1928, seventy-five per cent of emigrants from Indian ports went to Ceylon and Malaya; ten per cent to Africa; nine per cent to the Caribbean; and the remaining six per cent to Fiji and Mauritius.

The Maratha Deccan became cotton country; its black volcanic soil became 'cotton soil'. Following the Civil War boom, cotton farmers incurred such serious debt to finance cotton production that when prices dropped in 1876, riots broke out pitting farmers against non-Maratha bankers, especially Marwaris from Rajasthan. In the same year, cotton duties were abolished in Britain to further cheapen supplies from India, and a year later the biggest famine ever recorded struck the Deccan cotton-growing districts. Half the population also died in dry districts of Rayalaseema, in Madras Presidency. The coincidence of *laissez-faire* economic policy, imperial expansion, and famine sharpened government attention to capital investment in agriculture. In 1869, Lord Mayo reflected the imperial mind-set when he said, 'every measure for the improvement of the land enhances the value of the property of the State'. He went on to say, 'The duties which in England are performed by a good landlord fall in India, in a great measure, upon the government. Speaking generally, the only Indian landlord who can command the requisite knowledge is the State.'

From the 1880s, annual government publications document South Asia's massively increasing production of raw-materials for the world economy. By 1914, almost all the goods arriving at ports consisted of cotton, wheat, rice, coal, coke, jute, gunny bags, hides and skins, tea, ores, and wool that were heading overseas. Most cotton came to Bombay from Maharashtra. All tea came to

Calcutta and Colombo from British-owned plantations in Assam, Darjeeling, and the hills around Kandy. By far the most rice came to Rangoon. Wheat came primarily from fields under state irrigation in Punjab (60%) and the western United Provinces (Uttar Pradesh) (26%). Oilseeds came to Bombay from Hyderabad territory (Andhra Pradesh), the Central Provinces (Madhya Pradesh), and Bombay Presidency (Maharashtra). Coal, coke, and ores came from mines around Jharkhand into Calcutta and Bombay, where they stoked local industry as well as exports. Eastern Bengal (Bangladesh) produced almost all the world's jute, which went to Scotland and to Calcutta, where jute cloth output surpassed that of Dundee by 1908.

NATIONAL ECONOMY AND WORLD ECONOMY

Between 1880 and 1914, low prices prevailed in Europe and America as prices kept rising in South Asia. This encouraged investments in South Asia by firms producing for domestic and world markets, rather than primarily for markets in the West. This spurred the government to raise and spend more in India, resulting in the Local Self Government Act and a massive expansion of government irrigation from 1880 to 1900. The result was a new spatial pattern of capital accumulation, as imported industrial machinery was domesticated in regions of factory production in British India.

In 1853, the first Indian cotton mill appeared in Bombay, and the Factory Act (1881) imposed new rules of operation on Indian factories that were intended to reduce the advantages that Indian capitalists enjoyed over British competitors in virtue of low cost labour and raw materials in India. In 1887, J.N. Tata's Empress Mill arose at Nagpur, in the heart of Maratha Deccan cotton country. The Tatas became India's greatest industrial dynasty. Tata Iron and Steel Works at Jamshedpur consumed increasing supplies of ore and coal, which by the 1920s rivalled exports from Calcutta. Today, one branch alone of the Tata dynasty, Tata Electronic and Locomotive Company, is India's fourth largest corporation. By 1914, India was the world's fourth largest industrial cotton textile producer: cotton mills numbered 271 and employed 260,000 people, forty-two per cent in Bombay city, twenty-six per cent elsewhere in Bombay Presidency (mostly Nagpur), and thirty-two per cent elsewhere in British India, at major railway junctures. Coal, iron, steel, jute, and other industries developed at the same time, producing specialized regional concentrations of heavy industry around Bombay, Ahmedabad, Nagpur, Kanpur, Calcutta, Jamshedpur, and Madras. Jute mills around Calcutta multiplied from one to sixty-four, between 1854 and 1914; the number of looms and the scale of employment increased twice as fast.

The First World War further stimulated industrial policies to make India less dependent on imports; and the Great Depression (1929–33) again boosted incentives for industrial growth by reducing the price of farm output more than that of manufactures. As a result, industrial output in India grew steadily from 1913 to 1938 and was fifty-eight per cent higher at the end of the depression than at the start of World War One; compared with slower and more uneven rates of growth in the UK and Germany. By contrast, plantations languished from the early 1900s to the 1940s. The partial exception was rubber, which benefited from war booms.

By 1920, South Asia had complex, diversified, national economies – dominated by agriculture, but including a large public sector, major industries, and finance capital – in which investors were concerned with state policies to support capital accumulation in a changing world economy. Native states and non-British firms participated in this trend. The Mysore government built the high Sivasamudram dam at the headwaters of the Kaveri river, and in 1902 installed an electric generator built by General Electric using techniques and equipment pioneered at Niagara Falls. Bangalore was the first South Asian city with electrical street lights. In 1921, one-third of India's industrial production was driven by electricity, and Mysore had a higher proportion of electrified industry (33%) than the presidencies of Madras (13%) or Bengal (22%).

As South Asia's internally differentiated regions were collectively and individually integrated into the world economy by networks of investment, migration, communication, and cultural activity, London was losing ground as a world economic power; South Asia revolved less and less tightly around its imperial metropolis. British India was a land of opportunity for world trade. In 1914, the US consul at Bombay, Henry Baker, called India 'one of the few large countries of the world where there is an "open door" for the trade of all countries'. In 1914, the UK sent sixty-three per cent of British India's imports and received twenty-five per cent of its exports; and by 1926 these figures stood at fifty-one per cent and twenty-one per cent, respectively. In 1926, trade with the UK (including imports, exports, and re-exports) averaged thirty-two per cent of the total for five major ports (Calcutta, Bombay, Madras, Karachi, and Rangoon), and only fifty-seven per cent of trade with Europe. Bombay and Rangoon did forty-three per cent of their overseas business with Asia and the Middle East. Calcutta did one-quarter of its business with America.

The movement of people also expanded and diversified. The Suez Canal, undersea telegraph cables, larger and faster steamers, and eventually telephones and aircraft cheapened world travel and communication. Transnational migration increased and more British families came to South Asia, but few stayed for long: new immigrants represented an average of half the British resident population in census years 1891, 1901, and 1911. In 1911, British citizens were sixty-two per cent of the Europeans in British India, and fifty-four per cent in native states and agencies. Four times more immigrants came from Asia than Europe: seven of ten came overland from Nepal (54%) and Afghanistan (16%). In 1911, Nepalis entering British India (280,248) exceeded the British resident population by fifty per cent and Asian immigrants altogether numbered three times the British population in India. By 1921, emigration also far exceeded immigration: a modern diaspora was underway. Emigration was regionally particular. From 1896 to 1928, eighty-three per cent of 1,206,000 emigrants left British India from Madras (a port that accounted for only ten per cent of total overseas trade), and they mostly went to work in Ceylon (54%) and Malaya (39%). Bombay emigrants went mostly to East and South Africa; Calcutta emigrants to Fiji and the West Indies.

By 1920, British citizens still controlled the highest echelons of South Asia's economy, but the process of capital accumulation in South Asia that sustained the rise of British imperialism had always escaped British control. South Asia's economy became independently established in a world of national economies. A turning point came during the world war in 1914–18. Before the war, London's political position in South Asia seemed secure. After the war, London declined visibly in relation to other metropolitan powers and also to cosmopolitan powers in South Asia that were mobilizing for national control of the highest echelons of economic and political power.

MODERN IMPERIAL SOCIETY

As imperial governance and economic order evolved in the nineteenth century, the urban networks that connected cities, towns, and villages provided a scaffolding for modern regions. The British empire's urban hierarchy became a feature of everyday life as the urban ranks became cultural ranks in imperial order. At the apex of empire in England, imperial society was all English. In the major cosmopolitan centres that were the crux of empire in South Asia, British and regional cultures mingled most intensely. At empire's base in South Asia's towns and villages, where most people lived, imperial society had a distinctly local appearance.

The metropolitans

Most people in Britain may have thought the empire ran by remote control. It was rarely in the news, except in times of war, famine, or plague, when public pressure perked up to get normality re-established. Reassuring news came in reports of imperial Durbars and world exhibitions that dramatized the global richness of Pax Britannica. At most ten per cent of families in the United Kingdom would have had any direct personal contact with British territory in South Asia. Though some British elites cared intensely about empire, most did not, and they kept national interests close to home. When British eyes looked abroad, they looked primarily to white, temperate climes in Europe, Canada, Australia, and South Africa. Empire was a profession for bureaucrats in the India Office and Colonial Office, for the military, for diplomats, for Crown appointees in positions abroad, and for office workers, business-men, academics, missionaries, doctors, engineers, and others working overseas on British projects. Empire was a part-time concern for politicians. Few others in Britain cared or did much about it.

And few British citizens involved in empire ever spent much time in Asia. The tropics were never a popular place for them to live. South Asia was too hot, dirty, crowded, distant, and alien to attract many British citizens. At the peak of their numerical strength, in 1911, British residents in British India numbered 185,434, under one per cent of Britain's population and about 0.06 per cent of British India's population at the time. They lived in British enclaves, doing their jobs and maintaining British-style households and communities, trying to live as comfortably as possible until they could go home, hopefully better-off than when they arrived.

The Cosmopolitans

British territories in South Asia were too large and complex to be ruled from Britain. In 1871, British India had 256 million people, while England, Scotland, and Wales together had thirty-two million. By 1947, India was ten times bigger than Britain with over four hundred million people. Travel time between London and Calcutta diminished from six months to six weeks to three weeks in the nineteenth century; and undersea cable links made the telegraph a critical tool in government and business. The number of British residents in South Asia rose steadily after 1860, and resident British families became more common in British enclaves. But periods of residence were typically short, and faster communication and transportation made them shorter. Better technology improved remote control governance but left everyday controls in the hands of people in South Asia. Metropolitans involved in governance lived and worked in cosmopolitan cities.

Imperial government lived in South Asia's cosmopolitan cities, though supreme authority lived in London. Great cities in South Asia dramatized The Raj with their monumental buildings, ethnically segregated residential quarters, and grand public events. Their businesses, bureaucrats, lawyers, doctors, soldiers, educators, engineers, journalists, and other professionals made the empire work. In 1911, seven cities – Calcutta, Madras, Bombay, Hyderabad, Lucknow, Delhi, and Benares – each had many more residents than the total number of British citizens in British India. Calcutta and Bombay stood out above all other cities; they both held over one million people in 1921. Madras was half their size; and Delhi half again as big, about the size of Colombo with less than one-half million people. Outside the biggest cities, scores of lower-tier centres along railways contained most of the remainder of the empire's assets and ninety-five per cent of South Asia's urban population, which still amounted to only ten per cent of the total population in 1921. The vast majority of people in South Asia lived in rural settings into which very few British officials ever ventured. Imperial power lived in cities and towns.

Empire grew around big cities. Capital cities were core sites for investment and central nodes for transport and communication. Even today, international travellers typically arrive in South Asia by landing in one of the great cities of The Raj. The imperial transportation system laid the template for all modern infrastructure. After independence, cities maintained the advantages they enjoyed under British rule, so that nineteenth-century central places remain central today. Old cosmopolitan cities remain pre-eminent, though Karachi, Delhi, and Dhaka surged ahead after independence to join Calcutta and Bombay in the list of the world's biggest cities. The Mughal legacy also remained: cities in the Mughal heartland held half the population of the twenty-five biggest cities in British India. Most places that were physically remote and politically marginal under the Mughals remained remote and marginal under the British, and still do today: they form the majority of locales in the mountains and in poor, dry regions; they spread across high altitude regions from Baluchistan to Burma and cluster all across Central India, Jharkhand, Orissa, and the Deccan. Today, South Asia contains twenty per cent of the population of the world's top twenty-five cities. The legacy of the British presence is barely visible outside major cities; far from the railway, it is negligible and always was.

English became South Asia's cosmopolitan language in 1833, when it became the official imperial language for British India and Ceylon. Learning to read and write English fuelled social mobility everywhere in imperial society and English-educated people concentrated in major cities. In 1911, Delhi and Calcutta together had more residents counted by the census as being literate in

English than there were British citizens in South Asia. English schools boomed with funding from various sources. Official data in the 1920s indicate that ninety-seven per cent of the all the schools in British India were privately funded, though more than half of these received some government aid and more than a third were managed by local or district boards that were established in the 1880s. Endowing schools became a cultural enterprise comparable to endowing a temple or a mosque. Many aspiring social groups founded English schools. The government concentrated funding on colleges and universities and most South Asian governments have continued this practice since independence.

Literacy in general and English literacy in particular became the hallmark of social status and mobility. The seven million students reportedly in school in the 1911 census comprised about two per cent of the Indian population. Overall literacy then probably did not exceed the official figure of six per cent; and less than ten per cent of these literate people were officially counted as being literate in English, about one-half of one per cent of the total population.

English literacy was concentrated in cities in British territory. The 1911 census shows much smaller proportions of English literates in native states than in British provinces. In Calcutta, one-third of the total population was reportedly literate in 1911, and forty-four per cent of these were counted as being literate in English. Similar high overall literacy rates appear for Dhaka, Bangalore, Benares, and Delhi. Though Madras, Bombay, and Hyderabad had more typically low overall literacy rates, they shared high big-city figures for the percentage of literates who were literate in English, ranging from twenty-two per cent in Bangalore to forty-eight per cent in Madras. In 1911, Calcutta surpassed all cities with an English-literate population of 127,234 that was half again as many as in Delhi (80,947) and five times as many as in Madras and Bombay combined (25,628). The stature of the capital cities of British India is clearly reflected in the size of their English-literate populations.

Other important features of imperial society also appear in the 1911 census, and one to which we will return below needs underlining here. Official documents describing societies in South Asia employ a very particular kind of imperial framework of analysis, which had considerable influence on how people in society viewed their own identities and those around them. Census returns divided the population into religious groups, separating Hindus, Muslims, and Christians; and also divided Hindus on the lines of the *varna* classification scheme. Thus though literacy was very high among Muslim urban elites, literacy figures for Muslims are low, because most Muslim peasants and workers were not literate. Though literacy among urban elites in general was high compared with all other groups, statistics on literacy in the census do not reveal the social identity of most literate ethnic or caste groups.

One group stands out for its literacy: Brahmans. All Brahmans in British India combined to form about six per cent of the 1911 population and as an official census category they had exceptionally high rates of literacy: forty per cent in Bengal and Madras Presidencies and in some native states, like Baroda; and thirty per cent in Bombay Presidency and among Kashmiri Pandits. English literacy was also more common among literate Brahmans. More than twenty-five per cent of all literate Brahmans were literate in English in Madras and Bengal Presidencies; and the figure hovers around twenty per cent in Bombay, Kashmir, Baroda, and Mysore territories. Brahman stature in imperial society is reflected in high Brahman English literacy.

Though English literates were the most prominent members of imperial society, they numbered less than one per cent of the total population in the early twentieth century. Most were men from high status social groups, many were Brahmans, and they mostly lived in big cities. Most literate people who participated in public life read and wrote in other languages. Only fifteen per cent of all the books officially recorded as being published in British India in the 1920s were in English. The proportion of vernacular books was highest in Punjab (94%) and in the United Provinces (90%), but it was still above eighty per cent in Madras, Bengal, and Bombay Presidencies. Regional languages were the most prominent vehicles for communication among participants in imperial society.

People who participated most visibly in cosmopolitan imperial society pursued various occupations and professions. Most were civilians. English literates may have comprised about one-quarter of the one per cent of population that was employed in the armed forces and public administration. The army built the empire but civilians maintained and controlled it. In 1911, British India's standing army was very expensive to maintain in its far-flung posts, but also quite small by per capita measures compared with European armies, with one soldier for every one thousand people, a quarter the ratio in Britain and one-tenth that in Germany. Government employment in British India was also proportionately small compared with Western Europe, with about three working officials for every one thousand people.

The British empire's capacity to concentrate power and wealth in government hands remained limited. From beginning to end, the empire was organized to deliver benefits to private interests; thus the vast majority of imperial society worked outside government. In the 1920s, British India's state income was *five* per cent of British India's national income, compared with *nineteen* per cent in the UK and *twenty-nine* per cent in Japan; and *per capita* government revenue in British India was less than one pound sterling, compared with twenty-four in the UK and five in Japan. By such measures, the imperial government seems small compared with its charge. Only its military budget was large because it included expenses for imperial wars fought in China, Africa, and the Middle East. Civilian interests kept state revenues down: British businesses kept tariffs down; Indian business kept the income tax down; and landowners kept land taxes from rising even in nominal terms, which reduced them in real terms during steady inflation from 1855 to 1929. After 1880, nationalists sought to drive down government taxation and to shift expenditure away from the bloated military into civilian hands.

Regionalism

Cosmopolitan cities and regional networks around them provided most personnel for imperial governance and also organized its everyday operation. Britain's imperial administration included a tiny London elite, small British enclaves in South Asia, and soldiers, police, and bureaucrats among whom English-educated elites were most prominent, but all of these people added up to less than two per cent of the total of several hundred million people who lived in South Asia in the early twentieth century.

Honours, entitlements, and powers conferred, confirmed, authorized, and protected by the imperial state defined the vast majority of imperial society. In this respect the British empire was like earlier empires, but its scope was much wider and its influence much deeper. Modern empire disarmed the population and protected the state from internal military challenges. The legal system arrogated to the empire the universal ownership of all land, justified by the British interpretation of rights enjoyed by Mughal emperors under what they called 'Oriental despotism'. The imperial state's legal status as supreme landlord – referred to by Lord Mayo in the quotes above – allowed officials to assign entitlements to property everywhere; it gave bureaucrats vast legal authority over resources that everyone needed in everyday life. The imperial state retained as public property all the land that it did not assign to private owners. This included all rural and urban residential sites and also roads, rivers, reservoirs, forests, deserts, and any other land that private owners did not buy from the state with taxes.

Thus the small imperial bureaucracy had vast legal power. Officials used it to benefit politically important private interests. They gave forest land to British entrepreneurs for plantation development. They gave tracts of new farm land to Sikh military veterans in agricultural colonies favoured with government irrigation in Punjab. They took managerial control of huge tracts of 'reserved' forest under the Forest Department. In some mountainous regions, these forests comprised most of the land, which hence became available to loggers, miners, and others operating under contracts with the government. Virtually all the 'public land' thus allocated had been occupied by pastoral nomads, hunters, and forest dwellers who were displaced or brought under state administration. Separate tribal territories were carved out for administrative management in mountain regions.

In farming villages, private property rights were conferred on individuals in return for tax payments, and as farmers expanded the area under private land ownership, they pushed into forested areas. The expansion of private and public control over forest and open scrub land pushed nomadic and shifting populations aside. Most lost autonomous rights to land that they had worked for centuries. Among these groups, there were many fighters who had flourished in the eighteenth century who were now classified as 'criminal castes and tribes'. Most social groups who had lived migratory lives for countless generations before 1850 – fighting, hunting, and shifting cultivation from one place to another – became suspect thereafter, and many were placed under intrusive police surveillance and subjected to various 'rehabilitation' programmes intended to make them docile sedentary citizens of modern society.

The modern property system and administrative structure produced a more all-inclusive order of entitlements than ever before. As a result, imperial society grew beyond all previous bounds to embrace local landed groups as well as urban elites. But it still left a vast population of landless workers and poor people outside the imperial system of entitlements, disenfranchised, with rights that depended on their ability to gain support from influential groups. Their struggles to gain that support and to establish legal entitlements for themselves became increasingly prominent in modern politics.

All property entitlements were legalized and managed in the separate regions of imperial governance. All the regions were legally and administratively incorporated into an imperial scheme, where British imperial bureaucrats manned higher official echelons. But regions retained their own legal systems, their own administrative rules and procedures, and their own distinctive elites. The wider circles of imperial society were defined in regions where most civilians who participated in the everyday operation of the imperial order were not government officials but rather people with entitlements authorized, protected, taxed, and regulated by the government. Most of these people knew little or no English, lived outside big cities, and did not identify personally with the British or even with The Raj. They rather lived their lives within old environments of social identity and social experience. They constituted the vast majority of imperial society: they were ordinary people whose everyday lives were necessarily bound up with government despite their social distance from British elites and their cultural exclusion from the imperial spotlight.

The grandest regional elites did actually enter the imperial spotlight, now and then. They were native state dynasties established by treaties during the century of British conquest. Aggressive imperial expansion put many native state dynasties in harsh light and deposed a good number. All the old ruling families fell under increasing bureaucratic control and surveillance. But major dynasties remained powerful in their regions. Dynastic families, allies, and subordinates retained substantial control over forty per cent of the land area of British India and twenty per cent of its population. Native states held ninety-four million people in 1947. The largest, Hyderabad, had twice the population of Ireland and Scotland combined. Kashmir was the size of France. Mysore, Travancore, Sikkim, and Rajasthan states were also like small countries. Indirect rule through native monarchs allowed the empire to tap resources in native states while giving old elites a stake in the imperial system. As in centuries past, subordinate regional rulers held fast to honours that defined their nobility. In 1903, when King Edward VII was proclaimed the emperor of India at a Delhi Durbar, and again in 1911, when King George V attended a second Delhi Durbar to mark the transfer of the capital, India's 'native princes' marched in the ceremonial ranks to display their honoured place in imperial society.

Also dating back to the century of conquest, Zamindar landlordism defined local agrarian elites in Bengal, Bihar, the United Provinces of Agra and Oudh (Uttar Pradesh), and in scattered regions in the peninsula, Punjab, North-West Frontier, and central India. As we have seen, the term '*zamindar*' goes back to Mughal times, when it designated the lowest layer of sovereignty. The Company granted the title to tax payers who became private owners of landed estates called Zamindaris. Some new Zamindars were old rajas. Many were descended from eighteenth-century revenue speculators and military adventurers. Others came from rich farming families and elite tribal lineages. Their tenants numbered from dozens to many thousands, and under imperial law had to pay rent to Zamindars to retain rights to their land. Zamindari tenants thus became permanent underlings in the political structure of imperial society. As the Company's hunger for revenue and its passion for bureaucracy grew, it squeezed many Zamindars for taxes and shifted state policies in newly acquired territories toward 'settlements' for land revenue with peasants in local communities. But the folly of trying to eliminate Zamindars from the local ranks of imperial society in lands along the Ganga basin became clear in the 1857 rebellion, after which vast new landed estates were signed over to super-rich Zamindars, called Talukdars, in Awadh (Oudh).

The character of Zamindari landlordism changed significantly in the nineteenth century. In 1793, Lord Cornwallis had given Zamindars full powers to set their own rents and define tenures on their estates in the Permanent Settlement with Zamindars in Bengal and Bihar. At the same time, he had fixed Zamindar tax rates in perpetuity, to stabilize state revenues, to give landlords unrestricted rights to increasing rental income, and thus to secure the Zamindars' loyalty. In the early nineteenth century, however, the Company's rigorous annual cash tax demands crushed many Zamindars and caused a huge turn-over of Zamindar estates, which provoked complaints against the Company's ill-treatment of its agrarian aristocracy. Still, for every Zamindar who defaulted, another came forward to buy the land, producing a circulation of Zamindar families rather than a secular decline of the Zamindar class.

When the Company died, the Zamindars lost support. Though they collectively wielded tremendous local power, and though their wealth increased with the value of their land, their legal and economic position as landlords weakened. The government supported their rights but changed the rules of entitlement, abandoning permanent tax rates for periodic reassessments when this was legally possible. Government irrigation did often benefit Zamindars, but wealthy tenants invested much more heavily in land, a trend that the government also encouraged by enacting tenancy reforms after 1870 that circumscribed Zamindars' power to define conditions of tenancy. Bankers absorbed more and more Zamindar rental income.

By 1900, Zamindars could not prevent police from pursuing suspects into their estates and had to abide by new laws that favoured tenants. Many estates had been re-organized by the managerial bureaucracy of the state's Court of Wards. Squeezed by rising tenant resistance and by government restrictions, many Zamindars lost the power to collect rents. They secured their wealth by financing tenant investments and investing their own rental income in non-agricultural ventures in cities and towns.

Zamindar rental and banking incomes moved into urban education, business, and professional careers. In many large and small
urban centres, Zamindar families and employees became leaders
of society. In the countryside, Zamindars remained powerful elites
and many still remain so today, despite the abolition of most
Zamindar tenures in the 1960s.

The shift in government policies on land entitlements began in
Madras in the early 1800s and reached a milestone in 1813 when
Thomas Munro convinced parliament to authorize a Ryotwari
settlement with individual farmers. Thus after 1813, the ranks of
imperial society extended down the social scale as London sought
to increase tax revenue and to spread private property rights more
widely than the Zamindari system allowed. In London, Munro
convinced parliament that alien Muslim sultans had imposed
Zamindari landlordism in south India, and that private peasant
property in land was the authentic, ancient form of entitlement
everywhere in village India. Charles Metcalfe captured the new
official view of rural tradition most memorably in 1830:

> The village communities are little republics, having nearly every-
> thing they want within themselves, and almost independent of any
> foreign relations. They seem to last where nothing else lasts.
> Dynasty after dynasty tumbles down; revolution succeeds to
> revolution; Hindoo, Patan, Mogul, Mahratta, Sik, English are all
> masters in turn; but the village communities remain the same . . . If
> a country remain for a series of years the scene of continued pillage
> and massacre, so that villages cannot be inhabited, the scattered
> villagers nevertheless return whenever the power of peaceable
> possession revives. A generation may pass away, but the
> succeeding generation will return. The sons will take the place of
> their fathers; the same site for the village, the same position for the
> houses, the same lands, will be occupied by the descendants of
> those who were driven out when the village was depopulated.

Following on this official revelation – which was a very far cry
from historical reality but served the empire well – the government
henceforth settled for land revenue primarily with village landowners, either individually or collectively, first in Madras and
Bombay Presidencies, and later in Punjab and central India. As a
result, Zamindar middlemen between the state and farmers were
eliminated in much of British India. Ryotwari settlements with

individual Ryots and Mahalwari settlements with villages (*mahals*) vastly increased the population of local patriarchs with official status in the empire.

The rising social status and aspirations of village landowners and Zamindari tenants became a significant political force, particularly in regions where commercial farming produced farming families with assets to invest in the land. Wherever tenant farmers were most active commercially, they had the most success in raising legal challenges to Zamindar rights over their land. Munro had been right to argue that Ryotwari landowners would pay the state handsomely for private property rights, and they paid higher per capita taxes than all other landowners. But Ryotwari landowners also proved extremely adept at preventing tax rates from rising in proportion to the increasing value of their land. During the inflationary decades, 1870–1929, when commercial agriculture expanded most dramatically, real tax rates declined as incomes grew among landed families who invested in wells, bulls, and agricultural finance.

AGRARIAN SOCIETIES AND IMPERIAL ENTITLEMENTS

The imperial system of land rights was anchored in existing social relations of rank and power in rural society. It provoked and organized agrarian conflicts that had long-term, wide-ranging political effects, as we will see. All of these conflicts emerged in contexts that were shaped by old ethnic and social formations in the countryside as well as by the imposition of a new imperial order. Numerous conflicts emerged during the transition to the new entitlement system. The most dramatic example is the 1857 rebellion in regions around Lucknow and Agra and in nearby Bundelkhand, where old warrior clans fought to prevent the Company from reducing their rural stature. Some families lost out in the process; others won; but overall, formerly dominant social groups, including Rajputs and Thakurs in Bundelkhand, re-established their dominance on new legal grounds under the British.

Struggles between the groups that held official entitlements and those that did not became enduring features of agrarian politics. In each region, tenant struggles evolved in their own social context.

Each region had its own collection of politically privileged groups, its own cultural profile of social rank and conflict, its own ethnic flavour.

- Uttar Pradesh and Bihar had the highest percentage of Brahmans at every level in agrarian society. Uttar Pradesh contains roughly forty per cent of all Brahmans living in India today. The great Zamindars and Talukdars of Uttar Pradesh and Bihar included Brahmans, Muslims, Rajputs, and Bhumihars. Their most prominent tenants were Goala (Ahir), Kurmi, Yadavs, and Lodis – almost all Hindus. As we will see, the political progress of tenants in this region would include substantial recourse to idioms of Hindu devotionalism and caste status.

- In western Uttar Pradesh, Rajasthan, Punjab, Sind, North-West Frontier Provinces, Malwa, and the Central Provinces, the various Brahman, Jat, Rajput, Brahman, Maratha, Sikh, and Muslim landowners each had their own tracts. The spatial pattern of separation among Sikh, Muslim, and Hindu Jats would have particular importance for the binding of religion to agrarian politics in Punjab.

- In Bengal, the urbane *bhadralok* came substantially from the families of high caste Hindu Zamindars and their retainers. Zamindar tenant farmers and labourers were low caste Hindus and Muslims. Three major tenant castes dominated localities in nineteenth-century West Bengal: Sadgop, Kaibartta, and Aguri. These groups had colonized their territories before permanent settlement, and in the twentieth century their power was challenged by upwardly mobile caste groups (Mayra, Chasadhoba, Jogi, Namasudra, and Pod). Menial workers in the homes and factories of Calcutta were largely low caste Hindus and poor Muslims from Bihar. Almost all Zamindari tenants in eastern districts of Bengal were Muslims, and most of their landlords were Hindus. All of these ethnic distinctions in Bengal would take political forms in the twentieth century.

- In Assam, prominent Ahom, Koch, Kalita, and Rajbansi families controlled territories that received waves of immigrant Bengali peasants looking for land. Conflicts between indigenous peoples and foreign colonists would separate the hill farmers, lowland farmers, plantation owners, and Bengali peasants into competing ethnic factions in the twentieth century.

- In other regions, locally dominant landed castes – Gujarati Kunbis, Maratha Kunbis, Malayali Nayars, Telugu Kammas, Kapus, and Reddys; Kannadiga Vokkaligas, Lingayats, and Boyas; and Tamil Vanniyas, Vellalas, Kallars, and Maravars – controlled their own territories and lorded over low caste workers and poor peasants. All of these groups became locally dominant as the modern political system evolved.
- In native states, dynasties and their allies formed ethnic elites, some very small, like the Muslim dynasty in Hyderabad and the Hindu regime in Kashmir. The ethnic minority status of the Hyderabad and Kashmir dynasties provoked them to enact landlord policies that favoured small ruling cliques and caused widespread resentment among tenants whose struggles for land rights became political opposition to the dynasty. Both states witnessed severe violence as their native state dynasties ended in 1947.

Power relations between landlords and tenants changed over time, in part because regional state officials played an increasingly prominent role in enforcing and revising land laws, and in part because tenant power grew as tenants expanded commercial crop production. The main issue pitting tenants against landlords was who had rights to new wealth from the land. When tenants did the work to increase farm production, they fought hard for rights to keep the proceeds. Struggles among farmers, financiers, and landowners embroiled state officials who necessarily took sides in disputes.

Some struggles became violent and turned against the imperial state when it blindly backed up landlords against powerfully organized tenants. One telling case comes from Malabar in northern Kerala. The region was conquered by Tipu Sultan and then absorbed into Madras Presidency after Tipu's final defeat in 1799. A rapid shift in social power relations then occurred as British administrators reinstalled Brahman (Namboodri) and high caste Nair *jenmi* landlords who had declined in power or had been expelled under Tipu's regime. The autonomy that Mappillai

Muslim farmers had enjoyed under Tipu Sultan was then dramatically erased by the British. Mappillai farmers became Muslim tenants whose interests opposed Hindu landlords backed up by the British, whose mistake was to imagine that *authentic local tradition* had been prescribed by Hindu law. We consider the origin of this imperial mindset in the next section of this chapter.

As a result of British land policy, mosques in Malabar became centres for sermons against landlords and money lenders, and also against the police and British administrators who backed them up with force. Twenty-two local Mappillai revolts occurred between 1836 and 1854; more broke out in 1882–5 and 1896; and several more erupted before 1919. Altogether, these revolts involved only a few hundred activists; but they left a lasting impression. The rebels inspired folklore with bold attacks on temples and police stations and with their fearless self-martyrdom as *shahid*s destined for heaven. Madras government compiled hundreds of pages of reports on these 'Moplah outbreaks', filled with contemptuous awe for Mappillai *shahid*s. Madras officials wrote thousands of pages on Malabar land tenures in an effort to address tenant problems without disturbing the landlords. Yet nothing much was done in practice except to increase police power.

A large number of agrarian conflicts over entitlements to land arose in areas where farmers were rapidly pushing intensive agriculture into jungles, swamps, and mountains during the nineteenth century. Such regions were numerous in and around Bengal. In 1800, observers guessed that only about thirty per cent of cultivable land in the huge expanse of Bengal Presidency was being farmed. By 1900, farms had filled all the lowlands and were moving into Assam and into the hills on all sides of the deltaic tract, from Chhotanagpur and Orissa to Sylhet and Chittagong.

Conflicts during this rapid transformation of the agrarian landscape were of two major kinds, both etched in heavy ethnic tones. One pitted settled farming communities and landlords against tribal communities practising shifting cultivation, called *jhum*. Conflicts of this kind occurred across all mountainous lands from Gujarat to Bastar. The biggest outburst of violence involved a large, diverse group of forest cultivators, the Santhals, who had for centuries farmed uplands on the fringe of settled villages in the eastern Ganga basin and in adjacent regions. Santhals interacted regularly with farming communities in the lowlands. They cleared land in the jungle with fire and axe, making the extension of perennial farm cultivation much easier for lowland farmers. Before the nineteenth century, it appears that Santhal groups did not participate in rituals of rank in agrarian states; so they did not obtain official entitlements to land based upon ranked subordination in official hierarchies. Like other tribal groups, they maintained their separate social structures and hierarchies, their own rituals of rank.

In the nineteenth century, as revenue-paying farmers and Zamindars moved into *jhum* lands to expand agriculture, Santhals were steadily pushed into the forest. By 1850, they had moved out of districts in Orissa, Chotanagpur, Bihar, and Bengal, following skirmishes with Zamindari farmers in 1811, 1820, and 1830. In 1823, large Santhal settlements, formed under official state protection, ringed the Rajmahal hills in the Daman-i-Koh, 'the skirt of the hills', where by the 1840s, 83,000 Santhals lived in government territory, legally free of Zamindar control. Santhal leaders sought to establish a permanent homeland here, free of constant meddling by foreign money lenders and Company officials. Under the full moon on 30 June 1855, ten thousand Santhals are said to have heard a young leader named Siddhu declare his vision from god that Daman must be 'cleared of all outsiders, that moneylenders and policemen be immediately slaughtered, and that Superintendent Pontet be also slain'. In the ensuing war, Company troops and Zamindars massacred Santhals and their low caste peasant allies.

Mundas around Ranchi and many other smaller groups also waged similar wars to create independent territories in the nineteenth century. None succeeded, but their legacies live today in the political movement for autonomy in Jharkhand, 'the land of jungles'. As Santhals were driven back from the moving borders of Zamindari land, the state instituted tribal territories to segregate forest peoples in Bastar, other parts of the central mountains, and regions of the high mountains. This officially segregated the regional histories of the high mountains of the north-east and created the basis for separate national identities in Nagaland, Manipur, Mizoram, and the Chittagong hill tracts. As farmers pushed from Bengal into Assam, conflicts pitting farmers against plains tribals also occurred, and today conflict is raging in Assam which pits Ahoms against Bengalis in the plains and Bodo warriors fighting for a homeland in the hills.

Also in the nineteenth century, however, conflicts between Zamindars and tenants occurred inside the framework of imperial property law. In Zamindar territory, farming was primarily the work of peasant families and of superior tenants who combined labour and finance to create new farmland and to expand commercial production. Zamindars had many ways to exert power over tenants – legally and otherwise – but cultivation always entailed two distinct moments of power: the *physical* activity of farming and the *political* extension of Zamindari property rights over new production. By extending and intensifying cultivation, tenants made claims to property that Zamindars also claimed. Collecting rent from tenants was always a political activity that reinscribed ranks into rural society, season after season. Struggles over rights to farm land could allow tenants to entrench their legal position, as they increased the value of their own land, resisted Zamindar claims to rent, or bought tenures.

Legal activity thus formed a basic feature of agrarian politics in Bengal and Bihar from the 1760s onward. The comparative strength of tenants in different Zamindari territories is indicated by their relative success in getting rights recorded and payments acknowledged in receipts. In Bihar, tenants were relatively weak and Zamindars remained supreme. In Bengal, however, the relatively open frontier of agricultural expansion strained Zamindar power. Zamindars always met resistance when they endeavoured to extend their rights over new cultivation, and where open land for peasant colonization was most abundant, Zamindars faced the most difficult challenge. In such areas, a rent-seeking Zamindar might most profitably acquire new revenues by allowing effective ownership to devolve into stratified farming communities in which money lenders and larger tenants established superior rights over farming families. This was typical in Bengal, particularly in the east, north, and south.

Acts of the Bengal Government revised the terms of Zamindar property law in 1819, 1822, 1859, 1865, 1869, 1876, 1884, 1885, 1886, and 1894. At every step, pressure from tenants pushed reform. In 1859, the Bengal government insisted for the first time that tenant rights be recorded, which gave tenants new leverage. In 1873, a district judge's ruling encouraged a group of tenants in Yusufsahi to form an Agrarian League to defend tenants in Pabna District against additional rent claims, 'illegal cesses' (*abwab*s), and threats to their occupancy rights. The League led demonstrations in town to raise support for their cause. Their activity evoked critical reactions from Zamindari interests in Calcutta. But Pabna landlords who fought the League impoverished themselves in court and the number of perpetual leases jumped up from 627 to 1633 in the years between 1873 and 1877. This was the beginning of a long movement among Bengal tenants to secure tenures and lower rents and to restrict Zamindar power. Tenant activists and Zamindar allies occupied opposing positions in legal battles that became political positions in regional and national politics in the twentieth century.

FIVE

Origins of Nationality

National identities evolved inside modern imperial society. National experience became a defining feature of modern life. So entrenched are national identities today that they seem to be natural or even eternal, but they came into being as a result of historical innovations in the nineteenth century.

Nationality became a new kind of collective identity in old regions that made their own distinctive impact on its substance and meaning. Regions had their own vernacular languages, literatures, religious institutions, and cultural legacies. Empire brought all the regions into one political system but also enhanced their distinctiveness. Regions developed their own imperial institutions, urban hierarchies, bureaucracies, and legal and educational systems. Print media, schools, and public activity standardized regional languages. In official publications like the census, each region had a standard list of caste, ethnic, and religious groups; and thus each region attained a distinctive social profile, officially codified and enumerated every decade after 1871.

The empire never homogenized all its official statistics the way national states have done since 1950. Each provincial volume of the imperial census has distinctive features, most of all in social categories that describe the population. Imperial statistics did not embrace all native states until the 1930s. Each regional government printed its own manual of administration. Beginning with legislation that established local governments in the 1880s, political institutions also developed distinctively in each region. All the regions also had their own cultural politics. Activists, artists, and scholars worked to recuperate and reinterpret distinctive regional traditions; they developed new literary genres; and they engaged in projects of social uplift and reform – all in regional idioms. Imperial modernity gave old regions new life.

INVENTING NATIVE SOCIETY

Regional identities spawned national identities as cosmopolitan elites developed shared ideas about native society. The intellectual substance of national identity arose initially in the definition of native society by authors in cosmopolitan centres who stood forth as representatives of the native population and who became exemplars of national identity.

The empire's cultural hierarchy had a profound impact on cosmopolitans who invested native society with modern meaning. For the British, the most essential division in imperial society was that separating the 0.06 per cent of the population who were British from the 99.94 per cent who were not. The 99.94 per cent became 'natives'. Marking and reinforcing this ranked cultural division flattered and strengthened the class-conscious British ethnics whose small numerical force needed all the help it could get. Making British officials seem all-powerful was a cultural project that resembles the painting of halos on sultans and the Mughal concoction of the emperor's omnipotence. But the British empire was not a shifting set of ethnic and military alliances filled with layered sovereignties; rather, it reduced all its subjects to the official status of unarmed civilians. The whole population that ranked beneath the British 0.06 per cent officially comprised a native society under British authority.

The intellectual activity that defined native society began in the early days of British rule. Initially, Company governance rested on the legal premise that the Company ruled India on Indian principles. Native authorities legitimated early British legislation and judicial decisions; and the Mughal emperor himself had authorized the Company Raj in Bengal. After 1820, British ideas became dominant, but they still needed native authority for legitimacy. Property law needed to be justified with precedents and principles from old texts and old regimes. Personal law needed to be anchored in native codes and practices. In the eighteenth century, therefore, Company officials began their quest for indigenous codes and authorities to guide their law making. Indo-Persian scholars of Arabic, Persian, and Sanskrit stepped forward to provide the needed information. Based on that information, Company law makers and judges divided imperial society into legal 'communities' defined by religious laws that seemed to govern South Asia and Europe alike. Sacred texts attained legal authority. Religious texts and experts became part of government policy making and public debate. In Company courts, native tradition became religious tradition defined and composed by the local learned elites who controlled sacred texts in classical languages.

The politics of law making thus included legal reasoning based on the authority of native tradition. Defining tradition became an integral feature of imperial governance. For example, when British missionaries pressured the Company to outlaw *sati* – the immolation of a widow on her husband's funeral pyre – proposed legislation to ban *sati* produced opposition from local groups who claimed *sati* had religious sanction. When the legislation passed, in 1929, it rested on the authority of the Chief Pandit (Hindu religious expert) who was employed by the Calcutta Supreme Court, and who had opined in 1817 that *sati* was not sanctioned in the officially recognized Sanskrit legal texts (*sastras*). Similarly, Company courts initially followed orthodox Brahman opinion in Calcutta to declare that a remarried widow did not have a wife's legal right to inherit property. But after extended debates and public efforts by social reformers to reinterpret tradition, widow remarriage was legally recognized, in 1856. Beginning in the early nineteenth century, social reform movements led by cosmopolitan intellectuals strove to change social practices through innovations in religious interpretation that also facilitated reformist legislation.

After 1858, under Crown rule, basic principles for legal judgements had been established; there was no further need for courts to consult official Pandits and Maulvis (Muslim legal experts), as Company judges had done. But legislation that touched religious sensibilities still sparked controversy. For example, proposals to legislate a minimum 'age of consent' for a girl's marriage provoked conflicting interpretations of authoritative texts. Many such disputes produced reports and petitions to courts and legislators, because people in countless groups had disputes about marriage, inheritance, and ritual practices. Common law recognized tradition as authoritative. What tradition was in reality became a matter of debates recorded and propagated in newspapers, tracts, and public meetings. An official archive composed of authorized official knowledge about native tradition informed the composition of imperial law on all civil matters. Official studies of traditional practices gave rise to the modern discipline of ethnography, as official texts on administration and law came to include information on traditions among 'castes and tribes' and filled official ethnographic encyclopaedias for each region.

The government needed native authority to determine what native tradition *should be*. This made native experts prominent public figures in cosmopolitan circles where interpreting native tradition became a professional activity for public intellectuals. In these same intellectual circles, learned members of urban society were interpreting tradition, working to understand the world around them, and striving to change that world at the same time. Cosmopolitan disputes about tradition reflected changing social and cultural conditions even as disputants portrayed tradition as being fixed and unchanging. Empire provoked endless disputes about the legitimacy of practices deemed to be traditional. In this disputation, recognized authorities in imperial society constructed tradition as the ancient inheritance of native cultures.

Thus the rhetorical and analytical opposition of change and stability, reform and orthodoxy, Europe and Asia, and modernity and tradition became ingrained in imperial society. This set of oppositions structured public discourse. Traditionalists sought to protect what they claimed to be ancient rights. Modernists fought for what they imagined to be universal rights. Reformers worked to reinterpret and change tradition on what they saw as modern lines. Meanwhile, out in imperial society, people gained new entitlements based on ancient rights, people sued for new rights by invoking tradition, and people used sacred texts to fight for and against innovations in law and social practice.

LANGUAGE AND AUTHORITY

Native social identity first became a national identity for cosmopolitan activists who were literate in English and who spoke to one another and to imperial officials as representatives of the people among whom they ranked as natives. Three activities were most influential: (1) defining tradition, (2) reforming society, and (3) influencing government. All these activities required cultural authority. Old elites were most prominent early on, but as societies changed, authority shifted into various professional niches, particularly in higher education and legal chambers. All these activities were also contentious; they fostered debate and conflict that became more and more vocal and visible in civil society. All these activities preoccupied a wide variety of people inside and outside cosmopolitan settings. Many people engaged in all three. But they were distinctive and they became professional specializations. Broadly speaking, religious experts defined (and redefined) tradition; improving society fell to social reformers, and speaking for the nation became a job for politicians.

Cosmopolitan activities that built national identities always involved mediations between English and other languages. In 1833, English became pre-eminent. But scholars had to document and translate authentic native traditions by using non-English texts. Reformers needed to propagate their ideas in vernaculars and to influence government in English. The vast majority of people who wanted their voices heard in government did not know English and needed English interpreters and publicists. Mediators between English and other languages wrote, debated, and interpreted policy, law, tradition, and political programmes. They structured public debate as they constructed nationality inside imperial modernity. The regionalism of all vernaculars gave nationality many languages and many multi-lingual orientations. In the early days, the old imperial languages, Persian and Sanskrit, held positions of special privilege; and this gave the remnants of the Indo-Persian elite special prominence in the formative phase of imperial legislation.

The first generation of linguistic mediators lived in eighteenth-century Calcutta. Under Company authority, they developed a methodology for writing laws for British India by compiling authentic indigenous traditions from native texts in Sanskrit, Arabic, and Persian. To apply their methodology, which was called Orientalism, they needed classical language expertise. To write native law, Orientalist scholars and officials established that Hindus and Muslims formed separate legal communities with their own separate laws, cultures, and histories, documented in their separate classical languages. Defining legal canons on religious grounds suited British ideas about the separation of Christianity from Islam and Hinduism; it also provided a template for multi-cultural accommodation of cultural difference. Ideas from European legal history underpinned legal theory and policy making in British India, and these same ideas gave old texts and textual expertise in India a new legal authority. In light of Sanskrit *sastra*s, for example, officials determined that Hindu society was permanently divided into traditionally fixed castes according to *varna* and *jati*; this principle was applied legally and bureau-cratically across British India to reinvent caste as a modern legal and administrative category.

Elaborating these principles led census enumerators to count Jains, Sikhs, Parsis, Jews, Buddhists, and other religious groups in the category of minority communities. The census counted as many non-Muslims and non-Christians as possible under the category of Hindus, dividing them into caste (*jati*) or 'sub-caste' rankings inside the four *varna*s (Brahman, Kshatriya, Vaisya, and Sudra). Divisions between Hindu and Muslim were most scrupulously maintained in the official mind even after Orientalist methods for writing and interpreting law were abandoned, in the 1820s, in favour of legal methods that gave more weight to local precedent and to universal principles of individual rights. The classification of people in society according to religion and caste organized imperial activity to the end of British rule. Hindu and Muslim personal law remained separate. Hindus and Muslims were treated as statistically separate native communities for many official purposes. After 1871, imperial census enumerators who found that many people did not identify themselves as either Hindu or Muslim were instructed by their superiors to assign people to one of these two categories anyway.

Orientalist methods for law making had diffuse long-term effects and gave the British empire in India a distinctly Brahman flavour, because Brahmans were native experts in Hindu law. The official definition of India's majority population as Hindu gave Brahman experts vast influence. Cosmopolitan Brahmans guided official interpretations of native tradition and gave Sanskrit texts unprecedented authority. This trend had old precedents and was not unique to British India. As we have seen, Brahman authority prevailed in legal administration under the Peshwas in eighteenth-century Maratha country. Religious codes also became popular among other eighteenth-century rulers, including many Muslims and Portuguese and French Catholics. Brahmans became arbiters of law and political power in Nepal, where the Ranas enacted Caste Codes in the 1850s to regulate a society that included many Buddhists. In the native state of Jammu and Kashmir, Brahmans wrote the laws for a Dogra dynasty, established in 1846, whose subjects were mostly Muslim.

After 1833, when English became the language of the empire, cosmopolitan bilingualism focused less on mediations between English and Persian, Arabic, and Sanskrit; and more on mediations between English and regional languages: Tamil and Sinhala in Colombo, Bengali in Calcutta, Tamil and Telugu in Madras, Marathi and Gujarati in Bombay, Punjabi and Urdu in Punjab, and Hindustani across the Gangetic plains. This shift made language a political issue, because different literati specialized in different regional languages and on different texts defining what native society should be understood to be. Schools and printing presses standardized regional languages, which made them more distinct. In everyday speech, people typically combined elements from various languages, and in non-literate social life, language difference was not sharply marked. But in print, language difference becomes visible, and when people become literate, script, grammar, and vocabulary separate the languages they learn to read. South Asian scripts are phonetic, so that almost any language can be written in almost any script with a few adjustments. In modern printed texts, each language attained its own script. Script thus became an iconic representation for literate language communities.

Modern print culture separated vernacular language communities, particularly in urban centres where literacy was most widespread, but also more generally for people who became literate during upward social mobility, which often led them from village to town. This separation of social identities on linguistic lines produced conflict over the representation of native society by people in diverging communities. Though Hindi and Urdu blended into one spoken language called Hindustani, they were typically printed in different scripts: Sanskrit Devagari and Persian Nastaliq, respectively. With mass machine printing, Hindi and Urdu literary cultures generated activists using Hindi and Urdu who propagated different ideas about native society. They strove to separate their respective languages by writing with vocabularies and literary styles evoking Sanskrit and Persian classical forms, respectively. As a result, Hindi and Urdu texts became respectively associated with Hindu and Muslim ideas about native society, and their different scripts became associated with officially separate religious identities.

INDIA IN CALCUTTA

Bengal was the oldest province in British India. During the nineteenth century, Bengal Presidency was by far the biggest province; it stood head and shoulders above others in its imperial influence. Its capital, Calcutta, was the capital of British India. Bengal contained most of the assets of British India until the 1860s, when roads and railways up the Ganga basin and imperial investments in the United Provinces and Punjab rapidly shifted the empire's centre of gravity into regions around Delhi. Even then, however, Bengal remained several times larger than other provinces, until 1905, when Bihar, Assam, and Orissa were detached. The upheaval caused by that reduction in Bengal's size became a watershed in the history of nationalism, as we will soon see. When New Delhi became the imperial capital, in 1911, Calcutta became a regional capital; and after 1947, Calcutta's region shrank by more than half, when eastern Bengal became East Pakistan. But in the nineteenth century, Calcutta's stature was supreme.

Calcutta was British India's home town. On its streets, people spoke Bengali, as did most people in the surrounding Bengal region. Its eighteenth-century elites were Indo-Persian literati, both Hindu and Muslim. As it became a sprawling imperial capital, its urban population came to include a larger proportion than any other of English-literate professionals and office workers, many belonging to upwardly mobile families from the countryside, including Zamindars and their employees. In 1911, Calcutta's English-literate population was half again as large as Delhi's and five times that of Madras and Bombay combined. Calcutta was a regional city that spoke directly to London. Laws were made in Calcutta for all of British India. For the empire's metropolitan elite, Calcutta's English-literate public activists represented Indian native society most immediately and forcefully. Calcutta intellectuals thus attained a special native status to speak for, about, and to India. They were also people with high caste identities formed inside a Bengali *bhadralok* ('respectable people') culture; their particularly inventive construction of native society and nationality formed a creative counterpoint to imperial Brahmanism.

Indian native society first took intellectual shape in Calcutta in the days of Ram Mohun Roy (1772–1833), often called 'the father of modern India'. Ram Mohun grew up in a stronghold of Indo-Persian intellectualism, which included, in his day, a number of Englishmen, most prominently, the great Orientalist, William Jones (1746–94). Jones had learned Latin, Greek, Hebrew, Arabic, and Persian at Oxford and he was called to the bar, in 1774, and knighted, in 1783, before he came to Calcutta as a Supreme Court judge. There he studied Sanskrit and founded the Asiatic Society, in 1784. Jones pioneered Orientalism by using classical learning, legal training, linguistic skill, and command of local experts to compile Hindu and Muslim law codes. Another of Ram Mohun Roy's contemporaries, Mirza Abu Taleb (1752–1806), was born in Lucknow to a family from Isphahan, and he also moved to Calcutta for government work, but failing to find it, sailed to England with a Scottish friend. He returned to publish an account of his travels that argued in classic Persian style that Europe was steeped in materialism, whereas in India (religious) truth prevailed. He agreed with Ram Mohun Roy and William Jones that Indian and European cultures rested on distinctive, coherent traditions that could be reconciled by keeping each in their proper place.

The idea that Indian tradition was recorded in sacred tenets guided Ram Mohun Roy's education. He was twenty-two when Jones arrived and thirty when Abu Taleb returned from London.

At thirty-two, he published his first book on the essence of monotheism. He wrote in a Persian style that was indistinguishable to many at the time from that of Shah Wali Allah (1702–63), a renowned Sufi scholar in north India who strove to return Islam to Quranic essentials. Roy undertook a similar task for Hinduism. In 1828, he formed the Brahmo Samaj to promulgate a faithful interpretation of Vedic truth, congregational worship, and rational discussion. His Vedic purism rejected idol worship and caste divisions in society, which are not described in the Vedas. His religious mission entailed a reformist approach to prevailing Brahman social practices such as child marriage and the prohibition of widow remarriage. In practice, his cultural innovations were designed to make Brahman ideas more relevant for urbane Bengalis who worked alongside Europeans in Calcutta and who formed the beginnings of what would become India's urban middle class.

In the 1820s, in Ram Mohun Roy's later life, British national power expanded dramatically and imperialists became more nationally self-conscious and aggressive. British missionaries attacked Hinduism, Utilitarians denounced Orientalism, Company taxation ruined prominent Zamindars, British tariffs ruined Bengali weavers, and British businessmen cut Calcutta merchants out of the export trade. Aggressive British ethnic chauvinism fostered a new brand of cosmopolitan society in which natives stood more squarely on the underside of a racial divide. The separation of Indian and British cultures became starker. One of the merchants who lost out in the process was Ram Mohun's friend, Dwarkanath Tagore, a prominent Zamindar and businessman. Dwarkanath's son, Debendranath (1817–1905) succeeded Roy as leader of the Brahmo Samaj, repudiated the Vedas and declared reason and intuition to be the basis of true Brahmanism. Keshab Chunder Sen (1838–84) opened a new branch of the Samaj that sponsored temperance, encouraged the education of women, and campaigned for the remarriage of widows and for legislation to prevent child marriage. But when Keshab Sen arranged for his young daughter to marry a child prince of Cooch Behar, another new branch of the Samaj was formed, in 1878, which embraced Upanishadic mysticism.

Over the years, social reform faded in the Brahmo agenda amidst a rising sense of separation and opposition between Indian and British culture. In this context, Calcutta's growing middle class employed in clerical jobs, schools, businesses, professions, and government service flocked to hear Shri Ramakrishna (1836–86), who led a middle class spiritual revival. Born Gadadhar Chattopadhyaya, Ramakrishna was a poor Brahman with little formal schooling. He spoke only Bengali and knew neither English nor Sanskrit. A talented mystic, he had visions of Muhammad, Jesus, and Krishna. He preached that all religions are one. His large audiences included Europeans, for whom he represented a distinctively Indian spiritualism. He never published. He foreshadowed Mohandas Karamchand Gandhi (1869–1948) – India's national *mahatma* (great soul) – in seeing god everywhere. He proclaimed that all religions are merely different *ghat*s (steps) leading to the same water. 'Hindus call the water *jal*,' he said, 'while Muslims call it *pani* and Christians call it water; but it is all the same substance, no essential difference.' Ramakrishna inspired middle class individuals who sought to encompass the manifold diversity of their cultural environment, transcending the West's materialism and Christianity, and incorporating Islam into a larger cultural essence in the idiom of the Upanishads.

Also in Ramakrishna's lifetime, however, *jal* and *pani* were becoming linguistic markers for diverging cultural identities among activist Bengali Hindus and Muslims. Ideas hardened about the separation of religious groups. As Ramakrishna called the mystical transcendence of religious difference India's cultural essence, other activists turned religious division into a defining feature of Indian society.

1857 had raised and crushed the last vestige of Mughal authority, and in its aftermath the idea spread that alien Muslim invaders, now definitively defeated, had once conquered Hindu India. In the old Mughal heartland, defensive efforts ensued to revive Muslim culture. Muhammad 'Abid Husayn founded the Deoband School, in 1868, to inculcate ideas of Shah Wali Allah and of north Indian Wahhabiyah sectarians into a modern brand of Islamic puritanism. Then Syed Ahmad Khan founded the Muhammadan Anglo-Oriental College at Aligarh, in 1875, to foster Western learning among the Muslim intelligentsia. In Punjab, the Brahmo Samaj spawned an aggressively anti-Muslim, anti-Christian Arya Samaj, founded by Swami Dayanand Sarasvati, who invented the *suddhi* ritual of re-conversion to Hinduism. In Kashmir, Raja Ranbir Singh enacted Brahmanical law codes called the *Ain-i-Dharmath* in a native state inhabited mostly by Muslims whose public piety became politically suspect. In Bombay Presidency, Brahmans in Pune promulgated a new Hindu orthodoxy harking back to the Peshwas to counter challenges to Brahman caste privilege by Jotirao Phule, whose *Priestcraft Exposed* appeared in 1869. At the same time, a new generation of European Orientalists, led by Max Mueller, compiled texts to document the Hindu golden age. In 1870, H.H. Cole, Superintendent of Archaeology, announced that his department would seek to rediscover India 'before the Mohamedan invasions'.

Representing the intellectual trends dividing religious traditions in Ramakrishna's Calcutta, the first Bengali novelist, Bankim Chandra Chatterjee (1838–94), composed an essentially Hindu Bengali nation in which Muslims were antagonistic outsiders. Raised in an orthodox Brahman family and educated in English at Presidency College, Bankim Chandra was one of the first graduates of the University of Calcutta and served as a deputy magistrate from 1858 until 1891. His novels are historical fictions. The first, *Durgesh Nandini*, featured a Rajput hero and Bengali heroine; and Debendranath Tagore recalled that it took 'the Bengali heart by storm'. *Kapalkundala* (1866) described gruesome Tantric rituals and indicates the same cultural trend toward dividing urban middle class Hinduism from rustic Hindu cults that we see in the Brahmo Samajis and Ramakrishna. *Mrnalini* (1869) depicted a Muslim invasion of Bengal. *Rajsimha* (1881) had Rajput heroes fighting Muslim oppressors. *Anandamath* (1882) showed Hindu ascetics (*sanyasi*s) fighting Muslim armies. *Sitaram* (1886) described Hindu struggles against Muslim tyranny.

Bankim Chandra's historical fiction became prophetic. The song 'Bande Mataram' ('Hail to the Mother') – taken from *Anandamath* – became a nationalist hymn in 1905 and inspired national activists with religious fervour. In the 1920s, the anti-Muslim implications of the same song became a focal point for Hindu nationalists in the Rashtriya Swayamsevak Sangh (RSS), founded in 1925, whose members still sing it today. Looking back from the vantage point of 1926, one leading Bengali national politician, Bepin Chandra Pal, said that the image of a woman in *pardah* killing a Muslim warrior (in *Durgesh Nandini*) raised the 'larger national or racial issue [of] the contest for supremacy over the Hindu populations of West Bengal between their own king and the Moslem invader'.

If he could have walked into Calcutta in 1890, Ram Mohun Roy would have seen a city transformed. The capital of the Indian empire then bustled with a literate middle class that thrived on print media. In its English and Bengali books, tracts, magazines, and newspapers, he might have discerned three new kinds of social sentiment that were defining what it meant to be Indian in Calcutta. These were all components of emerging Indian nationality: we can usefully call them religious, linguistic, and political.

He might have been proud – though a little surprised – to see Calcutta's modern style of Hindu religiosity. Like his own, it was individualist, intellectual, pious, and often reformist; but unlike his, it was mystical and sought a broadly popular following. Like his own, it claimed to represent Indian culture but it also excluded Islam. It was self-consciously better than village religion and old styles of Hinduism, even as it imagined itself to be truer to ancient principles. Swami Vivekananda (1863–1902) announced this modern Hinduism to the world. Born Narendranath Datta into a wealthy Kayastha family, and educated in English, he joined the Brahmo Samaj and later became Ramakrishna's leading disciple. In 1893, he represented Hinduism at the Parliament of Religions in Chicago, where one journalist called him 'an orator by divine right and undoubtedly the greatest figure at the Parliament'. In 1897, after a long lecture tour, Vivekananda returned to Calcutta with Western disciples to found the Ramakrishna Mission.

Ram Mohan would have certainly noticed the prominence of Bengali language media. Popular concern with Bengali regional issues would have been a novelty for him, and the stature of authors writing in Bengali would have seemed astounding. The rise of a middle class Bengali literati represented very distinctly modern trends and accelerated with immigration into the city from the upper ranks of rural society. Among writers like Bankim Chandra, Ram Mohan might have detected a creeping cultural opposition between Hindus and Muslims that paralleled divisions on many Zamindari estates, where owners and managers were mostly high caste Hindus while tenants were often Muslims, particularly in the eastern districts. Among literate classes, however, he would perhaps have most admired a burgeoning pride in Bengali literature, heritage, and culture that crossed religious and caste lines and in which high caste Hindus like Bankim Chandra were leading lights.

He would have marvelled at the small but publicly prominent meeting of the Indian National Congress in Calcutta, in 1896, where Bengalis accounted for 605 of 784 delegates. This was the twelfth annual meeting of an organization that represented a totally new kind of national sentiment and activity, unimaginable in Ram Mohan's day. The Congress first met in Bombay, in 1885, and then met every year in late December in a different city of British India. Delegates who came at their own expense to these meetings from all the provinces discussed government policy and issued public statements that received wide press coverage. Delegates eschewed topics of religion and social reform that divided them and concentrated on what they all had in common as prominent leaders in urban societies in all the regions. They first came together after famines in the 1870s provoked an imperial Famine Commission to call for more state investments to improve economic security that could prevent future famine. One major inspiration had come in 1879 from Dadabhai Naoroji (1825–1917), a brilliant economist from Bombay who spent most of his life in England. His influential *The Poverty of India* documented the negative impact on India of imperial policies that enriched people in Britain. Naoroji presided over Congress meetings in 1886, 1893, and 1906.

The immediate stimulant for convening the Congress was public outcry over the Ilbert Bill, in 1884. The proposed legislation empowered Indian judges to try Englishmen in court and provoked resistance from British residents in India, who heaped racist insults on Indian judges and lawyers. By this time, everyday expressions of white supremacy were standard features of imperial society; they were visible in rules for Indian Civil Service (ICS) exams and quotas, in clubs and railway carriages 'for whites only', and in countless petty indignities that stung cosmopolitan Indians with exclusion and inferiority. The Congress came together as a forum to express united Indian public opinion in the face of vehement British opposition to Indians obtaining higher official authority. But in addition to seeking more Indian membership in the ICS at higher ranks, its annual meetings argued for reduced land taxes and increased state funding for economic development. Early Congress meetings brought together many Brahmans and lawyers, who each comprised forty per cent of all delegates before 1911.

Major Congress leaders came from Calcutta. Two of the most important were Romesh Chandra Dutt (1848–1909) and Surendranath Banerjea (1848–1925), who travelled together to London as young men to take the ICS exam. R.C. Dutt's father worked as a government surveyor and he himself rose as high in the ICS as Indians could do in his lifetime to become divisional commissioner in Orissa. He published the first academic study of peasant poverty in Bengal (1874), one of the first modern text books on ancient Indian history (1896), and the first Indian history of British India (1908), which followed Naoroji to describe the negative impact of imperial policy on Indian industry and agriculture – all in English. S.N. Banerjea came from a distinguished Brahman family and served briefly in the ICS in Sylhet before undertaking a long career in education, journalism, and politics. He founded Ripon College in Calcutta and, in 1876, helped to found the Indian Association, an early nationalist venture in Bengal and precursor of the Congress. His newspaper, the *Bengalee*, became a leading nationalist venue. He was twice elected Congress president.

SHAKING THE EMPIRE

Events in Calcutta in 1905 changed imperial society forever. They produced a new kind of Indian politics that Congress delegates could not have imagined at their small, sedate meeting in Calcutta, nine years before. Like the formation of the Congress itself, the new politics expressed public controversy over imperial policy. But now the drama moved into the streets and sometimes became violent. Calcutta was ground zero and centre stage for this radical innovation. India's first national agitation spread out from Calcutta to other Indian cities and even to small towns and villages, mostly in Bengal. The new public agitation combined all three kinds of national sentiment – religious, linguistic, and political – that were prominent among urban middle classes in Calcutta by the 1890s. The outburst occurred when the Viceroy, Lord Curzon, proposed to partition Bengal Presidency and then publicly insulted Congress critics of the partition plan, calling them 'effete Bengali Babus'. What followed more than proved him wrong.

In 1905, Bengal Presidency included Bihar and Orissa (since 1765) and Assam (since 1865). Curzon claimed it was too large to manage effectively and that this caused poor regions in the east to be neglected. He redrew provincial boundaries to separate Orissa and Bihar; and his plan also called for uniting Assam with fifteen Muslim majority districts in eastern Bengal to create a new province with thirty-one million people, mostly Muslims, with its capital at Dhaka. When Congress petitions against the provincial partition fell on deaf ears, public mobilization began. An outburst of agitation ensued that expressed apparently widespread pent-up hostility against British ruling elites.

Public meetings, marches, speeches, singing, posters, and pamphleteering against state policy were not themselves new. Even street violence and state repression had many precedents. Skirmishes between urban protesters and armed police had a long history – to which we shall return – arising from battles among groups over public space owned by the state but lived in by increasingly diverse populations. In the 1890s, city streets had seen demonstrations around Congress meetings organized by a younger generation of Congressmen who mobilized support for their leadership with popular festivals and marches. In Maharashtra, Bal Gangadhar Tilak had revitalized an old festival to the god Ganesh and invented a new festival to celebrate the Maratha hero Shivaji. His political promotion of explicitly Hindu political identity occurred at the same time as anti-Muslim riots erupted in cities in the United Provinces (Uttar Pradesh), as a result of agitations against cow killing. These agitations in Bombay and in Uttar Pradesh were distinctly regional in their tone and scope; and the 1905 agitation against the Bengal partition also had regional origins. Anti-partition agitations mobilized pre-existing public sentiments in Bengal around an issue that most immediately riled influential people in Calcutta.

But 1905 agitations in Calcutta against partition spread more widely than any before because Calcutta's stature as imperial capital and as India's national city turned Calcutta's anger into Indian national outrage. Calcutta's local Indian identities became national as agitations expressed Indian opposition to British domination. Opponents of partition argued that partitioning Bengal hacked apart a Bengali nation that symbolized India. The rallying cry and popular song 'Bande Mataram' hailed a mother goddess who stood for the motherland and was identified with India, Bengal, and the goddess Kali (invoked by *mataram* in the Bankim Chandra novel *Anandamath*, where the song originally appeared). Kali devotion thus acquired a new political meaning. Now the goddess became Bengal and a victim of British atrocities. Bengal became a homeland of Indian tradition ripped apart by cruel foreigners. Religious fervour combined with political protest in bombings of government buildings and assassinations of British officers by inspired young patriots.

The movement's missionaries travelled to agitate other parts of India. Aurobindo Ghosh (1872–1950) inspired many to mystical revolution. He had studied at Cambridge and returned to official work in Baroda and Calcutta before turning to the study of yoga and Sanskrit. In 1905, his advocacy of terrorism landed him in prison; then he fled to safety in the French colony of Pondichery, where he spent the rest of his long life teaching philosophy and making his spiritual commune (*ashram*) an international cultural centre. By 1918, his national ideas were serialized in 'A Defence of Indian Culture', published in the journal *Arya*, where he said, 'It is only if we have a just and right appreciation of . . . Indian religion that we can come to a true understanding of the sense and spirit of Indian culture.'

The 1905 movement also popularized an economic nationalism based on the writing of Dadabhai Naoroji and R.C. Dutt. Its radically new Swadeshi movement promoted indigenous (*swadeshi*) products and the boycotting of foreign goods. Bonfires of British cloth became festival occasions for chanting anti-British slogans, expressing patriotism, and demonstrating local support for the Congress.

Unable to stop the movement, the government agreed to rescind partition, which it finally did in 1911. Assam became a separate administrative territory, as did Bihar and Orissa. But Bengali-speaking districts were re-united. At the same time, the capital of British India was moved to New Delhi. This move was clearly intended to give the empire a firmer political foundation in its capital city. The Government also enacted constitutional reforms that clearly showed the 1905 agitation had demonstrated beyond all denying that Indian national politics was a potent force. This official recognition was a new departure, and Curzon's style of autocratic arrogance became a thing of the past. The Morley-Minto constitutional reforms established provincial electorates and assemblies with limited powers, which were convened in 1911 and provided a template for future reforms that would further increase Indian participation in government.

ACTIVISM, IDENTITY, AND NATIONALITY

1905 was a watershed. When the upheaval ended, official representatives of native society sat in the halls of government. The public expression of collective identity in civil society had become part of imperial politics. This original opening of the modern state to the influence of popular pressure pushed not only toward widening the scope of representative democracy but also toward the political redefinition of social identities by their public mobilization. Political activism expanded the embrace of national identity.

We have already seen how collective *social* entities were entrenched in eighteenth-century regions, and how they entered modernity as the new empire gave old groups new status. Rustic patriarchs became modern private property owners and anchored the evolution of agrarian *social* identities that we shall consider in more detail later in this book. We have also seen above that modern empire produced new kinds of *official* collective identities by defining religious communities and castes inside native society. Before 1905, government used *official* identities only as legal categories and treated all subjects as exemplars, experts, petitioners, and pleaders. Many subjects had pleaded for *official* identity groups before 1905. In eighteenth-century Madras city, leaders of caste groups allied under the label of Left and Right castes pleaded with the Company to recognize rights to conduct public festivals in the city. Violence between them posed an official problem. Law and order always dominated the government's handling of such cases; and in this respect, the British government modernized Akbar's strategies of ethnic divide and rule, by balancing demands from competing groups on the scale of state supremacy. Thus in the 1890s, when riots broke out between caste groups in southern Madras over the exclusion of wealthy but low caste Nadars from temples controlled by locally dominant Maravas, and when riots broke out between Hindu and Muslim groups in Gangetic cities over their respective rights to conduct public festivities, the government cracked down with police force and balanced the respective rights of *official* identity groups.

Official collective identities became a legal meeting ground for petitioners, judges, bureaucrats, and legislators; they became part of *social* identity in imperial society. Expanding imperial bureaucracy gave more people a stake in the definition of their official identity. Nadars and many other upwardly mobile caste groups petitioned census bureaucrats to improve their place in the caste ranks. Aspiring peasants in north India petitioned to be listed as Kshatriyas in the census. Tenants petitioned for the status of secure tenure holders. As upwardly mobile groups strove to improve their official identity, established groups sought state benefits and protection. Government officials strove to balance their distribution of rewards to various officially recognized groups so as to maintain the state's supreme stature as the arbiter of social status.

Until 1905, government viewed the Indian National Congress as one of many groups in civil society organized to influence government in favour of elite businessmen, landowners, and professionals. Lord Curzon often said that the Congress spoke for '*special interests*' whereas his government represented '*the Indian people*'. In 1899, during famines and plagues that killed countless poor people, Curzon countered critics by saying that he did immeasurably more than his nationalist critics did to help the poor. He tossed off critics of his 1905 partition plan the same way. But the prospect of partitioning Bengal aroused more public fervour in and around Calcutta than his Victorian imperial mind could imagine.

1905 agitations expressed *public* identities in civil society with more political vigour than ever before; and their mounting force

despite heavy police repression forced the government to acknowl-
edge that times had changed. Bombings of government buildings
and assassinations of British officers (which coincided with
outbreaks of revolutionary terrorism in Russia) helped to convince
metropolitan authorities that coercive force was not sufficient to
restore law and order; it needed to be supplemented with
institutional change. Thus the plan emerged to bring official
representatives of the Indian public into halls of state decision-
making on metropolitan terms. People who officially represented
native society would be granted official authority.

The new legislative bodies convened under the Morley-Minto
reforms would represent *official* identities in native society,
including Hindus and Muslims. This method of representing
official constituent identity groups was called 'communal representation'. Congress opposed it and spoke for all native society.
Other organizations spoke for native society through its *official*
identity groups, or 'communities', as they were called. Native
society included countless *social* identities that were not represented officially, but *social* identity in general was increasingly
influenced by *official* categories, as they became *public* identities in
political mobilization and electoral activity. A cultural shift thus
occurred toward the formation of *social* identities shaped by the
combined force of *official* categories used in government legal,
administrative, and electoral operations, and of *public* categories
used in mobilizing support for political causes and in discussing
issues in civil society. This shift began in earnest in 1905, when
Indian politicians still used all the old tools of petitioning and
pleading, but now, in addition, mobilized public agitations to
demonstrate that they, not the British, represented native society.

The 1905 agitations generated *public* identities that influenced
social identities first of all in Calcutta, then in other big cities, and
to a lesser extent in smaller cities and some parts of rural Bengal.
Spreading agitations demonstrated the expanding geographical
scope of public activism; they diversified the groups involved in
politics to include a wider variety of people; and they put Congress
nationalism into the imperial spotlight. The idea spread that
Congress represented *all* of native society.

1905 spread national ideas well beyond official and elite circles.
Agitations were formative experiences for students and teachers

who gave nationalism new populist, idealist, progressive, even revolutionary meanings. News, debates, and lore from 1905 entered public culture in most major urban centres. Police repression produced Indian martyrs and British demons portrayed in stories, songs, poems, cartoons, editorials, and public oratory, where Victorian racism merged with British brutality to oppose Indian national aspirations. Nationalism became a political movement, which, though small compared with the vast population of imperial society, moved decisively beyond cosmopolitan petitioning; and it attracted attention overseas. Several million Indians had settled abroad and some became involved in the movement. In far-away California, activists among Punjabi Sikh farmers launched newspapers and raised funds to support the Indian cause.

1905 also produced a schism in the Congress between Extremists who promoted public agitation and Moderates who opposed it. These factions did not reconcile and join forces until 1916. The activist wildfire of 1905 indicated Moderates were right to believe that political leaders, however astute and influential, could not control a popular movement filled with energetic young people who would fly unpredictably in various directions. The aftermath of 1905 also showed that Extremists were right to believe that public protest brought pressure on government that legal action could not. Both beliefs remained part of the new political environment that emerged in 1911, when Indian lawyers, educators, and other professionals became a national political force.

The new generation of Indian politicians that emerged in the movement came primarily from Bengal, Punjab, and Maharashtra. One major leader, Gopal Krishna Gokhale (1866–1915) left his chair in history and political economy at Fergusson College, Pune, in 1902, to enter full-time politics. In 1905, he led the Moderates as Congress president, and like most Moderates, he advocated social reform measures that were lost in the Extremist agenda. He founded the Servants of India Society, whose members took vows of poverty and of service to the poor, especially to the poorest 'untouchable' *jati*s in Hindu society, who remained excluded from imperial society and national politics. Also from Maharashtra, Bal Gangadhar Tilak (1856–1920) led the Extremists. A Brahman lawyer and teacher, Tilak founded the Deccan Education Society (1884); ran two nationalist newspapers, *Kesari* ('The Lion') in Marathi and *The Mahratta* in English; made Ganesh and Shivaji festivals venues for popular politics; and opposed social reform as a distraction from national goals. His ally, Lala Lajpat Rai (1865–1928), also a lawyer, was from Lahore in Punjab. Lajpat Rai followed Dayananda Sarasvati, who was the founder of the Arya Samaj and of Cow Protection Societies that treated Muslims as adversaries of Hindus, as we will see. Lajpat Rai established the Dayananda Anglo-Vedic School and his 1905 radicalism got him deported to Mandalay, without trial, in 1907. On his return, his campaign to become Congress president provoked the split between Moderates and Extremists.

Though Congress nationalism spoke for everyone in native society, its public agitations also invoked and provoked other *official* and unofficial *social* identities. As we have seen, Curzon lit the 1905 wildfire by torching high caste *bhadralok* Hindu

TABLE 5. WATERSHED YEARS: 1905–18

1905 Partition of Bengal. Anti-partition agitation. Swadeshi movement.

1906 All-India Muslim League founded at Dhaka.

1907 Surat Congress. Moderate–Extremist clash. Tata Iron and Steel Company founded.

1909 Morley-Minto reforms. V.D. Savarkar, *The Indian War of Independence*. M.K. Gandhi, *Hind Swaraj* in Gujarati (English, 1910). Punjab Hindu Sabha.

1911 Delhi Durbar: Bengal partition revoked. Delhi made capital of British India.

1913 Nobel Prize for Rabindranath Tagore. Annie Besant publishes *Wake up India*.

1914 Mohandas Gandhi returns from South Africa. World War One: Indian troops overseas.

1916 Lord Chelmsford Viceroy to 1921. Lala Lajpat Rai publishes *Young India*. Lucknow Pact between All-India Muslim League and Indian National Congress.

1917 Tamil non-Brahman movement launched with publication of *The Dravidian*.

1918 *Ghadr* movement. Besant and Tilak Home Rule League.

Congress leaders in Calcutta who spoke to and for the cosmopolitan English-literate youth whose professional prospects would be curtailed in partitioned Bengal. Calcutta's English-educated youth, who had come from villages and towns in Bengal, went home to spread wildfire in the countryside. The popular appeal of Hindu devotionalism fanned the flames. Cosmopolitan literati invoked the passion of devotees excluded from the temple of patriotic love by tyrants who abused their goddess. Their vernacular verse expressed regional linguistic identities that were identified with the Indian nation.

As the movement spread, it took distinctly regional forms. In Madras, for example, Aurobindo Ghosh inspired the poet Subrahmanya Bharathiyar (1882–1921), who had made his living as a translator and in 1906 declared he would never again write English. Bharathiyar opened nationalist rallies on the beach in Madras with rousing choruses of '*Bande Mataram*', recomposed in Tamil as a mystical song praising Kali, the mother (goddess) of the Indian homeland. He also popularized Swadeshi with a song praising Chidambaran Pillai, who founded the short-lived Swadeshi Steamship Company in Madras and became in Bharathiyar's verse a national hero. The Tamil language itself became an icon of native identity in Bharathiyar's time; and in the next decade, a regional non-Brahman movement evolved that identified Brahmans and Sanskrit as equally foreign elements in indigenous native society in southern India. When the periodical *The Dravidian* appeared in 1917, it announced a new *public* identity in Madras Presidency based on the regional distinctiveness of people who spoke Dravidian languages (Tamil, Telugu, Kannada, and Malayalam) and on the aspirations of activists who spoke for the ninety-five per cent of the population who were not Brahmans.

In eastern Bengal, Muslim leaders with various *social* identities – from various regions, ethnic groups, and sects – came together to make an old *official* identity a politically *public* identity when they met in Dhaka, in 1906, to form the All-India Muslim League. The League supported Curzon's partition plan and stood against the Congress as representatives of India's Muslims.

Curzon courted support from Muslim leaders for his plan by defining the proposed East Bengal province as a Muslim majority province, and also by citing the old organization of Bengal province as an impediment to progress in eastern districts, where Muslims formed a majority. Curzon's cunning had a Victorian legacy going back to 1871. Then, the first Indian census quantified Bengal's Muslim majority in the eastern districts; and in that year, the Viceroy, Lord Mayo, commissioned a Bengal official, W.W. Hunter, to answer the question, 'Are Indian Musalmans bound in conscience to rebel against the Queen?' Mayo took this to be the 'burning question of the day' in the aftermath of the 1857 rebellion and during British wars in Afghanistan, where Muslim fighters sought supporters in British India. Hunter's answer was a resounding 'no', but he also indicated the need to court Muslim support in British India, where he said Muslims were poor, uneducated, discriminated against, and susceptible to irrational calls to their faith.

British India's most prominent Muslim leader, Sir Syed Ahmad Khan (1817–98), strove vocally after 1857 to enhance official support for Muslims. In doing so, he underlined the division of Indian native society into 'two prominent nations, which are distinguished by the names of Hindus and Mussulmans'. He went on to provide a vivid natural imagery for India's major *official* identities, saying, 'Just as a man has some principal organs, similarly these two nations are like the principal limbs of India.' Thus for Viceroy Lord Curzon, a Muslim province in East Bengal would be a boon to all of India's Muslims. Leaders of the Muslim League agreed.

By 1905, moreover, Muslim leaders from Punjab to Bengal had experienced organized Hindu animosity against their own native society. For several decades, Cow Protection Societies protested to implement a government prohibition of beef butcher shops, a predominantly Muslim business. In the 1890s, violence ensued in cities across the Ganga basin when militant Hindus attacked Muslims who conducted sacrificial cow killing during Muslim festivals. Hindu militants also took umbrage at Muslim population numbers in the census, and the Arya Samaj organized re-conversion campaigns to 'bring Hindus back' to the fold. Religious identity, population figures, and conversion became more incendiary issues as the government proposed to calculate 'communal representation' for various groups in each region in accordance with census population figures. During the 1905 agitations, the fears of Muslim leaders increased when Tilak and Lajpat Rai rose to the Congress leadership and Congress rallied support around devotion to Kali. The origin of the 1905 slogan, '*Bande Mataram*', in a novel depicting Hindus fighting Muslim oppressors supported their fears.

In 1906, it was also not lost on the Aga Khan (leader of Ismaili Muslims) or on the Nawab of Dhaka (a major Zamindar), who sponsored and hosted the League's first meeting in Dhaka, that the proposed creation of an East Bengal province would directly benefit aspiring Muslims in Bengal and Assam. It also seemed that Congress opposition to the plan derived from its derogatory economic implications for high caste Hindu elites in Bengal. Even so, Muslim leaders were not of one mind. Mohammed Ali Jinnah (1876–1948), who became the League's most important leader, did not join until 1913. Until then, he like many other Muslims believed that the Congress represented Muslim interests. Jinnah was already a prominent lawyer, educated at an Islamic school (*madrassah*) in Sind. He had followed the Moderates in Congress and recognized Gokhale as his political guru. His opposition to the 1905 agitations followed the Moderate line.

In the decade of the First World War, Indian politics entered a new phase of institution building. The Congress agreed to support the British war effort in return for British promises to expand Indian control of government after the war. Politicians joined and formed organizations that represented the national movement and at the same time participated in imperial governance. Jinnah, for example, was elected to the Imperial Legislative Council under the 1909 Morley-Minto reforms; and in 1915 he also joined the Bombay branch of the Indian Home Rule League, which Tilak founded on the model of the Irish Home Rule League; and in that context, in 1916, he signed the Lucknow Pact that brought the Moderates, Extremists, and Muslim League together in the national cause.

The unification of disparate political identities being shaped by public activism now preoccupied national leaders. Calcutta remained a heartland of national sentiment, even as groups in Pune, Bombay, Ahmedabad, Delhi, Lahore, Lucknow, Allahabad, Madras, and other cities entered national politics. In this context, in 1913, Debendranath Tagore's son, Rabindranath (1861–1941), won the Nobel Prize for literature for his *Gitanjali* (1912) – his own English renderings of his Bengali devotional poems – with support from W.B. Yeats and André Gide. Educated in England, Tagore had spent the 1890s in eastern Bengal, managing his family's Zamindar land. In 1919, he wrote a story that looked back on 1905 with the insight of the next decade, and with national unity on his mind.

The story, '*Ghore Bhaire*' ('Home and the World') – later made into a film by Calcutta's own Satyajit Ray (1921–92) – reinterpreted 1905 as a trial for the country with lessons for later generations. The story concerns the family of a young Zamindar in eastern Bengal. His old mansion was designed to provide for the seclusion of women in *pardah*, but he had undertaken his own version of domestic social reform by making his wife learn English literature, music, and dance, so she could be a modern woman. He had also tried his hand at Swadeshi industry with a failed soap-making enterprise. One day, all of a sudden, the young Zamindar's college chum arrives from Calcutta, fired with 1905 enthusiasm. A romance (*prem*) ensues between wife and friend, suggesting that modern women face peril when freed from family discipline, and also indicating that well-meaning social reform can spoil domestic harmony. Tragedy strikes when the Zamindar's friend agitates for a Swadeshi boycott of foreign goods in the local market, provoking local activists to attack Muslim shops. Riots break out and the young Zamindar dies trying to bring peace to his estate.

This story was intended as a national allegory. The British are missing. The Indian nation is, in effect, on its own, looking for itself. Moderates and Extremists have disappeared. The new dilemma is to find common cause among forces pulling the nation in various directions. With this goal in view, Mohandas Karam-chand Gandhi (1869–1948) had written *Hind Swaraj* in Gujarati in 1909 (and in English, 1910), but at the same time V.D. Savarkar's *Indian War of Independence* had projected a more militant Hindu view of nationalism that was followed by the Punjab Hindu Sabha, also founded in 1909. When Gandhi returned to India from South Africa in 1915, Home Rule Leagues were forming in major cities to propagate the idea of Indian independence. Calcutta's premier unifying politician of the day, Chitta Ranjan Das (1870–1925), tackled the dilemma of defining the nation with vigorous pragmatism. As a lawyer, he defended people accused of political crimes during the 1905 crackdown and he opposed continued British rule. He rejected the idea that India must develop on Western lines and he advocated a vision of Indian uniqueness based on India's distinctive, all-inclusive national culture. Tagore's allegory haunted the end of his life: in the year after his death, Hindu-Muslim riots broke out in Calcutta that irreversibly alienated eastern Bengal politicians from the Congress.

Creating Nations

Nationality became universal in the twentieth century. Its meaning and substance remained particularistic, however, and they changed significantly every decade. British imperial nationality expanded to its global limit with the Treaty of Versailles, in 1919, but Britain's power had been irreversibly weakened by the long war. In the next decades, an unpredictably rocky, riotous road led to the empire's end. In South Asia, British control declined steadily until Britain lost India and Ceylon in the aftermath of World War Two. In the 1950s and 1960s, it lost most other colonies. British national identity shrank back into Britain. English cricketers even began losing to West Indians, Pakistanis, Indians, and Sri Lankans, not to mention Australians and South Africans. Some members of the imperial intelligentsia interpreted all this to be a civilized transfer of power, but in South Asia and elsewhere, lowering the Union Jack and raising national flags signalled victory after bitter struggles for independence.

In South Asia, nationality changed dramatically as it encompassed peoples more numerous and diverse than in all of Europe and Russia combined. National histories divide roughly into four periods, two on either side of 1947. The history of nationalism before 1947 divides into two periods that pivot around 1920. Before 1920, national movements in India and Ceylon fought for official recognition inside the empire; national identity remained a feature of specialized public activism. In the 1920s, India attained fiscal autonomy; the governments of India and Ceylon included elected national representatives; and nationalism became a mass movement. After 1920, nationalists mobilized vast public support to expand native authority in government. Nationality became a widespread, diverse social identity expressed in countless petitions, agitations, print media, films, songs, visual arts, elections, legislation, social movements, and educational institutions. In the 1930s, a major expansion of nationalist activity occurred as a new constitutional framework came into being. In 1947 and 1948, India, Pakistan, and Ceylon won independence.

The history of nationality and collective identities in the decades since independence divides roughly into two periods that pivot around 1970. The first two decades after 1947 witnessed the building of new national states. Nationalities were radically redefined by new official boundaries, legal systems, political systems, and cultural institutions in new national state territories. By 1970, a contemporary period had begun, whose historical contours remain imprecise because they are still changing. It is certain, however, that social and political trends have transformed nationality and social identity in the past three decades. We consider this contemporary condition in the next chapter. We focus in this chapter first on the political movements and constitutional change that gave nationality its political form before 1947; and then on the forging of national states that reinvented nationality as national citizenship. But before we begin, we must outline the stark novelty of the twentieth-century environment, whose unprecedented qualities have conditioned all politics and social experience during the past century.

A NEW TWENTIETH-CENTURY LANDSCAPE

Everyday living conditions changed more rapidly in the twentieth century than ever before, and change accelerated after 1947. Each new century after 1500 altered the landscape significantly, but the twentieth century literally changed it entirely. People crowded together with more intensity than societies had ever accommodated. Population density in Bangladesh surpassed two thousand people per square mile in 2001. South Asia's total population in 2001 was greater than the total number of people who had ever lived in South Asia over all the centuries before 1900.

Tranquil, bucolic scenery disappeared forever at an ever-quickening pace. India's urban population increased by just over *one* per cent (from 11% to 12%) in the first three decades of the century, by *six* per cent during the next three (1931–61), and by *eight* per cent during the next three (1961–91). This accelerating upward trend appeared in all regions except Sri Lanka, which started with a relatively big urban population (12% in 1901) that less than doubled (to 22%) by 1991; whereas India's 1991 figure (26%) was 2.4 times what it was in 1901 (11%). Pakistan urbanized at a quicker pace, seventy per cent faster than India after 1961, to reach thirty-three per cent in 1991. Nepal's small urban population (9% in 1991) grew as fast as Pakistan's after 1961. Bangladesh urbanized faster still: its 1961 population was only five per cent urban, only double the 1901 figure; and after 1961 it quadrupled to reach twenty per cent in 1991.

In the first half of the century, economies actually became slightly more agricultural despite the growth of industry: cultivators and labourers in undivided India increased from sixty-nine per cent to seventy-three per cent of the male workforce between 1901 and 1951. Heavy national government investments in economic development reversed that trend with a vengeance. In the 1990s, farming accounted for only fifty-seven per cent of the workforce in Bangladesh, sixty-three per cent in India, fifty per cent in Pakistan, and forty-three per cent in Sri Lanka. Industrialization and urban growth deforested mountains and pushed farmers to produce more on less land. During the *three* decades after 1950, livestock, net cultivation, and built-up land increased as much they had during the *seven* previous decades, and forest cover declined at about the same rate as the population grew: about fifteen per cent faster.

Vast areas were transformed in a short time. After 1950, a million people moved from Bihar into the Chhotanagpur jungles to turn tribal farm land into industrial sites and mines. Rapid immigration by farmers and workers pushed out and absorbed tribal people in many regions and all of Assam, swelling the ranks of tribal insurgencies in the north-eastern region from Chhotanagpur to Assam to Mizoram. Urban unrest has also been fuelled by waves of people coming to town in seasons of distress and dislocation. Famines brought millions of hungry families into Calcutta, Dhaka, and Patna in the 1940s, 1950s, 1960s, and 1970s. Calcutta riots in 1946 helped to rush the partition of British India, which in turn uprooted Punjabis, who poured into Delhi, and Uttar Pradesh Muslims, who resettled in Karachi and Lahore. Mass resettlements fuelled ethnic strife.

Upward mobility also enriched cities. One small but useful example is Nellore District, just north of Madras, where improved irrigation and urban demand for rural products pushed up land rents by a factor of nine between 1850 and 1927, and then doubled rents again from 1927 to 1982. The proportion of rent to output also increased, especially after 1940, and this rental income fed social mobility. For rustic rent receivers, occupational change was a one-way street leading away from the farm to urban business, education, and employment. Families receiving higher rents moved from village to town to the big city. The concentration of wealth in cities exaggerated urban–rural differences and made cities even more attractive places to live and work.

Migration extended overseas. Millions and millions of South Asians went to live and work for long and short periods and to resettle permanently overseas; they typically retained and cherished their national identities. The overseas dimensions of Indian nationality early in the twentieth century are most famously embodied in Mohandas Gandhi's career in South Africa, where he defended Indian nationals' rights in a context that included ethnic–national divisions among Europeans, Africans, and Indians. On his return to India, Gandhi served to unify nationalist forces from 1915 to 1925; and this in part testified to the distinctive cultural unity that India had attained among overseas Indians. After 1947, national citizenship stamped in South Asian passports went with migrants wherever they travelled. The idea of 'diaspora' emerged and carried the identities of 'non-resident' nationals from all the separate countries into many other national environments. Virtually every political and cultural movement in South Asia since 1970 has involved overseas nationals. At the same time, overseas earnings have been invested in South Asian localities to attach them economically to widening circuits of migration that came to form a new kind of home in the world for national identity.

AN OVERVIEW OF EMPIRE'S END: 1919–47

No one could have predicted the future of nationality in 1919, when the Great Powers met to finalize plans for peace in Paris and to create the League of Nations. No one could have imagined India's partition in 1947. It was a different age then, another world of nationality. New nationalities would arise in later decades.

By 1919, the Lucknow Pact had united Moderates, Extremists, and the Muslim League. The Viceroy had promised constitutional reforms to widen Indian power in government. Gandhi had employed his method of peaceful non-cooperation to settle disputes between landlords and tenants in Bihar and between factory workers and owners in Gujarat. Gandhi attracted wealthy businessmen who were becoming Congress supporters. Home Rule Leagues were spreading the word that Indians should rule their own country. Nationalism had entered the mainstream of political activity in imperial society.

Then unforeseeable events opened the rocky and riotous road to empire's end. Each decade brought dramatic events that changed the history of nationality. In 1905, Curzon's partition plan had triggered unpredictable upheaval. In 1917, the Bolshevik revolution stirred British apprehensions of revolution in India, which were stoked by memories of 1905 and gave nationalist demands for home rule on Irish lines frightening overtones in London. Home Rule Leagues were active in major Indian cities, where various activists also protested government restrictions on the press and on public assembly as well as new taxes and economic controls imposed by the government to support the war effort. More urban organizations were now involved in political activity, including labour unions. Indian business supported the national cause and sought to remove British constraints on Indian capital accumulation. The press indicated that the public expected the government to accommodate Congress demands for Indian self-government. Indian troops fought loyally for Britain in the war, but returning soldiers also posed a threat, particularly in Punjab, from which most recruits came. Many soldiers were Sikhs and in far-away California, an expatriate Sikh *Ghadr* revolutionary movement promoted the overthrow of the government. The threat of revolution in India was made more real by

Communists. One Calcutta revolutionary, Narendranath Bhatta-charya (1887–1954), had joined a plot to smuggle arms into India, gone abroad to seek arms, travelled to San Francisco (where he changed his name to Manabendra Nath Roy), and helped to establish the Communist Party in Mexico before he joined the executive committee of the Communist International in Moscow. (M.N. Roy left the Comintern in 1929, to oppose Stalin, but led India's Communist Party until 1947.)

In the face of all this promise, anxiety, and pressure, Parliament passed the Montagu-Chelmsford (Montford) Reforms, in 1919, which expanded the power of elected governments in the provinces of British India. At the same time, it also passed the Rowlatt Acts to maintain martial law restrictions on public activity. The Rowlatt laws allowed police to imprison people without trial. This two-handed imperial strategy became a routine in London. For the next thirty years, the British government measured increments of power for elected governments in India with one half-open hand, while it used a mailed fist to crush illegal opposition with constitutional emergency powers, soldiers, police, censors, and judges.

By the time Jawaharlal Nehru (1889–1964), India's first prime minister, announced the new dawn of independence, at midnight, 15 August 1947, he and most national leaders had spent years in jail. Their struggles engaged countless people not only in elections and provincial governments but also in street demonstrations, riots, and pogroms that shaped national identities that were also embedded in constitutional reforms. In 1947, London took credit for establishing democracy in South Asia and blamed all the violence on indigenous hatreds, Communists, and greedy, recalcitrant politicians.

Though many nationalists would trace their struggle back to the wars of 1857, national activists did not in general see British rule as alien and tyrannical before 1919, when Congress leaders judged the Montford reforms grossly inadequate and opposed the Rowlatt Acts' blatant violation of civil rights. Mohandas Gandhi led the way. With backing from businessmen and old Congress leaders, he rose quickly in the Congress leadership. Using techniques of disciplined street action he had developed in South Africa, Gandhi launched a *satyagraha* campaign of peaceful, nonviolent public gatherings, which violated the Rowlatt laws, to demand the restoration of civil liberties. One peaceful meeting at Jallianwalla Bagh in Amritsar was massacred by imperial troops under the command of Punjab's military administrator, Colonel Dyer, who was never brought to book for his crime.

The Amritsar massacre sealed the fate of the Montford reforms, which the Congress then rejected absolutely. Congress called for self-government, *Swaraj*. It organized a mass campaign for complete non-cooperation with British government. In 1920, Gandhi turned Congress into a national organization for mass mobilization. Congress national leaders formed an All-Indian Congress Committee (AICC) and provincial Congress committees organized district committees throughout British India. Congress activists covered the country using regional languages to recruit new members and to propagate the Congress platform. They called for a total boycott of Legislative Assembly elections under the Montford 'dyarchy' system. In alliance with the Muslim League, the Congress non-cooperation campaign also supported the Khilafat movement's demand that the British reinstate the Caliph.

Dyarchy gave provincial assemblies partial power over regional administration and gave the Imperial Assembly no power beyond advising the Viceroy. Officially, dyarchy ended in 1935, when the Government of India Act transferred provincial administration to elected legislatures and established a central legislature in New Delhi. But dyarchy effectively continued to 1947, because the outbreak of World War Two, in 1939, interrupted the formation of a central legislature in Delhi. National law and order and central administration thus remained in the hands of British appointees to the end of the empire. In 1920 and 1935, provincial politicians gained increasing control over regional governments. By 1920, India's central administration was autonomous financially and in its powers to make internal policies and was effectively a national government in British hands. Thus the withholding of power by the British became more intolerable for nationalists, and the Congress effectively became a national opposition party. At the same time, the reality of Indian national governance was coming into being in the provinces.

In the 1920s, more unpredictable events occurred. The Congress non-cooperation campaign petered to an end as regional political parties formed provincial ministries and conflict broke out among participants in the national movement, including riots in Calcutta following the death of C.R. Das, which alienated Bengal Muslims from Congress. In 1928, an All Parties National Conference convened in Calcutta, at which Jinnah made impassioned pleas for Congress to adopt constitutional proposals to protect Indian Muslims. He reasoned thus:

> Every country struggling for freedom and desirous of establishing a democratic system of Government has had to face the problem of minorities wherever they existed and no constitution, however idealistic it may be and however perfect from [a] theoretical point of view it may seem, will ever receive the support of the minorities unless they can feel that they, as an entity, are secured under the proposed constitution . . . Otherwise no proper constitution will last but [will instead] result in a revolution and a civil war.

After all but one of his proposals were rejected, Jinnah felt sure that Congress would not write constitutional protections for Muslims into its plan for new government reforms. When he left the meeting, he told a friend, 'This is the parting of the ways.'

In the next year, another unpredictable event rocked imperial society: the start of the Great Depression. In the depression years, new conflicts broke out among groups on opposite sides of economic schisms. Tenants confronted landlords. Debtors fought money lenders. Unions fought factory owners with organized workers. Radicalism and discontent increased in many quarters. Jawaharlal Nehru became president of the All-India Congress Committee in 1930 and announced its radical turn with these words:

> the great poverty and misery of the Indian People are due, not only to foreign exploitation in India but also to the economic structure of society, which the alien rulers support so that their exploitation may continue. In order therefore to remove this poverty and misery and to ameliorate the condition of the masses, it is essential to make revolutionary changes in the present economic and social structure of society and to remove the gross inequalities.

In 1932, a determined Congress organized another non-cooperation campaign to protest the British exclusion of Congress from plans for a new government re-organization; and also to

TABLE 6. A CHRONOLOGY OF EMPIRE'S END

1. Nationalism becomes a mass movement

1915 Home Rule Leagues active. Gandhi returns from South Africa and tours Indian cities gathering support.

1916 Lucknow Pact unifies Extremists, Moderates, and Muslim League.

1919 Montagu-Chelmsford reforms. Jallianwallah Bagh massacre. All-India satyagraha. Ceylon National Congress formed. Third Afghan War. India enters League of Nations.

1920 Non-cooperation movement. Khilafat movement. Reorganization of Congress at Nagpur. Gurudwara reform movement to 1925.

1921 Dyarchy established. Provincial governments formed. Moplah rebellion. Indian fiscal autonomy.

1923 V.D. Savarkar, *Who is a Hindu?*

1925 Death of C.R. Das. Founding of Rashtriya Swayamsevak Sangh (RSS) and Shiromani Akali Dal.

1927 M.K. Gandhi, *An Autobiography, or The Story of My Experiments with Truth.*

2. Imperial politics redefines nationality

1928 Simon Commission. The journal *Pukhtun* launched by Abdul Ghaffar Khan.

1929 Depression to 1933. Congress call for Purna Swaraj. Jinnah's 'parting of the ways'.

1930 Round Table Conferences 1930 and 1932. Salt satyagraha.

1931 Donoughmore constitution in Ceylon. Ceylon State Council elected by universal suffrage.

1932 Second civil disobedience movement. Communal Award. Separate representation for Sikhs. Gandhi's Poona Pact with B.R. Ambedkar.

1933 'Pakistan' coined in Rahmat Ali, *Now or Never, Are We to Perish or Live for Ever?*

1934 Muhammad Iqbal, *The Reconstruction of Religious Thought in Islam.*

1935 Government of India Act.

3. Struggles to shape national governance

1937 Burma separated from India. Indian elections. Congress provincial ministries in seven of the eleven Indian provinces. Muslim League reorganized at Lucknow session. Sinhala Mahasabha founded by S.W.R.D. Bandaranaike.

TABLE 6. CONTINUED

---

3. Struggles to shape national governance continued

1939 World War Two to 1945. M.S. Golwalkar, *We, or Our Nationhood Defined*. Congress ministries resign. Muslim League celebrates 'day of deliverance'.

1940 Muslim League declares for Pakistan in Lahore.

1941 Foundation of Jamaat-I-Islami by Syed Abul Ala Maudoodi.

1942 Quit India movement. Maudoodi's *Tehreek-e-Azadi-e-Hind aur Musalman*.

1943 Bengal famine to 1944.

1944 Tamil Congress founded in Ceylon by G.G. Ponnambalam.

1946 Cabinet mission. Violence in Bengal and elsewhere. Elections. Muslim League wins Muslim majority areas. Cabinet mission proposal for federal India. Sikh deputation calls for an independent Punjab. Great Calcutta killing. Lord Mountbatten sent to India.

1947 Independence of India and Pakistan. Punjab massacres. Mass dislocations and forced migrations. Accession of Kashmir to India. Naga secessionist movement. United National Party under D.S. Senanayake forms government in Ceylon.

1948 Ceylon independence. Gandhi assassinated. Telengana war. Indo-Pakistan war over Kashmir. UN truce line in Kashmir. Jinnah dies. Integration of the native Indian states within India.

---

protest the British proposal to retain communal representation in the new electoral scheme. Congress itself split over a demand by Dr. B.R. Ambedkar (1891–1956), to include communal representation for India's lowest caste, so-called 'untouchable' groups; but Gandhi conducted a fast-unto-death that forced Ambedkar to withdraw his demand. Separate representation for Muslims became a touchstone of Muslim League opposition to Congress, for the League believed that only separate elections for Muslim legislators could protect Muslim interests. In 1933, agitations by various groups in the context of depression distress led to riots in the rowdy industrial city of Kanpur. The animosity between the League and Congress increased when the Congress committee that convened to investigate the riots blamed the Muslim League for causing violence and raising opposition to a unified national struggle in tacit connivance with the British.

When the 1935 Government of India Act brought elections for new ministries in the provinces, Congress took control of most regional governments, but failed to win enough seats to gain a majority in Bengal and Punjab. As we will see, events in these two provinces would create an unpredictable and insurmountable dilemma for the British when, after the Allied victory in the Second World War, the Labour cabinet rushed to extricate Britain from India.

Before the 1935 constitutional plans were fully implemented, World War Two brought more unpredictable events. Japan conquered British Burma and made India critical strategic territory for the Allies. The Congress refused to stand behind the British in the war effort and instead launched a massive Quit India movement, in 1942, to drive the British out. Again, war brought the spectre of revolution to British India and made the British more brutal in their suppression of the Quit India movement.

War brought disaster in Bengal. Non-Congress ministries headed the provincial government in Calcutta, which was also the centre of Allied operations. When food prices sky-rocketed in 1943, administrative measures to secure provisions for the city deprived villagers of food and millions of people in rural Bengal died in the next year. Congress blamed the British and its foes in Bengal. Desperate people flooded Calcutta. Under these incendiary conditions, massive riots broke out in 1946, when, as the war ended, the idea of again partitioning Bengal came into public view. The plan would separate West Bengal, where Congress would be in control, from East Bengal, where Congress had no prospect of winning elections. Eastern districts held a largely Muslim electorate filled with aspiring tenants who fought for land rights against Zamindars who backed Congress and prevented Congress from promising land reforms. The 1946 riots again pitted Hindus against Muslims for reasons having nothing whatever to do with religion but fuelled with passions stoked by religious activists.

The fear of revolution haunted the British during the war. One leading Congress figure, Subhas Chandra Bose (1897–1945), formed the Indian National Army (INA) in Japanese-occupied Burma. He planned to invade India to fight for liberation at the same time as Quit India battles for independence raged on the streets when the transfer of power was being further delayed by war, and when police routinely attacked protesters and imprisoned national leaders. The final push for independence after the war was embittered by British punishments of treasonous nationalists. When the war ended, Britain kept tight control of the transfer of power but London also set a precipitous 1947 deadline for its escape from the now unbearable burden of empire in South Asia.

THE INVENTION OF CONSTITUTIONAL IDENTITIES IN THE 1920S

The *official* and *public* identities that guided *government* thinking and *political* mobilization in the first decades of the twentieth century merged in *constitutional* identities in the 1920s. This merger had a powerful impact on social identities and national politics.

In Ceylon, reforms in 1920 gave an elected legislature authority over the whole island, which was the size of a small Indian province (Table 7). The Ceylon legislative assembly worked like Indian provincial assemblies, where legislatures and ministries controlled portfolios and budgets for education, health, and public works, using provincial taxes and imperial allocations. These official responsibilities remained in the hands of provincial governments under the 1935 Government of India Act and in the hands of state governments under India's 1950 constitution.

In Ceylon, British officials kept more control of the administration after 1931, when the Donoughmore constitution instituted a universal adult franchise. Regional and minority group politicians – Tamils, Kandyans, Muslims, and Christians – competed for influence in the central legislature, which after 1931 was dominated by Sinhala leaders of the Ceylon National Congress, who demanded a total transfer of power from London to Colombo. In British India, the franchise never included more than ten per cent of the adult population before 1947, and electoral competition focused entirely on provincial assemblies. In Ceylon and India alike, debates about constitutional reform revolved around transfers of power from British to native representatives and civil servants. In British India, however, debates also involved the definition of the electorate itself, an issue that was settled in Ceylon by 1931.

As in Ceylon, where the appointment of the Donoughmore Commission in 1927 to write a new constitution spurred political parties to mobilize their influence on government, also in India the arrival of the Simon Commission, in 1928, triggered political efforts to affect official decisions that would have lasting influence on the character of government. The Ceylon Congress called for a universal franchise and a unitary central government. The Kandyan National Association (KNA) proposed instead to establish a federal system to better represent Kandyan people who had lost their separate government in 1833. Ceylon's other minority politicians agreed with the KNA that the British were mistaken to treat all the various peoples of Ceylon as a 'homogeneous Ceylonese race'. But the Congress plan prevailed because it meshed with the official line in the Colonial Office.

In India, constitutional reform stumbled on the same problem of how to represent group interests in an electoral system. The problem in India was immensely complicated by the existence of *official* identity groups like Hindus and Muslims; by the political mobilization of *public* identities, including Hindu and Muslim in various parties; by provincial differences in the distribution of various groups; and by disputes in and among parties and government about the principle of 'communal representation'. This principle was officially established in 1911 and maintained in 1919, and thus became a legitimate basis for political strategy and planning. Like the Ceylon Congress, the Indian National Congress opposed this principle because it broke the electorate into particularistic ethnic blocks rather than uniting the population under the banner of a single national party, represented by each Congress. But official tradition in London, New Delhi, and provincial capitals favoured the communal principle in British India.

Indian elections complicated matters further. In 1921, the Congress–League non-cooperation campaign reduced election turn-out to less than a third of the small electorate, but this did not prevent politicians from standing for elections and forming provincial governments. The result was a two-tiered national system. In New Delhi, a central administration under the Viceroy controlled national policy-making and the Indian Civil Service. The Congress and the Muslim League spoke to the central administra-

TABLE 7. IMPERIAL REGIONS IN SOUTH ASIA, 1947 (DESCENDING ORDER OF POPULATION)

	Area (square miles)	Population
Bengal Presidency	77,442	60,306,525
United Provinces	106,247	55,020,617
Madras Presidency	126,166	49,341,810
Bihar	69,745	36,340,151
Punjab	99,089	28,418,819
Bombay Presidency	76,443	20,849,840
Central Provinces and Berar	98,575	16,813,584
Hyderabad	82,313	16,338,534
Rajasthan native states	132,559	13,670,208
Assam	54,951	10,204,733
Orissa	32,198	8,728,544
Mysore	29,458	7,329,140
Travancore	7,662	6,070,081
Nepal	54,000	5,600,000
Ceylon	25,332	5,312,548
Sind	48,136	4,535,008
Kashmir	82,258	4,021,616
North-West Frontier Province	14,263	3,038,067
Delhi	574	917,939
Ajmer-Merwar	2400	583,693
Baluchistan	54,456	501,631
Coorg	1593	168,726
Andaman and Nicobar Islands	3143	33,768

tion for national constituencies and their allied boycott of the 1921 elections enhanced their national stature. Elected provincial governments *also* represented legitimate Indian nationality, however; and they controlled budgets for education, agricultural development, and public works, as well as most civil administration. The politicians and parties that joined Legislative Assemblies and formed provincial ministries in the 1920s were regional parties that defied the Congress–League call for non-cooperation. They worked inside a constitutional system where separate 'communal' electorates – designated seats allocated in proportion to the

FIGURE 1. THE COMPARATIVE SIZE OF SOUTH ASIAN REGIONS BY POPULATION IN 1947

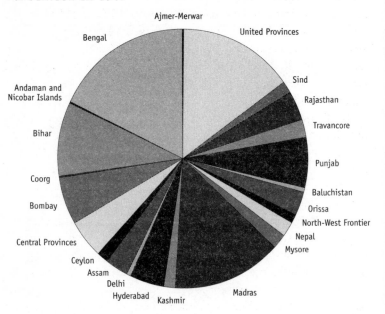

population of specified groups – were an established feature of *national* politics *in the provinces*. Thus the national political system made the communal principle not only legitimate and officially sanctioned but also intensely important for politically mobilized sectors of the public that exercised influence over popular sentiments. In the provinces, Indian nationality included regional *public* identities mobilized by politicians committed to their continued *constitutional* recognition.

THE DISTINCTIVENESS OF BENGAL AND PUNJAB

The provincial *public* mobilization of national identity around *official* identities produced strident opposition to Congress calls to end communal representation, most of all in Bengal and Punjab. Bengal spawned many parties other than Congress. A number of these represented Zamindar tenants. Legal struggles for tenant rights took off with 1859 reform acts in Bengal, and escalated in

1873 when tenants formed the Agrarian League to resist rent increases, illegal cesses (*abwabs*), and threats to occupancy rights. A more sweeping tenant reform act appeared in 1885. In the decades that followed, tenant representatives carried their struggles into regional politics; in the 1920s, they sat in government. Because many tenants were Muslims, communal representation benefited politicians who struggled to secure tenant rights to land.

In Punjab, activists among the Sikh, Muslim, and Hindu populations also won Assembly seats in the 1920s. Their separate interests combined religious and secular elements. Old Muslim elites were prominent Zamindars. Muslim Jats were the most numerous farmers in Punjab, particularly in the west. Muslim Paxtun clans also controlled the neighbouring North-West Frontier Provinces (NWFP) region between Punjab and Afghanistan. Muslim religious leaders received considerable patronage in Punjab and NWFP, which they used to run schools and to expand their social influence. Their influence became more politically important as the numerical weight of Muslims gained official recognition. Meanwhile Muslim Kashmiri politicians, banned from expressing their views publicly in Kashmir, made Punjab their base of operations.

Sikh soldiers formed powerful regiments in the Indian army and Sikhs were prominent commanders. Sikh farmers had the reputation of being the most productive and modern in India. Thus the government policy of giving most land in the newly irrigated canal colonies to Sikh veterans served economic as well as political ends. Because of their position on the north-west border, Punjab and NWFP played a central role in British military planning; Punjab received the lion's share of military investment in British India. In the 1920s, Sikh religious leaders successfully organized a movement to bring all Gurudwaras under an officially unified Sikh administrative control, which increased their political influence among Sikhs. Meanwhile, Hindu Banias and Khatris who lived in the major cities had become the financial backbone of Punjab's thriving commercial economy. Many merchants from north India also arrived in urban Punjab during the boom decades after 1880, when Punjab became the most profitable region for agrarian business in British India. Merchants became prominent patrons of

Hindu revivalist organizations like the Arya Samaj, whose influence was greater in Punjab than anywhere else.

This mixture of politics with business and religion proved volatile. Government concern for the productivity of Punjab farmers and for the political stability of the region caused official anxiety as many farmers fell deeply in debt to finance commercial production. Officials feared an explosion of violence like that heaped by indebted Maratha cotton farmers on Marwari money lenders in 1875. Fearing upheaval in Punjab and also committed by their own official tradition to the people they called 'martial races' and 'sturdy yeomen' in Punjab, the government passed the Land Alienation Act in 1900. The act prohibited the transfer of land for debt default to what it called 'non-cultivating tribes', who were mostly Hindus. This law expelled merchants from markets in agricultural credit and enriched the landed groups who moved into money lending, mostly Muslims and Sikhs. Landowners large and small rallied around the law. Merchants opposed it. For Sikhs and Muslims in Punjab, numerical strength in communal electorates protected economic interests. The fact that *official* ethnic identities coincided with religious identities made religious leaders more influential in election campaigns and thus in debates about contending constitutional proposals in the 1920s and 1930s.

The distinctiveness of Punjab and Bengal stands out when we compare them with Madras, where another non-Congress regime came to power under dyarchy in the 1920s. In the sprawling Madras Presidency, the Justice Party was assembled in 1921 as a motley assortment of non-Brahman politicians, mostly Tamil-speakers, who controlled the Legislative Assembly in the 1920s. The Justice Party used its government powers to benefit constituents in the same manner as parties in Punjab and Bengal. But in Madras, there was little unity of interests among constituents, except that they collectively sought to displace Brahmans from dominance in higher education and administration. One thing that all the Tamils had in common was their passion for the Tamil language as the medium and icon of their native cultural identity. Because Brahmans were most prominent in Congress, the Justice Party became a regional collection of politicians who competed with a nationally dominant imperial elite represented by Brahmans in Congress. With its patronage for

Tamil scholarship and education, the Justice Party established a political culture of regional nationality in Madras. But its organizational powers dissipated. When faced with all-out Congress electoral campaigns in Madras, in the 1930s, it collapsed. Congress took power in the 1937 elections. Congress held power in the land of Tamil nationality until a stronger Tamil Non-Brahman party, the Dravida Munnetra Kazhagam (DMK) took power in 1967.

By contrast, Congress never won provincial elections in Bengal and Punjab. That political fact laid the constitutional basis for the partition of India and Pakistan in 1947.

With this in view, it is important to note that the administrative partitioning of states along linguistic lines in independent India, in 1956, made the DMK ascendancy possible. By separating regions that were formerly in Madras Presidency, where Tamil, Telugu, Kannada, and Malayalam were respectively the dominant languages, the ruling Congress government in independent India, under Prime Minister Jawaharlal Nehru in New Delhi, effectively turned Tamil linguistic identity into a *constitutional* identity and made Tamil an *official* identity in a separate 'communal' electorate that was now available for *public* mobilization. In the officially Tamil political environment in the new Indian state of Tamil Nadu, Congress steadily lost support to explicitly Tamil political parties, which have dominated state politics since 1967.

THE RECONSTITUTION OF NATIONALITIES: 1931-47

In 1931, when deliberations for a new constitutional system for British India went into high gear, the Indian National Congress, led by Nehru and Gandhi, vehemently opposed communal electorates. Dividing the electorate by official religious categories violated the Congress ideal of Indian unity. Congress called it a British strategy to 'divide and rule' India forever. Perhaps it was. But communal electorates were already in place in the provinces, where Indian politicians embraced them. Indian politicians sought not only to maintain them but to expand their political importance by expanding government authority in the provinces. Congress, by contrast, strove to capture national authority in New Delhi and to expand the power of the central government in independent India.

In national debates, the Muslim League identified itself most prominently with Indian demands for communal representation. The League held but a pittance of seats in provincial assemblies, however, and Congress gained strength in all the regions after it dropped its non-cooperation programme, entered elections, and took many regional politicians into its ranks. Jinnah's personal 'parting of the ways' with Congress in 1928 over the issue of minority rights thus had little political force in the early 1930s.

Dr B.R. Ambedkar presented a more potent challenge to the Congress position. At the same time as Jinnah argued for increased Muslim representation based on the 1931 census figures, Ambedkar argued that all of India's so-called 'untouchable' castes merited separate electoral representation. Gandhi conducted a fast-unto-death to force Ambedkar to drop this idea. Ambedkar settled instead for a small number of reserved seats for 'depressed classes'. Gandhi called the untouchables *harijans* ('children of god') and promoted their uplift by voluntary charitable action along the model of Gohkale's Servants of India Society. Gandhi won wide support for his belief that even the severest inequities of caste society could be ameliorated without the separate political mobilization of the poor and of low caste groups. Nehru and other Congress leaders on the Left determined that broad government action would be needed to erase India's 'gross inequalities', and peasant and workers organizations allied with Congress pushed for more radical action than Gandhi could ever condone, including massive land reform. But in the Congress before 1947, this kind of government action remained a promise to be fulfilled after independence had been won by a unified national movement under Congress authority.

Arguments against communal representation did not impress Jinnah and the League. They stuck to the position that Muslims needed separate political representation to safeguard their minority interests in a majority Hindu electorate led by a predominantly Hindu Congress. Ambedkar recognized the legitimacy of this position even as he rose in the Congress ranks and he eventually guided some of its ideas into the writing of India's national constitution after 1947.

In 1932, constitutional debates among lawyers gave way to hard politics, when government announced its 'communal award', that is, the legislative seat allocations reserved for elected representatives of officially defined groups in the population. Based on 1931 census returns, these reservations comprised a large majority of seats in the North-West Frontier Provinces (82%), Punjab (75%), Sind (68%), and Bengal (68%); and a smaller majority in Assam (59%). In NWFP and Sind, Muslims got most reserved seats (72% and 57% of total reservations, respectively). In Punjab, Muslims got forty-nine per cent and Sikhs eighteen per cent of reserved seats. In Bengal and Assam, Muslims got forty-eight per cent and thirty-one per cent of the total, respectively; and additional reservations were made for British plantation owners. 'Depressed classes' got small reservations in all the provinces, and other reservations went to representatives of 'backward areas', Indian Christians, Anglo-Indians, Europeans, universities, organized labour, and big business.

The second Congress non-cooperation campaign, launched in 1932, succeeded in raising the national stature of Congress but failed to alter substantially the allocation of reserved seats, let alone to dislodge the principle of communal representation. When elections under the 1935 Government of India Act were held, in 1937, Congress candidates obtained huge majorities in Madras (74%), United Provinces (59%), Bihar (63%), Central Provinces (63%), and Orissa (60%). Congress did well enough to become the most powerful party in Bombay (48%), where it also formed a government.

Congress candidates did not win enough seats to form governments in Bengal (24%), Sind (13%), Punjab (10%), and NWFP (38%), where Congress refused to join coalition governments. The League fared worse than Congress in Muslim majority areas, where it failed to win most Muslim reserved seats. Congress received many more Muslim votes than the League but provincial parties got many more than both combined and formed coalition governments in Bengal, Punjab, Sind, and NWFP. Congress controlled all other provinces; among these, the United Provinces in particular had many Muslim majority areas, mostly in cities.

The League responded to this election debacle with dramatic efforts to attract Muslim voters and allies among provincial parties. Jinnah re-organized the League on lines similar to the Congress and conducted similar mass campaigns to attract Muslim politicians who faced the prospect of being swamped by Congress in any head-to-head competition for national political power. In the 1940s, the League reversed its electoral fortunes and came to lead coalition governments in Bengal, Sind, and NWFP.

In 1941, the leader of Bengal's Krishak Praja Party (Peasant and Workers Party), Fazlul Haq, joined forces with the Muslim League. He tabled the resolution for Pakistan at the League meeting that year in Lahore, calling for a separate territory called Pakistan reserved in its entirety for Muslim government. Pakistan represented a political territory in a League-proposed federal constitutional scheme that secured for Muslim-majority provinces maximum control over regions in which they counted as the majority. Creating this territory would require redrawing political boundaries to separate Muslim majority areas then included in Punjab and Bengal and uniting them with other Muslim majority areas. The promise of attaining constitutionally secure regional power in a national system that would surely be dominated by Congress attracted Muslim provincial politicians like Fazlul Haq to the League and to its demand for Pakistan.

In the League's campaign to become the party of all Muslims, it received inadvertent help from Congress. In 1941, Congress called for ministerial resignations to protest Britain's declaration of war in India. The British put India on the front lines of war without consulting Indian national leaders. Congress resignations led to by-elections won by League supporters. In 1942, the Congress declared its all-out Quit India campaign to drive the British from India, and the League supported the government to concentrate its attention on winning official support for Pakistan. As a result, when the war was over, the League was in a much stronger position than when the war began.

In 1945, negotiations began that determined the shape of independent India. The League had powerful electoral support in Bengal, Sind, Punjab, NWFP, and Baluchistan, and also had supporters in cities in the Ganga basin. Congress controlled all the other regions and was in a position to form a central government immediately. Congress had prominent supporters from all national groups, including Muslims. Congress sought to make its government a bastion of Indian unity and national strength, which could bring the country out of ruin caused by decades of war, depression, famine, and upheaval. With a legitimate claim to represent the Indian nation, Congress stood firm against Jinnah's less credible claim to represent all Indian Muslims. Congress appeared to the League as a domineering Hindu majoritarian party bent on reducing minorities to its authoritarian will. The League appeared to Congress as a threat to India, a divisive communal party of special interests that sought to hobble if not dismember the nation.

Pakistan remained constitutionally ill-defined when Lord Mountbatten arrived in New Delhi, in 1946, carrying a precipitous 1947 deadline for ending negotiations, set unilaterally by the British. In 1947, intransigence on all sides made the partition of India the only solution that all parties could agree upon. No one originally wanted partition, but no option could be found within the short time-frame available. On 15 August 1947 independent states of India and Pakistan were born at the bargaining table and agreements to transfer imperial power to national governments were signed at the same time as massive dislocations and rioting occurred in cities, towns and villages, where people were fighting for property and revenge. A civil war among the peoples of Punjab sent millions of refugees across the new international border. Countless thousands died.

INDEPENDENCE AND PARTITION

The new national states altered the meaning and substance of nationality. The partition of India and Pakistan produced a new geography of belonging and alienation that never existed before. Since 1947, the term 'India' has referred ambiguously to a national state, to a larger territory encompassed by British India, and to a region of culture and history embracing most of South Asia. After partition, national histories obscured the character of nationality before 1947. For example, Muhammad Ali Jinnah came to be known as the founder of Pakistan, and therefore as not Indian, even anti-Indian, by virtue of being a Pakistani, which he was for only one year of his long life. Before 1947, Jinnah was an Indian. He was a devoted Indian nationalist who fought for Muslim minority rights. Indian nationality before 1947 embraced peoples divided by nationality in 1947. Almost one-third of all Indians in

1946 had become Pakistanis by 1948. Indians in 1948 lived in a national state territory that was unimaginable a decade before.

Partition uprooted ten million people; most were forced to move to India or Pakistan. The pain of partition was very unevenly distributed and afflicted a small proportion of the total population. For most people, partition was a national trauma that affected people far away in other regions. Non-border regions had little disruption, though Muslims did leave urban areas of hostility and some violence in Uttar Pradesh, Gujarat, Bombay, and elsewhere to live in Pakistan, mostly in Lahore and Karachi. Almost all the pain fell on three historic regions that partition divided between India and Pakistan: Punjab, Bengal, and Kashmir. In each region, the new international borders were unprecedented; their local details were also quite arbitrary. All the regions produced expulsions, riots, killings, refugees, and new justifications for ethnic solidarity and hatred. The people of Punjab experienced by far the most violence and dislocation as an immediate result of partition. Battles for assets and revenge became a civil war. Bengal's partition was long, slow, and peaceful by comparison. Unregulated migration and everyday mobility continued for decades across the new borders. Kashmir was divided by a treaty that ended a war between India and Pakistan over the territory in 1947.

Kashmir remains disputed territory. The Raja of the native state of Jammu and Kashmir opted to join India. Opposition groups from his Muslim majority population argued for joining Pakistan. Pakistan claimed Kashmir because of its Muslim majority. The political polarization of the state on Hindu–Muslim lines originated in the Dogra dynasty's nineteenth-century installation of a Brahman and Kashmiri Pandit ruling elite of landlords, bureaucrats, and businessmen, and its institution of state Hindu rituals and law codes. Public Muslim activity in the observance of prayers and festivals was officially imbued with an air of dissent and even outlawed periodically. A Muslim political opposition arose that was banned in Kashmir and exiled to Lahore in Punjab, where Kashmiris and their supporters entered the fray of Punjabi politics. Political antagonisms among Hindu, Muslim, and Sikh groups in Punjab were embroiled in struggles over the rights of Hindus, Muslims, and Sikhs in Kashmir. Thus the external dimensions of Kashmiri politics were well established in 1947, when India and Pakistan went to war and then divided Kashmir to bring the major portion, including the Vale and its capital, Srinagar, into India, and a smaller portion, called Azad Kashmir, into Pakistan. The two countries went to war over Kashmir again in 1965 and hostilities continue today. Kashmir's borders remain contested. Extricating the people of Kashmir from hostile claims by both countries remains impossible.

War and violence have haunted Kashmiris since 1947. Partition's pain also continues to haunt other groups in partitioned regions. For example, thousands of Muslim Biharis left to live in East Pakistan; and when East Pakistan became Bangladesh, in 1971, they became 'stranded Pakistanis' living on the margins of another new national society. Along the current borders of Bangladesh, 1947's poorly defined borders between India and East Pakistan left tiny enclaves of foreign Bengalis on both sides, permanent hostages in hostile territory. Since 1947, Muslim Bengalis who have continued the long tradition of moving to farm land in Assam and to find work in West Bengal have become suspect, sometimes hated, foreigners.

FORGING NATIONAL UNITY

After independence, governments built nationality anew by constructing institutions that identified nationality with national states. Development programmes made economic prosperity a national project, led by government. Warfare nationalized militant patriotism. Educational systems turned national identities into social identities for most of the population. National boundaries became natural geographical features in the socialization of citizens. The shape of the national map itself became an icon. Historical sites became national treasures. History writing, films, songs, holidays, parades, and countless cultural events expressed national unity, which became an article of modern faith, as it did around the world.

After 1947, social change accelerated as new states governed the entitlements that people needed for social mobility and human security. New national governments consolidated control over their territories and became leading investors in economic

TABLE 8. FORMATIVE EVENTS IN THE EARLY HISTORY OF
NATIONAL STATES

1950 Constitution of India. Universal adult franchise. Indian National
Planning Commission.

1951 Fall of the Rana regime in Nepal. India's First Five Year Plan and
general election. Jana Sangh Party founded by Dr S.P. Mookerjee,
former head of Hindu Mahasabha.

1952 Bengali language movement in East Pakistan. Massacre of students.

1953 First linguistic state, Andhra Pradesh. Akali Dal demands Punjabi
Subha.

1954 Muslim League defeated by United Front in East Pakistan. United
Front government dismissed.

1956 Indian States Reorganization Act. Pakistan constitution introduces
presidential government. Militant Naga insurgency.

1958 Ayub Khan becomes martial law administrator of Pakistan.

1962 Third Indian general election. Indo-Chinese war on Tibetan frontier.

1963 Indian state of Nagaland created.

1964 Death of Jawaharlal Nehru. Vishwa Hindu Parishad founded by
Swami Chinmayananda.

1965 India–Pakistan war over Kashmir.

---

development. But old national movements had produced a broad
public feeling of participation in state activity and now politically
active groups mobilized to shape the constitution of national
governments. The result was a rapid shift of the social basis of the
political order. This shift bears comparison to others in earlier
periods following imperial collapse. The end of the Gupta and
Mughal empires opened the field of opportunity for local and
regional elites who then used powers inherited from old empires to
create new political domains. The end of the British empire also
accelerated upward mobility for politically active groups who
were positioned to establish themselves in a new institutional
framework.

India

Partition left the Congress with uncontested national power in the
Republic of India, which inherited most of the empire's assets and

institutions. The All-India Congress Committee quickly formed an elected national government. India's 1950 constitution kept most features of the 1935 Government of India Act: it gave the centre in New Delhi all the power of the old imperial administration under a new universal adult franchise; and it also maintained the old powers of the regional governments. India's national power and political unity increased with the incorporation of all the native states, Goa, Pondichery, and Sikkim. Military force became prominent in the early years of national consolidation. War with Pakistan secured the major portion of Kashmir. The army took more than a year to crush a revolution in the Telengana region of the former Hyderabad state.

Political mobilization in many regions reconstituted the Indian electorate along new territorial lines that gave old public identities new official status. The partitioning of Punjab between India and Pakistan was followed within two decades by the repartitioning of the Indian Punjab into two new states, Punjab and Haryana, in which Sikhs and Hindu Jats, respectively, held sway. In 1956, partitioning old provinces according to linguistic majorities gave Marathas, Rajputs, Gujaratis, Tamils, Telugus, Oriyas, Kannadi-gas, and Malayalis their own territories.

The Indian constitution erased communal electorates. In their stead, it defined official reservations in legislatures, government employment, and education for members of underprivileged groups listed on official 'schedules' of 'backward castes' and 'backward tribes'. Caste lists disappeared from the Indian census. Official classifications and enumerations of the population by religious categories remained.

Ethnic identities emerged quickly as public constituents of the electoral system, despite their unofficial status. Regional patterns of ethnic and caste mobilization expanded their role in govern-ment, even though a formally unitary Congress Party dominated national and state elections. Voting blocs developed in all the regions around social identities mobilized in public to win elections and to seek advantages for a widening variety of groups. These groups included workers, peasants, landlords, industrialists, Muslims, Sikhs, and various Hindu sects and caste alliances that formed distinctive patterns in each Indian state. Official religious and unofficial ethnic, class, and family identities remained a major public asset for candidates who represented local and regional identities under the Congress banner.

India's national Congress Party regime became a vast political umbrella under which many groups mobilized for entitlements and influence. Under the leadership of Jawaharlal Nehru, who remained Prime Minister until his death in 1964, Congress built a national system of alliances in villages, towns, and districts, based on loyalties inherited from the national movement and on the ability of the ruling party to provide patronage in return for votes. Congress leaders strove to balance change with stability by enhancing their leadership in local power structures. State development plans kept local elites in mind and encouraged state investments to strengthen Congress organization. India's national development regime invoked the ideals of socialism and expanded the public sector but also rested on a socially conservative local power base composed of Congress big men. Industrial policies favoured major businesses and urban voters. The Green Revolution gave rich farmers new funds and technologies.

After decades of dithering on the subject of land reform, Congress leaders led a drive to eliminate Zamindari tenures in a manner that would be least disruptive for local Congress supporters and was calculated to increase their numbers. Land reforms were enacted state by state and thus their impact was limited by the balance of power in each site. Charan Singh, the architect of Zamindari abolition in Uttar Pradesh, explained his strategy thus:

> The political consequences of the land reforms are . . . far reaching. Much thought was given to this matter since the drafters of the legislation were cognisant of the need to ensure political stability in the countryside. By strengthening the principle of private property where it was weakest, i.e. at the base of the social pyramid, the reformers have created a huge class of strong opponents of the class war ideology. By multiplying the number of independent land-owning peasants there came into being a middle of the road stable rural society and a barrier against political extremism.

Pakistan and Bangladesh

Reconciling social change and stability proved impossible in a united Pakistan. In West Pakistan, government immediately came into the hands of major landowners, industrialists, military men, bureaucrats, and business families, mostly from Punjab, but also from Sind, where many immigrants from India settled in Karachi. When formerly eastern districts of Bengal Presidency became East Pakistan, Bengalis in Pakistan found their government dominated by West Pakistanis. Separated by a thousand miles of hostile Indian territory, Pakistan's two wings had little in common. In the East, rapid social change was underway as Hindu Zamindars left for India and former rich tenants (*jotedars*) became powerful local politicians. In the West, landed elites prevented land reform. The West had a strong military legacy; the East had none. In the East, the drive for national independence included a widespread tenant struggle for property rights and the partition itself was not traumatic. In the West, ruling elites craved nothing more than order and stability after civil war in Punjab during partition. The same kind of regional mobilizations for political power in the new national government that produced India's re-organization of states, in 1956, produced a military coup in Pakistan. In 1958, General Ayub Khan became martial law administrator. During the next decade, the Pakistani military bureaucracy established firm control over the government.

In the 1950s, the East Pakistan capital, Dhaka, grew rapidly with the self-creation of a new Bengali middle class. Many aspiring East Pakistanis came straight from villages. Others came from Calcutta and from towns in West Bengal. Few knew Urdu, Pakistan's national language; more were in fact literate in English. Their common language was Bengali. Elite Muslim Bengali culture closely resembled that of Calcutta's *bhadralok*, with whom aspiring Bengalis in East Pakistan shared tastes, habits, and expectations. When Pakistan's Urdu-speaking state officials arrived in Dhaka, they were foreigners. When they tried to make Urdu the language of law, education, and administration in East Pakistan, in 1952, Bengali opposition spilled from universities into the streets. Bengali activists killed by soldiers became martyrs for their language. At the same time, government efforts to requisition grain to relieve food shortages that lingered for a decade after the 1943 famine triggered resentment among local landed elites. The Pakistan government's heavy hand not only failed to improve the food situation, it generated corruption, disrupted local grain markets, and provoked landowners (*jotedars*) to attack Hindu merchants, who fled the country.

By 1954, the combination of urban and rural resentment drove the Muslim League from power in East Pakistan. The Awami League became the national party in East Pakistan. In the 1950s and 1960s, Pakistan government controls over economic development widened disparities between East and West. The Awami League sought more provincial authority in the East to give Bengalis more economic and political opportunity. Military governments in Islamabad resisted (see Country Profiles). In 1966, the Awami League leader, Sheikh Mujibur Rahman, published his *Six Points: Our Demand for Survival*, advocating federal autonomy for East Pakistan. In 1970, when Pakistan held elections, the Awami League won an absolute majority in parliament, sweeping Bengali constituencies that contained fifty-five per cent of Pakistan's electorate. Euphoria in Dhaka gave way to horror when Sheikh Mujib was arrested and Pakistani troops arrived to subdue the rebel province. The Awami League declared independence. Freedom fighters fought the Pakistan army through 1971, chanting '*Joy Bangla*', 'Victory for Bengali'. Poorly armed villagers fought the Pakistani army to a stalemate. Pakistan received support from the United States. The army committed innumerable (still unacknowledged) atrocities among civilians. Eventually, India marched in to expel Pakistan from its eastern borderlands.

In December 1971, Bangladesh became an independent national state. Five years later, Bangladesh military officers assassinated Sheikh Mujib. The army then ruled Bangladesh until 1990, when a popular democracy movement forced the return of elected government.

Sri Lanka

In Sri Lanka, the early drive for national unity by the dominant national party also had extensive repercussions. The United National Party suspected immigrant Indian Tamil plantation workers, who formed a large population in the central highlands, of supporting the Trotskyist *Lanka Sama Samaya* Party, which had ten seats in parliament. The Citizen Act (1948), Indian and

Pakistani Residents Act (1949), and the Parliamentary Elections Amendment Act (1949) denied citizenship to most Indian Tamils and then disenfranchised the rest.

As in India and Pakistan, language became a volatile issue in Sri Lanka. Parliamentary elections in 1956 triggered national mobilization among Sinhala-speaking rural elites who sought more positions in a civil service that was still dominated by English-literates, and also among Buddhist monks who sought more influence in government on the 2500th anniversary of Buddha's enlightenment. In 1956 – the same year that riots also erupted in Madras when New Delhi tried to impose Hindi in the schools – the 'Sinhala Only' election slogan attracted votes from aspiring Sinhala speakers and Buddhist monks in Sri Lanka. In 1956, the most prominent public definition of nationality in Sri Lanka became Sinhala Buddhist. English-educated Tamils had been prominent in Ceylon's government, but now they were losing the advantages of their English literacy and official recognition of their native tongue. The 1956 Official Language Act in effect altered the 1947 constitution, which explicitly forbade language discrimination. In 1972, a new constitution gave Sinhala and Buddhism supreme official status. Anti-government riots ensued in the Tamil-majority areas in the north and east. Tamil demands for regional Tamil authority were opposed in Colombo and increasingly met with Sinhala hostility. In 1981 and 1983, political division and public hostility turned into civil war with the creation of Tamil fighting forces led by the Liberation Tigers of Tamil Eelam (LTTE).

Since 1983, Sri Lankan state military action in the Tamil north and east of the island has included several rounds of conquest and military occupation; also four years of collaborative efforts with India, during which Indian troops endeavoured to subdue Tamil rebels. In 1987, when the Indian Peace Keeping Force (IPKF) arrived, the *Sinhala Janatha Vimukthi Peramuna* (JVP, People's Liberation Front), launched a revolutionary war in the south – their second effort, the first being in 1971 – and national violence reigned from 1987 to 1990, as troops and rebels killed each other on two broad, ill-defined fronts. Civilian victims remain uncountable. Up to sixty thousand people officially 'disappeared' without a trace. Though the JVP revolution ceased, the LTTE continues to fight for Tamil autonomy and to garner financial support from far-flung locations around the world, where Tamil refugees have fled, resettled, and continued the struggle. Sri Lanka's ethnic national civil war continues today with no end in sight.

SEVEN

National Environments

Nationality was never the same after 1971. India's watershed years began in 1967, when the Congress lost control of state governments in Kerala, Tamil Nadu, and West Bengal. In each state, parties came to power with more radical, popular agendas than Congress could muster for constituents who demanded state action to improve social conditions. Decades of popular political mobilization had provoked aspirations that the dominant national party could not satisfy. Activists sought new solutions. Like Sheikh Mujib, Indian populists attracted voters with attacks on established elites. Revolutionaries found supporters in city and countryside. India's Congress system had rested on national loyalties that legitimized the Congress power brokers who managed the flow of patronage from New Delhi. Their legitimacy collapsed in the 1970s. When Nehru's grandson, Rajiv Gandhi, became India's prime minister, in 1985, he effectively signed a death warrant for the Congress system at celebrations for the party's one hundredth anniversary, by blasting 'cliques' that held 'the living body of the Congress in their net of avarice'.

Social change produced new forms of nationality that burst into politics. Pakistan's military regimes and war in Bangladesh expressed a dramatic state response to disorder in the nation. Faced with unpredictable upheavals, national governments acquired a more draconian substance elsewhere as well. In 1971, Sri Lankan armies massacred revolutionaries in the Peoples' Liberation Front and suppressed their public supporters. Sri Lanka's 1972 constitution strove to strengthen Sinhala Buddhist national dominance. In

1975, Sheikh Mujib was killed with most of his family in a coup that brought military rule to Bangladesh for fifteen years. When the Indian army expelled Pakistan from Bangladesh, in 1971, it also crushed a four-year-old Communist-led peasant revolution in nearby Naxalbari, in Darjeeling District in the Himalayan foothills of West Bengal; and at the same time, the army and police suppressed Naxalite support in Calcutta. Charan Singh's fear of rustic radicals proved justified as little revolts broke out in many Indian districts. As poor workers and forest peoples attacked elites supported by the army, police, and courts, subaltern wrath often turned against the state. In 1975, India's Home Ministry harked back to Jawaharlal Nehru's 1930 declaration when it reported that continued failure to alleviate severe inequalities in the country 'may lead to a situation where the discontented elements are compelled to organize themselves and the extreme tensions building up within . . . the Indian village may end in an explosion'. India's military victories in 1971 gave the Congress Prime Minister, Nehru's daughter Indira Gandhi, a brief popular supremacy; but in 1975, facing threats all around, her government declared a national emergency that suspended civil rights with constitutional powers retained from the 1935 Government of India Act.

By the 1980s, nationality came to include various struggles that pitted citizens against citizens and nationals against national states. New social movements arose among workers, women, farmers, tribals, and other underprivileged groups. Untouchables and Harijans now became known as *Dalits* ('the oppressed'). Ethnic regional autonomy movements erupted. Sikhs fought for Khalistan in India's Punjab. Tamils fought for Eelam in Sri Lanka. Kashmiris fought to free Kashmir. Mountain peoples fought for autonomy in Assam, Mizoram, and Nagaland. By 1991, democratic movements had won victories in Nepal and Bangladesh to establish elected governments. In the 1990s, a new Maoist revolution spread across Nepal to force the pace of change. India's electoral system remained intact throughout upheavals that ushered in new formations of national order and identity in the 1980s and 1990s. National identity as it prevailed in South Asia in 1965 was a thing of the past twenty-five years later.

Though the wider world has always been part of nationality in South Asia, and though global capitalism, socialism, and the Cold

War shaped nations before 1970, new external dimensions of national histories emerged from the 1970s onward. Financial pressure from foreign aid donors, the World Bank, and the International Monetary Fund (IMF) forced national governments to relinquish control over national economies. Emigration from South Asia dispersed its national identities more widely overseas. Foreign companies and overseas connections became prominent in national life. New social movements went global in struggles for human rights and for protections against the onslaught of world capitalism. The new term 'globalization' came into vogue to evoke a new context for contemporary history.

This new global context informed public reformulations of national identity in rapidly changing South Asian societies. Public activists came to concentrate with new force on the unity of national culture and tradition. Sri Lanka's 1972 constitution was a landmark. Soon after Bangladesh's independence, Sheikh Mujib declared to a gathering of non-Bengalis that 'we are *all* Bengalis'. In the 1980s, the cultural unity of Hindu India and Islamic Pakistan became a rallying cry for ascending political forces. New forms of religious nationalism captured the limelight with support from nationals overseas. Regional autonomy movements among Tamils in Sri Lanka and Sikhs in Punjab took root in diaspora communities in Australia, Canada, Europe, and the US.

Young people today live in social environments quite different from the ones that their parents knew when they were young. Collective identities have changed significantly in the past thirty years, as national environments have been transformed by local, regional, international, and global trends. Today's emerging social identities include regional, national, official, ethnic, caste, religious, and linguistic elements whose mixtures of meaning and substance are unstable and unpredictable. Identities are being constructed in diverse cultural idioms simultaneously, to constitute the mixed, varied substance of nationality for ordinary people in everyday life. New identity elements – particularly gender and social class – attained new prominence in new social movements, cultural politics, and international migration. Communications media – cinema, television, and now the internet – are expanding the influence and spreading the ideas of public activists more widely than ever before. More groups than ever are now mobilized to increase entitlements, secure rights, and turn popular support into political power. As a result, *public* identities promulgated by political activists influence *social* identity more widely.

This concluding chapter considers the recent history of *public* identities that influence *social* identity for people in five *official* religious categories: Buddhist, Christian, Sikh, Muslim, and Hindu. For each, we consider only a few major themes. This brief account is – like the rest of the book – a strategic simplification with two goals: first, to indicate prominent trends in the history of social identity; and second, to survey political history from a social perspective.

BUDDHIST REFORMERS, EXILES, RULERS, AND MAJORITARIANS

By 1900, new Buddhist organizations were being established by social reformers in British India to invent a cultural alternative to the Hindu caste ideology, which some reformers saw as the root of degradation and deprivation for poor people in the lowest Hindu caste groups. In 1900, a prominent Brahman officer in Madras, S. Srivinasa Raghava Aiyangar, submitted an official report saying that untouchable Pariahs in Madras could not make progress without leaving Hinduism.

Fifty years later – and twenty-five years after he relented to Gandhi on the question of separate electorates for Indian untouchables – B.R. Ambedkar converted to Buddhism and led a mass neo-Buddhist conversion movement in Maharashtra. Ambedkar had been the main author of India's constitution, in which he secured state recognition for 'scheduled castes', that is, the untouchable *jati*s listed on a constitutional schedule of groups needing special government assistance. By 1956, however, Ambedkar had concluded that government efforts and Gandhian voluntarism would never empower the poorest Hindus. He led several hundred thousand converts to Buddhism in order to provide them with the organization, visibility, and state recognition that came with being members of an officially recognized religious community. New Buddhists sought to gain political representation that they could not acquire by other means. Today, they number as many as four million, mostly among Mahars in Maharashtra, though their numbers remain hard to assess because of political resistance to their official enumeration.

Also in the 1950s, a very different kind of dissident Buddhist identity came into being when China conquered Tibet. Thousands of Tibetan Buddhist refugees, including leading *lamas* and the Dalai Lama himself, settled in exile communities in north India and Nepal. These countries became bases for the international movement to restore the Dalai Lama in a free Tibet, which continues today. New Buddhist visibility in Nepal energized Nepal's own Buddhist cultural identities in a country where the ruling class was mostly Brahman, the majority population was officially Hindu, and the law of the land enforced divisions among religions and Hindu castes.

By contrast, in the old Himalayan kingdoms of Sikkim and Bhutan, regional forms of Tibetan Buddhism remained state religions, as under the old lamas in Tibet. Sikkim was incorporated into India in 1975, when it became a Buddhist state in a vastly diverse, secular, multi-cultural republic. Bhutan remained an independent nation where state Buddhism sustained a substantial population of influential monks. In Bhutan's southern region, the large national minority of Nepali Hindus became politically suspect. Since 1980, Nepalis have been pressured to repatriate to Nepal or to adopt Bhutan's national dress, customs, religion, and language, as have the fifteen per cent of Bhutan's people who are from indigenous and/or migratory tribal groups.

Making Buddhism into a ruling Sinhala state religion became a political project for monks and allied activists in Sri Lanka, who endeavour to use Buddhism to unite the country against threats from Tamils, Marxists, and Western globalization. This recent political trend represents a much longer and quite varied tradition of Buddhist activism. Since the nineteenth century, many social movements with many political agendas have reinterpreted Buddhism and deployed its cultural authority on the island. As a result, Buddhism today means many things in Sri Lanka, as it does in South Asia more generally. The Siam Nikaya are a conservative, wealthy Buddhist sect in which membership is restricted to high caste Goigama families. The large Amarapura sect has grown over the years by reaching out to include lower castes. Various social reform sects have also emerged. The most prominent are the Sarvodaya groups that conduct social programmes like those of the Gandhian Sarvodaya movement in India, using volunteers among the middle class to serve the rural poor.

TABLE 9. DEFINITIVE MOMENTS IN RECENT HISTORY

1966 Indira Gandhi becomes Indian prime minister. Sheikh Mujibur
Rahman, *Six Points: Our Demand for Survival.*

1966 M.S. Golwalkar, *Bunch of Thoughts.* Militant Mizo insurgency.

1967 Fourth Indian general election. Dravida Munnetra Kazhakam
(DMK) victory. Congress dominance declines. Pakistan People's
Party (PPP) founded. Naxalbari revolution begins in north-east.

1970 Pakistan's first national elections. Zulfiqar Ali Bhutto becomes
president. Awami League wins absolute majority.

1971 Fifth Indian general election. Arrest of Sheikh Mujibur Rahman.
Bangladesh liberation war. India's war with Pakistan. Janatha
Vimukthi Peramuna (JVP) People's Liberation Movement
suppressed in Ceylon, where state of emergency declared, to
1977. Naxalbari revolution suppressed in Calcutta and north-east
India.

1972 G.M. Syed heightens Sindhi nationalism with *Sindhi Culture.*
Pakistan's third constitution. Riots following Sind Language Bill.
Ceylon becomes Sri Lanka.

1973 Insurgency in Baluchistan.

1974 Akali Dal passes Anandpur Sahib Resolution. Police violence at
Fourth International Tamil Conference in Jaffna.

1975 State of emergency in India, to 1977. Sheikh Mujib assassinated.
Military coup in Bangladesh. Chelvanayakam declares for a separate
Tamil state in Sri Lanka.

1977 Janata Dal government in India. Zia-ul-Huq martial law regime in
Pakistan.

1978 Anandpur Sahib Resolution. Foundation of All-Pakistan Mohajir
Students Organization. Liberation Tigers of Tamil Eelam proscribed
in Sri Lanka.

1979 Execution of Zulfiqar Ali Bhutto. Tehrik-I-Nifaz-I-Jafria founded by
Shias in response to Zia's state-sponsored Sunni Islamic law.
Prevention of Terrorism Act in Sri Lanka. Military occupation of
Jaffna District.

1980 Indira Gandhi wins general election. Jana Sangh becomes Bharatiya
Janata Party (BJP).

1981 Akali Dal launches Dharam Yudh Morcha for Punjab autonomy.
Mandal Commission report. Movement for the Restoration of
Democracy in Pakistan. Anti-Tamil riots across Sri Lanka; war with
Tamil separatists begins.

TABLE 9. CONTINUED

1984 Indian Army Operation Bluestar at Golden Temple at Amritsar. Indira
Gandhi assassinated. Delhi anti-Sikh riots. Rajiv Gandhi elected.
Formation of the Mohajir Qaumi Mahaz (MQM) by Altaf Hussain.
VHP calls for the liberation of the Ramjanambhoomi. *Khalistan News*
published in UK; *World Sikh News* and *The Sword* in North America.

1985 Partyless elections in Pakistan. Rajiv Gandhi's accord with Sant
Harchand Singh Longowal. Longowal assassinated.

1986 Shah Bano case. New social movements rise in India. Babri Masjid
Committee formed.

1987 VHP mobilizes liberation of Ramjanambhoomi. MQM triumphs in
Karachi elections. V.P. Singh forms Janata Dal government. Indian
Peace Keeping Force (IPKF) in Jaffna.

1988 Zia's death. Elections in Pakistan; Benazir Bhutto leads PPP
government.

1989 National Front wins Indian elections. BJP seats increase from 2 to 85.
Mandal Commission report accepted. Ram Shila Pujan programme.
Insurgency begins in Kashmir.

1990 L.K. Advani's *rath yatra*. *Kar sevak*s killed in Ayodhya. Secessionist
movement in Assam. Dismissal of Benazir Bhutto government. BJP
withdraws support from Janata Dal government. Democracy
movement changes constitution in Nepal.

1991 Nepal general elections. Nepali Congress majority. Elections in
Bangladesh. BNP wins. Rajiv Gandhi assassinated; P.V. Narasimha
Rao minority Congress government; BJP government in Uttar
Pradesh. Indian economic liberalization accelerated.

1992 Destruction of Babri Masjid, 6 December. Riots kill 1700, injure
5500 in four months.

1993 Dismissal of Nawaz Sharif. Benazir Bhutto comes to power after
elections.

1994 Karachi MQM violence. Caste violence in Tamil Nadu.

1996 Thirteen-day minority BJP government. Bhutto dismissed. Nawaz
Sharif returns. Awami League government in Bangladesh.

1998 Fall of Gujral government. BJP-led coalition government in India.

1999 Fall and re-election of BJP-led coalition government. Indo-Pakistan
conflict in Kargil. Parvez Musharaf military coup removes Nawaz
Sharif from power.

2000 War over Tamil Eelam continues in Sri Lanka. Maoists in power in
majority of Nepal districts. Caste wars in Bihar.

After the outbreak of civil war, in 1983, when Tamil fighters and Sri Lankan troops started killing each other, Buddhist nationalism attained broader public influence. This occurred at the same time as Hindu nationalism ascended in India. The two have much in common. They both endeavour to define and enforce allegiance to a national ethnicity defined by official religious categories established under British rule. Neither has a substantial theological base and both gloss over diversity within religious communities and ambiguities at their borders. Both combine a reverence for classical texts and modern language with support from religious activists to forge an ethnic-linguistic support for national cultural unity defined by religious community. Their nationalization of ethnicity involves an ethnic genealogy of the nation that dominates Sinhala Buddhist as well as Hindu nationalist (*Hindutva*) historical writing. The *Mahavamsa* is often cited and interpreted by Sinhala Buddhist activists to establish basic articles of faith: (1) Sinhala identity can be traced genealogically to the arrival of Vijaya in ancient times, when (2) Buddha chose Sri Lanka to be a pure island for his teaching (*dhamma dipa*). Thus (3) the Sinhala have been chosen as pure Aryans from Buddha's home territory to protect his *dhamma* for ever. (4) Sinhala Buddhists had been ruled by their kings and are today ruled by an elected government that continues the mission to protect *dhamma*. (5) Tamils are intruders from south India who are not Buddhist and not Aryans. Their language is Dravidian, whereas Sinhala is Indo-Aryan. Tamils occupy parts of a Sinhala Buddhist motherland (*mawbima*). *Hindutva* interprets Hindu history in a similar vein.

CHRISTIAN COMMUNITIES, REFORMERS, MINORITIES, AND TARGETS

In 1900, the size and diversity of South Asia's many small Christian societies were still increasing with the influx of Europeans, spread of English education, growth of ethnically mixed Anglo-Indian communities, and expansion of missionary education and medical facilities. As European residents declined in number in South Asia, the Christian population continued to expand. The vast majority of Christians and Christian missionaries in South Asia have always been South Asians, and after 1940 ethnically non-South-Asian Christians became insignificant.

Christian societies have ethnic and regional patterns like others. The oldest Christian communities began in medieval Kerala, where Syrian Christians remain a majority in northern districts and a potent cultural and political force in the state as a whole. After 1500, Catholicism spread around Portuguese and French settlements; and Protestantism around Dutch and English settlements. In Sri Lanka, numerous English-educated urbanites are from upper caste Sinhala (Goigama) and Tamil (Vellala) families. In the nineteenth and twentieth centuries, Protestant missionaries and churches became part of local societies in many urban centres but were most influential among the poor and in marginal areas where they provided education and medical care. Missionary schools and hospitals provided public service to many people who were served poorly or not at all by the state. India's poor north-eastern hill states are almost all Protestant.

Christians became most numerous in scattered localities along the coast from Goa to Madras, in Sri Lanka, and also in India's north-east mountains. Christian social elites include Catholics, Syrian Christians, and Protestants in Goa, Kerala, Sri Lanka, and India's north-eastern hill states (Meghalaya, Mizoram, Nagaland, and Manipur). But in these regions and others, the majority of Christians are poor people with low caste backgrounds, Anglo-Indians, and mountain people. Protestant churches in particular developed a reputation for social reform and local activism. In the nineteenth century, for example, missionaries built schools and communities of converts from low caste Shanars in southern Madras Presidency, whose English education allowed them to become the most prominent of all non-elite castes in local educational institutions and government. Today Protestant church groups are active in movements to improve living conditions among poor low caste and tribal peoples in many parts of India.

External perceptions of Christians by people in more powerful social groups have been important for Christian identities. The British government provided support for Christian activities. Though many social reformers in South Asia were influenced by Christianity, and though individual Christians did gain public prominence, particularly in Sri Lanka, Christians never became a national political force anywhere in South Asia. Their respected minority stature in Indian politics was established by national leaders like Ram Mohan Roy, Sri Ramakrishna, Sri Aurobindo, and Mohandas Gandhi, all of whom saw Christianity as one *dharma* or spiritual path among others inside India's all-inclusive culture.

Hindu nationalists made Christian conversion a political issue. In the early twentieth century, the Arya Samaj and Hindu Mahasabha began promoting the idea that Christians and Muslims took Hindus away from their native faith to bolster alien power, particularly in Punjab. More anti-Christian public energy emerged from the Rashtriya Swayamsevak Sangh (RSS), which was formed in 1925. Hindu nationalists kept their distance from national politics before independence and staked their claim to represent the nation on their militant defence of Hindu tradition. They took this to include fierce resistance to all Muslim and Christian influence. The Vishwa Hindu Parishad (VHP), Jana Sangh, and Bharatiya Janata Party (BJP) followed this strategy after independence, with increasing vehemence since 1980. Since the 1950s, politically prominent Buddhist monks in Sri Lanka have also attacked Christian influence in government. In the 1990s, Indian Christian schools, churches, and clinics have been burned to the ground in the name of Hindu pride; missionaries have been killed.

SIKH ELECTORATE, RELIGION, RIGHTS, AND TERRITORY

As we have seen, the 1932 communal award gave Sikhs separate representation in Punjab. In 1948, Punjab's mountain districts were made into the Indian state of Himachal Pradesh. In 1966, Haryana became a predominantly Hindu, Hindi-speaking state. Indian Punjab then became a primarily Sikh, Punjabi-speaking state.

High levels of public and private investments in agricultural productivity made the three regions of plains Punjab – Pakistani Punjab, Indian Punjab, and Haryana – the wealthiest agrarian regions in South Asia. The rising wealth of Punjab came with a combination of state and local investments that enriched Jat farming lineages and also helps to explain the territorial politics behind Punjab's three partitions. Sikh, Hindu, and Muslim identities in Punjab changed in relation to one another, and state policy combined with lineage power to produce an ethnically and religiously organized agrarian citizenry.

The rivers of Punjab flow down from Afghanistan, Kashmir, and the Himalayas; the long history of contemporary Punjabi politics has moved up and down these river valleys as well as down roads across the Indus and Ganga plains. In this strategic cross-roads of empire, solidarity among landed warriors sustained the official imperial idea of 'Indian village republics', which was most rigorously applied in Punjab. After the annexation of Punjab, in 1849, the Punjab village became a proprietary body composed of landed lineages. Village culture changed as collective arrangements for local defence became unnecessary and the joint interests of lineages focused on privatizing family control over land and labour. By 1900, Punjab landowners had privatized all the open, common land around their villages. As Jat lineages expanded their control over agricultural territory, their sons became the backbone of the Indian army. The imperial military was organized around ethnic regiments in which the so-called 'martial races' of Punjab were most highly valued, along with Gurkha recruits from Nepal. A preference for Punjabi soldiers combined with Punjab's location astride routes to Central Asia make Punjab politically central for imperial strategists. This paid huge local dividends. Road and railway building benefited cities where merchants sent commodities from Punjab and Kashmir to Karachi, Bombay, and the Gangetic basin. Lahore boomed as the regional capital. Military installations brought lucrative contracts for supplies and construction. From 1880 to 1930, the state built huge systems of irrigation dams and canals in Punjab and in western districts of the United Provinces (Uttar Pradesh), to water the land of Jat farmers stereotyped as being the most productive in India. In Punjab, canal colonies especially benefited military families. Farms were large and provided ample scope for investment at low rents. The Punjab government granted most land to families officially defined as 'peasant', owning one square of about twenty-seven acres each; larger tracts (with up to three squares) to 'yeomen' farmers and 'military' grantees; and huge tracts to 'capitalist' farmers with five to one hundred squares.

Heavy government investments in the land of old Punjab continued after 1947. In the 1960s, under the aegis of the Green

Revolution, public and private investments accelerated. As a result, the regions of old Punjab became powerful economically in India and Pakistan. In 1992, Punjab and Haryana together held nine per cent of India's population and eight per cent of its cultivated acreage, but seventeen per cent of its food grains. In India, only Punjab and Haryana have large food crop surpluses to export to other states: Punjab has proportionately six times as much food as it has people, and Haryana has three times. Since 1960, Punjab and Haryana have also had the highest growth rate in the value of agricultural produce (4.89% and 4.14%, respectively). Very substantial farmers own much of this prime farm land. In India as a whole, seventy-three per cent of all farmers work holdings of less than one hectare, but in Indian Punjab, this figure is forty-five per cent, and in Haryana sixty-one per cent. Some of Punjab's large farmers are capitalist tycoons. J.B.S. Sangha, for instance, has six thousand acres under potatoes; and A.S. Dhinda has seven hundred acres of flowers, which yield seventy tonnes of seed and half a million dollars in export earnings to the US.

The individual economic success of Punjab farmers is rooted in a long history of collective action. As we have seen, religious solidarities have been prominent from the eighteenth century. Soon after Punjab became a province of British India, the Brahmo Samaj became active, and the Arya Samaj emerged from it to pursue a similar reformist agenda but with stronger commitments to the sanctity of the Vedas and with a critical stance toward other religions. Muslim and Sikh activists responded in kind, as Christian missionaries became the most prominent providers of English education.

The Sikh Sabhas were first organized by large landowners and by Sikh native state rulers but were soon led by middle class activists who organized Sikhs to increase their employment and influence in government. At the same time, Sikh army regiments gave Singh families rising in the ranks more influence in shaping a Sikh identity that became a critical feature of the empire's military recruitment and discipline. In 1900, when the Punjab Land Alienation Act set in motion political opposition between merchants and farmers, it also fostered opposed solidarities between Hindu merchants allied with the Congress and the

Muslim and Sikh groups that were much more successful than Congress in elections.

The Shiromani Akali Dal was founded in 1925 to represent Sikh political interests after the Gurdwara reform movement succeeded in making representatives of the Sikh community official managers of Sikh temples (*Gurudwaras*). Thus religious institutions became centres of Sikh politics, which became more urbanized and religious in tone. During the partition of Punjab in 1947, violence forced Sikhs out of the canal colonies and into eastern Punjab and Delhi, where their numbers and influence increased. In independent India, the electoral success of Sikh parties led Congress politicians to pursue strategies to win Sikh votes and to keep the Akali Dal in check. Green Revolution policies favoured Punjab economically and a gleaming new capital was built in Chandigarh (after the loss of Lahore to Pakistan).

After Jawaharlal Nehru's death, in 1964, and the creation of a mostly Sikh Punjab, in 1966, the Akali Dal faced stiff competition from other parties in Punjab. But now the Congress was also weakening. National struggles for power would prove momentous for Sikhs in Punjab.

Until 1967, Congress controlled Indian state governments as well as the upper (Rajya Sabha) and lower (Lok Sabha) houses of parliament in New Delhi. But in 1967, regional parties began to beat Congress, beginning in Tamil Nadu, Kerala, and West Bengal. At this fractious time, Nehru's Oxford-educated daughter, Indira Gandhi (1917–84), ascended to the Congress leadership. She had been primed for the role by her father. She became Minister of Information and Broadcasting under his successor, Lal Bahadur Shastri, and then prime minister after Shastri's sudden death, in 1966.

Indira Gandhi struggled for the next decade to strengthen herself against Congress rivals, to maintain Congress power in the states against regional parties, and to prevent defections from Congress. Her political strategy centred on cultivating personal loyalties and on increasing her personal authority in Congress, and it succeeded for a time. But in 1975, faced with a challenge to her own election, she instituted a national emergency regime using martial law powers retained from the 1935 Government of India Act. Two years later, she lifted the emergency, held national elections, and lost. A non-Congress coalition government led by the Janata Dal and Jayaprakah Narayan (1902–79) a venerable Gandhian and former Congress man, came to power in Delhi. Under this government, which lasted three years, calls for regional autonomy became insistent.

The most famous of these was the Anandpur Sahib Resolution, a landmark in modern Sikhism. It was composed by a committee of the Shiromani Akali Dal, appointed in 1972, and adopted unanimously by its working committee, in 1973, at Anandpur Sahib, a town sacred to Guru Gobind Singh and revered as the birth place of the Khalsa. The resolution was proclaimed in 1978 by the All India Akali Conference at Ludhiana. Citing the centralization of national powers 'in the form of the Emergency, when all fundamental rights of all citizens were usurped', and proclaiming support from various non-Congress parties for 'the principle of State autonomy in keeping with the concept of Federalism', the resolution pressed the Janata government 'to take cognizance of the different linguistic and cultural sections, religious minorities as also the voice of millions of people and [to] recast the constitutional structure of the country on real and meaningful federal principles to obviate the possibility of any danger to National unity and the integrity of the Country'.

The Anandpur Sahib Resolution affirmed that 'the Shiromani Akali Dal is the very embodiment of the hopes and aspirations of the Sikh Nation and as such is fully entitled to its representation', and went on to assert that 'basic postulates of this Organization are Human progress and ultimate unity of all human beings with the Spiritual Soul', based on 'the three great principles of Guru Nanak Dev Ji, namely, a Meditation on God's Name, dignity of labour and sharing of fruits of this Labour'. Authenticated by the Akali Dal leader, Sant Harchand Singh Longowal, the resolution concentrated on an economic programme whose 'chief sources of inspiration . . . [are] the secular, democratic and socialistic concepts of Sri Guru Nanak Dev and Sri Guru Gobind Singh Ji', which are 'Dignity of Labour; An economic and social structure which provides for the uplift of the poor and depressed sections of society; and Unabated opposition to concentration of economic and political power in the hands of the capitalists'. Secular dimensions stand out in the resolution, which goes on to proclaim 'the need to break the monopolistic hold of the capitalists foisted on the Indian economy by 30 years of Congress rule in India'. It is well worth quoting at length:

> This capitalistic hold enabled the central government to assume all powers in its hands after the manner of Mughal Imperalism. This was bound to thwart the economic progress of the states and injure the social and economic interests of the people. The Shiromani Akali Dal once again reiterates the Sikh way of life by resolving to fulfill the holy words of Guru Nanak Dev: 'He alone realizes the True Path who labours honestly and shares the fruits of that Labour.'

> The Shiromani Akali Dal calls upon the Central and the State Government to eradicate unemployment during the next ten years. While pursuing this aim special emphasis should be laid on ameliorating the lot of the weaker sections, Scheduled and depressed classes, workers, landless and poor farmers and urban poor. Minimum wages should be fixed for them all.

> The Shiromani Akali Dal urges upon the Punjab Government to draw up such an economic plan for the State as would turn it into the leading province during the next ten years, by raising per capita income to Rs. 3,000 and by generating an economic growth rate of 7% per annum as against 4% at National level.

> The Shiromani Akali Dal gives first priority to the redrafting of the taxation structure in such a way that the burden of taxation is shifted from the poor to the richer classes and an equitable distribution of National income is ensured. The main plank of the economic programme of the Shiromani Akali Dal is to enable the economically weaker sections of the Society to share the fruits of National income.

In opposition to the secular and constitutional tone of the Akali Dal's resolution, a radical Sikh militant movement arose around a young mystic, Sant Jarnail Singh Bhindranwale, whose following grew after Indira Gandhi returned as prime minister, in 1980. Militant calls for an independent Sikh state, Khalistan, inspired Bhindranwale's militant followers to take up arms. A war ensued in Punjab. In 1984, the Indian army trapped the rebels in the Golden Temple, in Amritsar, and killed them all during Operation Bluestar, damaging the Golden Temple in the process. This provoked outrage even among Sikhs like Longowal who opposed

Bhindranwale. In apparent retaliation for Operation Bluestar, several of her Sikh bodyguards assassinated Indira Gandhi. In Delhi, riotous murders of Sikhs ensued and the police and local Congress activists were implicated in atrocities. When Indira Gandhi's son, Rajiv, became prime minister in the next elections and signed a pact with Sant Longowal, accepting basic Anandpur Sahib demands, Longowal was shot dead by three young Sikhs in the Akal Parkash Gurdwara at Sherpur in Sangrur District, where he had gone to address an Akali Dal conference.

Since 1985, the Akali Dal has pursued a strategy of optimizing its leadership within shifting political coalitions, and the power of the Congress has steadily declined with the rising political fortunes of the Bharatiya Janata Party, to which we turn shortly. Since 1998, the Akali Dal has worked in coalition with the BJP, but remains committed to Anandpur Sahib. Its Amritsar Declaration, of 1994, 'reiterates its commitment to pursue a democratic struggle for the creation of a separate region for the Sikhs, where they can enjoy freedom . . . [and] the practice of ideals enshrined in the Guru Granth Sahib of universal brotherhood and unity, humility, corruption-free politics and peaceful coexistence . . . [where] religious, economic, political and social institutions based on the Sikh way of life will uphold moral awareness, and also provide the Sikh people a place in history, hitherto unavailable'. The Amritsar Declaration concludes thus: 'In case such a new confederal structure is not accepted by Indian rulers, then the Shiromani Akali Dal has no option but to demand and struggle for an independent and sovereign Sikh state'.

MUSLIM SOCIETIES, POLITICS, MINORITIES, AND NATIONALITY

In 1900, Muslims lived in all regions of South Asia. They were part of all regional societies like any other group. Muslim communities, like others, were organized on ethnic lines within localities where religious institutions and leaders enjoyed prominence and respect. Islam was one feature of Muslim social identity among others. For most Muslims, belonging to the *umma* or community of believers in everyday practice meant participating in local religious activities; in theology, it evokes a spiritual community of all Muslims. This theological concept was part of a Muslim cultural ethos that travelled with Muslims across wide migratory circuits in Asia and Africa. Migratory Muslims continued to travel these old circuits in the nineteenth and twentieth centuries, creating social connections and cultural communication among dispersed Muslim communities. Among migratory groups, merchants, artisans, and manual workers were most numerous, though in and around Bengal especially, peasant migrations to settle new land also changed the social composition of local populations. Among migratory cultural activists, learned Muslim religious leaders were important as communicators of ideas about Islam and of information about Muslim societies in distant places.

South Asia has long been historically part of a wider Muslim world. Muslim societies are spread across countless political domains from Africa to the Philippines. Muslim Arabs had colonized the Kerala coast in the eighth century. Arab merchant communities later formed coastal enclaves all around the Indian Ocean, from Zanzibar to Indonesia. After 1300, inland migrations brought Turks, Afghans, and Persians into India, where they settled mostly in towns and cities; and local conversion and long-distance migration also produced large Muslim populations across Afghanistan, Baluchistan, Sind, Punjab, and Bengal. Urban Muslim societies spread from Mughal times across the Indian peninsula.

By 1900, primarily pastoral and agrarian Muslim societies covered Baluchistan, Sind, Afghanistan, and Punjab. Stratified village societies with Muslim farmers and landlords covered Sind, western Punjab, and eastern Bengal. Urban Muslim communities composed mostly of merchants, literati, aristocrats, and craft workers were scattered across the Gangetic plain, the Deccan, and coastal regions, including Sri Lanka. Muslim societies in all these regions have very different histories. Locally, these histories carry ethnic cultures that are often quite loosely attached to religion. For example, Sri Lanka's Muslims are mostly Tamil-speakers. Muslim Tamils in Sri Lanka and India have historically identified with Tamil culture. Muslim Tamil writers have made major contributions to Tamil literature. Muslims in Tamil Nadu became prominent Tamil nationalists in the twentieth century. Similar ethnic and regional affiliations define Muslim identities everywhere.

The British empire produced a new environment for South Asia's Muslim societies. The official classification of Muslims as a single religious community in the empire gave all Indian Muslims a common feature they never had before. Communications among diverse communities came to include public assertions that being Muslim meant being a different kind of Indian. Muslim society became a different kind of native society. Its difference was inscribed with various meanings. The 1857 rebellion made Muslim identity fearsome for imperial authority. In 1871, Muslims became a single *population*. As we have seen, Lord Mayo commissioned a report from W.W. Hunter to evaluate the *political* threat that Muslims posed *as a population*. In Bengal, Bankim Chandra Chatterjee's historical novels imbued Muslim difference with animosity toward Bengali Hindus. In Punjab, the Arya Samaj depicted all Muslims as foreigners in a Hindu land.

As Muslim communities became officially distinct from their social surroundings and as they became officially homogenized into a population of different Indians, Muslims developed more distinctively Muslim idioms of public activity. Muslim petitioners and representatives stressed the religion that defined their common *official* identity rather than stressing all the other elements in their diverse *social* identities. In this context, clerics, sufis, scholars, missionaries, mystics, poets, and other cultural activists – eventually including professional politicians – used Islamic idioms to address Muslim community issues. Problems that Muslims shared were addressed in Islamic idioms to mobilize people classified as Muslims for public action.

The concept of a Muslim political community thus emerged in the nineteenth century, when Muslims – like Hindus, Sikhs, Buddhists, and Christians – acquired official identities in government courts and administration. Even then, being a Muslim inside Muslim societies still meant belonging to the *umma*, which was not a political community. Islamic theology does not support the idea that Muslims constitute a political community. In 1930, Muhammad Ali Jinnah indicated that, by then, this distinction had been blurred by Muslim political history, when he said, 'I have a culture, a polity, an outlook on life – a complete synthesis which is Islam.' Then he clarified what he meant by saying that 'where God commands, I am . . . nothing but a Muslim', but 'where India is concerned . . . I am . . . nothing but an Indian'. On the verge of Pakistan's independence, many orthodox Muslim scholars chided the idea that Islam could be identified with a national state.

Muslim politics in British India had indeed blurred this distinction by 1930. As we have seen, Sir Syed Ahmad Khan and Muhammad Ali Jinnah were most adamant that Muslims comprised a separate community, a nation, with its own culture and history, and with its own political leaders and needs. The Muslim League underlined this assertion by its public alliance of Muslim leaders from various sects, regions, and ethnic groups. In 1920, the Khilafat movement won official Congress support for its drive to force the British to reinstate the Caliph in Turkey as the leader of all the world's Muslims. By this time, the mobilization of Muslim tenants to gain land rights in Bengal and Malabar had produced several generations of leaders for whom Islam imbued politics with theology and devotion. In 1921, the Khilafat movement inspired as many as ten thousand fighters – led by Muslim preachers but also including high-caste Hindu Namboodri and Nayar radicals – to attack British installations in Malabar. Mappillai warriors liberated two sub-divisions (*taluks*) in south Malabar for a few months. Nationalist leaders disavowed the revolt; its violence was indeed one reason that Gandhi cited when he called off non-cooperation. To suppress this revolt, police killed 2337, wounded 1652, and took 45,404 prisoners. Sixty-six prisoners were locked in a railway carriage and asphyxiated, perhaps by accident, recalling the 'Black Hole of Calcutta' without provoking similar outrage. Tenancy reforms later followed. The fearsomeness of Muslim outrage had received another affirmation.

Political differences between Muslims and others were sketched on a larger canvas in Bengal. As the upper caste Hindu *bhadralok* projected their own cultural identity out over all of Bengal, Muslim Bengali tenant leaders opposed Hindu Zamindars. Hindu Zamindar and Muslim tenant supporters rejected each other's claims to represent Bengal. After the death of C.R. Das, in 1926, possibilities declined for alliances between them. Indian National Congress national strategy called for accommodating landlords. In the 1930s, Congress gained strength and Zamindari power weakened during the Great Depression. In 1941, Fazlul Haq, the leader of the Krishak Praja (Peasants and Workers) Party, joined the Muslim League in calling for Pakistan at the League's meeting in Lahore. In 1947, what they called 'partition' in Calcutta was hailed in Dhaka as the arrival of a peasant utopia, a land free of Zamindars.

New national states put Muslim societies in a totally new political environment. But being Muslim still included all its old ethnic, class, sectarian, local, linguistic, and regional elements. In India, it lost its former constitutional substance but retained political meanings derived from decades of public activism. Most people who were Indian Muslims in the 1940s remained Indian Muslims in the 1950s, but now they were officially minorities everywhere in India. Anti-Muslim feelings and hostilities continued in some places, particularly in urban centres disrupted by agitations in the 1940s. Attacks on Muslims occurred periodically in the 1950s, 1960s, and 1970s; as we see below, they attained new political force in the 1980s. In everyday politics and social life, however, Muslims became one of the many ethnic identity groups that formed local community organizations and voting blocs in India's multi-cultural and constitutionally secular polity.

In 1947, being a Muslim in Pakistan came to include being a citizen in a state defined by its Muslim majority. In 1947, Pakistan included five major cultural regions. Very different regional political histories in old Sindhi, Baluchi, Paxtun, Punjabi, Kashmiri, and Bengali cultural regions had converged unpredictably. Nationalities and societies in each region remained distinct.

In Sind, a few prominent families owned huge Zamindar estates and became dominant politically. Leaders among them include the Bhutto family that would provide Pakistan with two prime ministers, Zulfiqar Ali and his daughter, Benazir. In Punjab, landowners much like those across the border in India provided Pakistan's economic, political, and military base in its most powerful province. Business families in Lahore and Karachi carved out new zones of national influence. In the hills above Sind and Punjab, Baluchi and Paxtun clan leaders had long-established domains of power that they strove to maintain. Most Kashmiri Muslims remained in India after 1947, and many exiled Kashmiri Muslim political activists lived and worked in Lahore. Kashmir remained such a burning issue in Pakistan because of Kashmiri activists and their supporters, primarily in

Punjab. In East Pakistan, being Bengali became an increasingly potent feature of Muslim identity and Islamic evocations of Muslim unity came to be associated with national loyalty to Pakistan over loyalties to the people and culture of Bengal.

After 1971, being Muslim in Bangladesh became consistent with national loyalty in a radically new way. Lingering suspicions remained among Bengali activists who had fresh memories of how Islamic rhetoric and loyalty had been deployed to support Pakistan over Bangladesh. During fifteen years of military rule after 1975, state-sponsored Islam became more prominent in Bangladesh. For a small but influential population, Islam represented national unity and cultural strength amidst the turmoil of domestic social change and globalization. Islam became one symbol of national unity in a Bengali Muslim nation where divisive struggles for national resources pulled Bengalis apart, and where social activism threatened elites who sought security in public invocations of a traditional moral order backed by state power. For many activists, however, Islamic politics threatened rights promised in the country's secular constitution but still insecurely established in society, particularly for non-Muslim minorities and women.

Islamic traditionalism emerged more forcefully under military rule in Pakistan, where disorder increased when war erupted in Afghanistan, in 1978. The war originally pitted US-armed Afghan guerrillas against Soviet forces. By 1992, more than a million Afghans had died. After 1992, the war pitted ethnically diverse Afghan militias against Sunni fundamentalist fighters, Mujahidin, most prominently the Taliban, who controlled most of the country until 2001 and began their career in Pakistan. The war spilled its influence across all the borders around Afghanistan. By 1992, five million refugees had fled along old routes into Punjab, Sind, and Kashmir. During the war, Sindhi activists began to assault Punjabi domination of the government. The Muhajir Quami movement, representing immigrants from pre–1947 India, also fought for power in Sind. In 1979, Zia-ul-Huq instituted Sunni Islamic state law in an Islamic Republic. This triggered a repression of the many minority Muslim communities in Pakistan, where Shia activists formed the Tehrik-I-Nifaz-I-Jafria to gain official recognition. Conflicts ensued between Shias and Sunnis, which have been most violent in Punjab. Drawing on intellectual activity going back to the eighteenth century Shah Wali Allah, state-sponsored Sunni orthodoxy is intended to unify diverse Muslim societies inside Pakistan and to maintain orderly state management of elite interests. In addition, however, it provokes the use of competing Islamic idioms in struggles among contending groups in all the regions. It has also produced a new kind of cultural opposition between idioms of secularism and religion, which has been most pronounced in public efforts to improve the rights of women.

HINDU SOCIETIES, MOVEMENTS, POLITICS, AND HINDUTVA

Over the centuries, cultural activism and diverse local patronage combined to establish many different Hindu societies. Though connected, they did not profess theological unity, as did Muslims, Christians, Sikhs, and Buddhists. Their many commonalities include the veneration of deities in the *Purana*s, above all, Siva and Vishnu, whose devotees form major sectarian divisions between Shaiva and Vaishnava. They all conduct *puja* rituals and other ceremonies led by ritual specialists who represent divinity in everyday life. Various kinds of temples house living deities. Social rituals make spiritual principles part of community. Rituals define collective *jati* or caste identities attached to specific regions. Castes are constructed internally, by rituals of marriage and family; and externally, by rituals that define each *jati* in relation to others.

Medieval Hindu kingdoms were complex ritual institutions. They were political and also religious domains where rituals of caste ranking focused on dynasties and deities at the same time. In medieval times, temple ceremonialism seems to have been paramount in definitions of social rank, including that of a king. Sacred texts and inscriptional records indicate that the ritually purest Brahman *jati*s played a paramount personal role in defining social rank, because their command of sacred texts governed ritual activity in the temple, state, and society.

The *varna* ranks of Brahman, Kshatriya, Vaisya, and Sudra provide a cultural template for social order in Hindu cultures. This order is often called 'Brahmanical' because Brahmans have special authority as interpreters of the Sanskrit texts that prescribe the *dharma* or sanctified path that each Hindu should follow in social life. Rituals of social ranking also provide a cultural template for disputation over social status; thus they are basic political institutions in Hindu societies. Because Brahmans uphold moral order, challenges to Brahman authority often attend social change when aspiring groups challenge Brahman rights to determine social ranks in ritual. In medieval centuries, devotional *bhakti* movements raised the stature of non-Brahman groups in deity worship. Socially mobile groups often formed new sects and communities based on spiritual principles and practices that denied, by-passed, or ignored Brahman authority.

One exemplary reformist Shaiva sect arose in the twelfth century Deccan, on the borders of Maharashtra and Karnataka. The Virashaivas ('heroic Shaivas') worship Siva in the form of the phallic *linga*. These Lingayats, 'bearers of a *linga*', wear the Siva image to make each male and female body a temple of god. Lingayats are thus all spiritual equals. They do not recognize Brahman authority. They do not marry their daughters before puberty to protect their purity. Lingayat widows are freely allowed to remarry. Lingayats also conduct burials rather than cremation. Each family has a guru or spiritual guide. A distinctive Virashaiva *jati* of Jangama gurus attain personal sanctity based on ascetic detachment. Monasteries (*matha*) for training Jangamas are central Lingayat institutions. Lingayat *ahimsa* ('non-violence') and strict vegetarianism also indicate the formative Jain influence among the original Lingayats, who were primarily merchants. Jangama ascetic gurus are teachers and spiritual guides who mediate between Virashaiva communities and the wider world, providing wisdom for changing times.

Virashaivism is one of many innovative religious movements organized historically around innovative spiritual leaders. Such movements have been pervasive vehicles of social and political change. Their style and influence has overlapped with Muslim, Jain, Buddhist, and Christian spirituality. The Brahmo Samaj, for example, has a Protestant flavour like the Jain flavour of Virashaivism. Such movements typically emerge around the moral authority of key individuals, typically styled as *guru*s (spiritual teachers) or *sannyasi*s (ascetic monks). Their followers weave networks of communication and teaching and build institutions for sectarian learning that constitute social movements. These movements articulate and generate new forms of community and social activism. They have suffused modern political environments, where leaders have often employed idioms of popular devotionalism and ascetic authority. These agents of change have worked in settings of social change to improve the powers of various caste groups to acquire honour, rank, and entitlements.

Hindu cultures never lived in a vacuum. In medieval times, warrior sultans provided new ways for Hindu groups to acquire honour and ritual status that supplemented those available in Hindu courts and temples. Expanding commercial economies provided new wealth for families who patronized new sects and invested in rituals to improve their social standing. Commercial wealth became noticeably more prominent in Murshid Quli Khan's Bengal, where new temples built by business families rose to a third of the total as the proportion built by landed Zamindars declined to around sixty per cent. This shift reflects a shift in social power over the honours that were being conferred by deities on pious individuals.

Hindu societies changed more dramatically in the nineteenth century. Most temples used today were built after 1800 with financial endowments from upwardly mobile groups. The influence of educated white-collar middle classes also increased. Modern urban reformulations of Hindu religion followed theological lines that we sketched in Calcutta, stressing personal piety and philosophy and downplaying caste and temple ritual. As a result, by the twentieth century, there were more different Hindu societies than ever. A new kind of cultural division had been established. In the villages, rustic ritualism bolstered dominant castes in the officially ordained agrarian power structure. In the cities, urbane spirituality detached itself from localism, absorbed diverse groups from surrounding regions, and became more literate in regional languages. As urbane Hinduism became more separate from village oral cultures, it also became more self-consciously Hindu as it mingled Vaishnava and Shaiva sectarian traditions and tuned itself to the formulation of national identity. Similar changes occurred in Muslim and Buddhist societies.

Social conflict often attended social change in modern times, as it had in previous centuries. Struggles for status and challenges to old patterns of caste ranking are clearly visible in records from medieval times to the present. In eighteenth-century Madras city, for example, two organized groups of *jati*s formed regional divisions between Left- and Right-hand castes. The Right-hand group had its base of power in land ownership. The Left-hand group featured merchant and artisan castes. They competed for state recognition of their rights to express their solidarity in public. They came into conflict over the use of city space to build temples and conduct festivals. British officials did not understand why people would fight on the streets and petition governors for exclusive rights to use religious insignia and carry idols along certain streets at particular times. But even as the Company puzzled over this problem in Madras, Nayaka rulers in Madurai galloped from one town to another to resolve similar disputes, asserting their own authority to resolve them. Such official activity was part of governance in societies where families achieved status through honours displayed and dispensed in public rituals patronized and authorized by rulers.

The British initially endeavoured to comply with such expectations, and to inform their decisions they consulted local experts, typically learned Brahmans. The new regime also continued to provide tax relief for temples and monasteries, which often owned substantial tracts of land. Centuries of pious endowments had made major temples vastly rich, for example, in Kanchipuram, where five temples owned thousands of acres of prime farm land in every Tamil district. Temples not only reflected prosperity, but also produced it, increasing their importance for the state. Temple precincts in Kanchipuram were also the site of silk production and merchants flocked to the city to engage in textile trades and endow temples at the same time. Peasants also looked to the state to support rituals that sustained their livelihoods. Living gods and social rituals were understood as fonts of prosperity. In 1811, Tamil peasants in the Tirunelveli District in southern Madras Presidency petitioned the British Collector to fund temple rituals to help prevent famine and, for them, the onset of Kali Yuga, the cosmic age of destruction. Government obliged, because panicky peasants could become lawless or might flee the country. With the advice of trusted Brahmans, the Collector paid for rain-making ceremonies in all the major temples 'with the view of inspiring the people with confidence and encouraging them to proceed with their preparations for cultivation'.

This state policy changed in British India, after 1830, under pressure from British missionaries. The government withdrew from religious patronage and settled into a bureaucratic routine of regulating temple finance and management. Legally, temples became a 'public trust'. In this regulatory capacity, the state established a new relationship with religion, which focused on the adjudication of rights to control the assets of religious institutions. Ritual activity became the private business of individual subjects of the state. The state was thus in a strong position to influence the definition of religious leadership, as it did in response to the Gurudwara reform movement in Punjab, where, in the 1920s, the Punjab government established a single Sikh authority to administer Gurudwaras. This administration officially recognized Sikh religious leaders as the leaders of their religious community.

The state also institutionalized official sectarian leadership in Hindu temples across British India in the 1920s. The imperial state thus withdrew from ritual participation in temple rituals, which distressed farmers in Madras districts deeply resented during famines; but at the same time, the state also became paramount in the official designation of religious community leadership.

As state officials formed new religious institutions, forces of change gained strength inside Hindu societies. Records abound to show intense sensitivity in higher ranking castes to upward social mobility from below. In early nineteenth-century Travancore, a public dispute soon broke out when low caste women took to wearing saris that covered their breasts, because such modesty marked higher status. In southern Tamil districts, high caste non-Brahman farmers fought on the streets and in the courts against insistent Brahman claims to own the land they farmed. Local caste elites argued to the British that caste ritual ranks should govern official allocations of rights and privileges. They met mounting public criticism from lower castes and from social reformers. In the 1850s, untouchables in Tirunelveli violated caste traditions that called for them to take their funeral processions through rice fields and irrigation ditches rather than along city streets. They were attacked on city roads by caste elites who claimed that public space belonged to them. Company troops suppressed the ensuing riot with public support from social reformers. The untouchables' procession passed through Brahman streets, and this signalled state control over public space and changed the rules of public life for everyone in Tirunelveli.

Government became permanently implicated in social conflict over the public rights and honours that mark social mobility in Hindu societies. After 1850, modern economies provided new avenues for social change; and modern politics provided new institutional means to resist it. State control over public space and private property introduced an important new element into conflicts over social mobility, by usurping domains of caste privilege and by making legal rights a matter of public dispute. Old regimes had left property matters and social regulation to local authorities, though eighteenth-century regimes increased the role of state power in everyday social affairs, as we have seen. Under British rule, Brahman influence initially supported conservative interpretations of custom by judges and policy makers. Brahmans became literate in English, assumed official authority, and became lawyers, judges, and politicians far out of proportion to their numbers. Struggles for social mobility thus often included attacks on government and Brahman authority. Social reformers who worked to abolish *sati* and to legalize widow remarriage criticized 'Brahmanical British laws'. In 1869, the old heartland of Maratha warrior peasant power in Bombay Presidency witnessed a dramatic assertion of opposition to Brahman authority when Jotirao Phule published his tract, *Priestcraft Exposed*.

The tension between rising social ambition 'from below' and social restraint 'from above' was not confined to Hindu society. As we have seen, the cultural politics of social rank and honour encompassed Muslims, Christians, Sikhs, and others as well. But struggles over social mobility sometimes pitted aspiring non-Hindus against high caste Hindus, especially Brahmans. Such instances became public symbols of religious difference. Mappillai Muslims in Malabar fought for rights against landlords, high caste elites, and British officials, all at once. The Raja of Jammu and Kashmir restricted Muslim public activity to maintain the supremacy of Brahmans and Kashmiri Pandits. But as Tagore's 'Home and the World' indicates, political activity could pit elite Hindus against poor Muslims unpredictably and unintentionally. In urban north India, such conflicts emerged in the 1890s; they resemble those between Right- and Left-hand castes in Madras a century before. When Muslim merchants, workers, and artisans in cities in the Ganga basin sought to display their piety more grandly by sacrificing cows for ritual feasts, rather than goats, Cow Protection Societies led by high caste landlords attacked them and sought a state ban on cow 'slaughter' to embrace even butcher shops that provided everyday protein for Muslim workers as well as sustenance for many poor Muslim butchers.

The government that made Hindu and Muslim into official legal categories and gave religious leaders official status also interpreted conflicts between any Hindus and any Muslims as battles between two opposing religious communities. Social conflicts of many sorts were thus homogenized under a single official heading as 'communal conflicts'. 'Communalism' became a modern term for the antagonistic mobilization of 'communal' sentiment by Hindus and Muslims.

Conflicts inside Hindu and Muslim societies were often the same kind as conflicts across religious borders. Struggles for rights by many different groups produced leaders who sought state support and faced elite opposition. Dr B.R. Ambedkar underlined the political similarity of Muslims and untouchable Hindus in his 1945 book, *Pakistan or Partition of India*. In it, he argues that separate electorates are a legitimate constitutional solution to the problem of securing collective rights for peoples who are struggling against entrenched elites and electoral majorities. Politicians in Madras Presidency made similar claims when they sought regional autonomy to secure power for a non-Brahman majority in a polity controlled by Brahmans in government and in the Congress. Their struggle resembles that of Bengali Muslims in Pakistan in four important ways. They stressed the primacy of language in their political identity. They identified official Hindu identity with the power of an alien elite, in their case, the Brahmans. Language riots marked a watershed in their movement. Four years after the Bengal language movement ignited Bengali nationalism in East Pakistan, language riots in Madras against the imposition of Hindi inspired the Tamil nationalist Dravida Munnetra Kazhagam, which took power in 1967. As in Bangladesh, contending versions of a distinctively regional nationality, embedded in a regional language, has animated politics in Tamil Nadu since then.

Thus elements of 'communalism' and of 'communal conflict' are dispersed in many contexts where struggles over state authority set groups seeking new rights against those fighting for established privilege. The cultural dimensions of such conflicts are religious, political, and economic, all at once.

As the modern state grew in size and wealth, and as it gained capacities not only to regulate the accumulation of cultural capital but also to produce new honours and symbols of status, the government became a dominant force in determining social status. The first imperial census, in 1871, is a landmark. It immediately generated heated disputes over official caste definitions and status. Activists representing upwardly mobile castes sought to have their caste names changed to indicate higher status. For example, a group of wealthy cotton merchants in market towns in southern Tamil Nadu petitioned to have their *jati* name changed from Shanar, which denoted low-caste toddy tappers, to the more prestigious name Nadar, used inside the *jati* to designate its elite. This change would make merchant Nadars leaders of the whole caste and also increase Nadar numbers in the census, thus their official visibility. Their census campaign was combined with funding for English schools and with petitions to the courts to grant Nadars the right to enter temples from which they were excluded by virtue of their low, Shanar status. The court case and demonstrations to support the Nadar temple entry campaign provoked riotous opposition from locally dominant Maravas. After riots in the 1890s, communal conflict between Nadars and Maravas simmered for decades.

The temple entry issue rose to the top of the political agenda for Hindu groups locked out of major temples. Their logic was the same as that which secured untouchables in Tirunelveli rights to use the city streets for their funeral processions; that is, all the public has a right to move peaceably in public space. The radical step was to call the ritual interior of temples 'public' by virtue of being a 'public trust' under government regulation. Though Nadars won their name change for the 1921 census, courts upheld the right of temple managers to exclude them. This legal right remained intact until 1947.

The drive to remove the right of elite castes to exclude low caste people from temples gained force after 1920. In Madras, M.C.

Rajah led an untouchable movement with the idea that the lowest caste people were Adi Dravidas, the original inhabitants of Dravidian language regions in south India. Their combined numbers made India's lowest caste people a potentially formidable electoral force for any political party. As a consequence, agitation to give them new rights as Indian citizens entered Article 15 of the Indian constitution, which says, 'No citizen shall, on grounds only of religion, race, caste, sex, or place of birth, be subject to any disability, liability, restriction or condition with regard to (a) access to shops, public restaurants, hotels and places of public entertainment; or (b) the use of wells, tanks, bathing ghats, roads and places of public resort maintained wholly or partly out of State funds or dedicated to the use of the general public.' Struggles to enforce this constitutional right continue in many Indian villages today, where local groups must still mobilize political force against entrenched elites to make the state enforce citizens' rights.

Major social movements in the middle ranks of Hindu societies embraced classical *varna* categories to improve social status. This cultural strategy became popular in Bihar and Uttar Pradesh among Kurmis, Yadavas, and Kushvahas. Organized under Vaishnava Ramanandi *sannyasi* monastic leadership, the Kshatriya movement spread all across north India and produced a new warrior style of cultural aspiration among upwardly mobile farming families. Activists invented warrior genealogies and ancestors, reinterpreted ancient texts, embraced Rajput customs, promoted strict Vaishnava social conduct, proclaimed racial equality among all Aryans, and, like Sikh activists, insisted on the dignity of manual labour. Their efforts reinforced solidarity among tenants who were also fighting for land rights against the claims of Rajput, Brahman, and Bhumihar Zamindars. At the same time, the movement promoted strict patriarchal authority over women and fed anti-Muslim activity among Cow Protection Societies.

Other movements initially embraced *varna* ranks and then rejected them as an impediment to mobilizing different groups who shared the same disadvantages. Swami Sahajanand Saraswati led a movement of this kind. An ascetic of the Shaiva Dasnami *sannyasi* order, Swami Sahajanand entered social reform in 1914 and devoted himself to defending the Brahman status of Bhumihar cultivators against denigrations by Maithil Brahmans and other elites in Bihar. Using Sanskrit texts, he showed that Brahmans did not have a monopoly on receiving charity and doing priestly work. He elevated the spiritual status of the manual labour done by Bhumihars, which Brahmans claimed lowered their status. To promote this work, he founded his Sitaram *ashram* (sanctuary) in Bihar, where he came to the aid of local Goala and other *kisan*s (peasant farmers), who sought his help in their struggles with Zamindars. In 1927, his movement became a broadly peasant rather than caste movement, and he became the leader of the Kisan Sabha, fighting for 'downtrodden people . . . regardless of their jati or religion [in a place where] the question of jati does not arise'. This struggle crossed caste lines, because some Bhumihars were Zamindars while others were peasants. Though most Bihar Kisan Sabha leaders in the 1920s and 1930s were Bhumihars, most of its members, like most peasants in the region, were Yadavas, Koeris, and Kurmis.

The Kisan Sabha led a broad trend away from caste, religion, and ethnicity as organizing principles in social movements in the 1920s and 1930s. The disruptions of the Great Depression and mass mobilization by the Congress led many activists to adopt secular socialist, democratic ideals that concentrate attention on inequality and injustice rather than caste and religion. All of South Asia's Left parties have followed this approach to politics, which gained strength when Jawaharlal Nehru made his 1930 proclamation (quoted above) that the 'structure of society' in India accentuated the 'poverty and misery of the Indian People' and demanded 'revolutionary changes . . . to remove the gross inequalities'.

This analysis led Nehru and the Congress to promote state strategies for social improvement and economic development that became official policy with India's first Five Year Plan, in 1952. Combined with a constitutional abolition of caste discrimination and with official lists of scheduled castes and tribes, government planning sought to address the poverty problem as a whole, which the Congress platform in 1947 analysed in this way:

> Though poverty is widespread in India, it is essentially a rural problem, caused chiefly by overpressure on land and a lack of other wealth-producing occupations. India, under British rule, has

been progressively ruralised, many of her avenues of work and employment closed, a vast mass of the population thrown on the land, which has undergone continuous fragmentation, till a very large number of holdings have become uneconomic. It is essential, therefore, that the problem of the land should be dealt with in all its aspects. Agriculture has to be improved on scientific lines and industry has to be developed rapidly in its various forms . . . so as not only to produce wealth but also to absorb people from the land . . . Planning must lead to maximum employment, indeed to the employment of every able-bodied person.

The abolition of Zamindar landlordism in independent India eliminated the most politically contentious 'gross inequality'. And as in East Pakistan, also in India, a new class of prosperous farmers emerged as a political force. In India, differences among them became pronounced. Between 1960 and 1990, the proportion of cultivated land in holdings over ten hectares shrank from thirty-one per cent to seventeen per cent, as holdings less than one hectare increased by roughly the same proportion, from nineteen per cent to thirty-two per cent. A huge number of small landlords and substantial farmers emerged from the ranks of former tenants and Ryotwari peasants. They became the bulwark of the Congress strategy of agrarian patronage announced by Charan Singh. They were a rising rural elite filled with former tenant middle castes who had won struggles for land rights and now aspired to supplant the political power of rural elites. Beneath them in rural society, however, a much larger population of poor people working tiny farms and owning no land at all also developed political aspirations. These two rising forces undid the Congress system in the countryside, where patronage could not flow fast enough to satisfy a rising middle class that faced political challenges from lower caste activists representing the rural poor.

Agrarian societies differ significantly across regions. Very small farms and relatively poor farmers typify the wetter regions in eastern and southern India, Sri Lanka, and Bangladesh; whereas larger farms cover drier regions of canal and tube-well irrigation in Pakistan, Punjab, Rajasthan, Haryana, and western Uttar Pradesh. In India, larger land holdings (over 2.6 hectares) comprise the highest percentage of farms in Rajasthan and Punjab (30%), and are also prominent in Gujarat, Madhya Pradesh, and Haryana

(20%). They are least visible in Assam (4%), Bihar (4%), Tamil Nadu (3%), West Bengal (1%), and Kerala (0.5%). Maharashtra, Karnataka, Andhra Pradesh, and Orissa fall in between, averaging ten per cent. Uttar Pradesh resembles Bihar in that only three per cent of the total holdings are bigger than 2.6 hectares, and the resemblance increases in the east, which has forty-nine per cent of all the farms in Uttar Pradesh that are smaller than one hectare. In this as in other respects, western Uttar Pradesh more resembles Haryana and contains forty per cent of all Uttar Pradesh land holdings between four and ten hectares.

Larger farms where the owners command substantial political and economic power at the local and the state level account for much of India's agricultural growth. Between 1962–5 and 1992–5, the highest annual rates of growth in farm output came in Punjab (5%), Rajasthan (4%), and Haryana (4%). These are also regions in which the dominant farmers, mostly Jats and Rajputs, make the strongest claim to represent their regions politically and culturally. India's north-west quadrant, with the most large farmers and highest per capita state investments in irrigation, had the highest overall growth rate, averaging three per cent. Eastern states averaged two per cent. Central (2.7%) and southern states (2.6%) fell in between, and Kerala (1.7%), Orissa (1.6%), and Bihar (1.0%) had the least growth. Everywhere in India, politically well-connected and organized farmers get state subsidies for capital-intensive cultivation, and their local capital accumulation depends on state-managed electrical supplies; on state prices for petrol, pump sets, tractors, pipes, fertilizer, and hybrid seeds; and on state procurement prices, transport costs, bank charges, and credit conditions.

Influential farmers have spurred political movements to represent farming interests. Sugar growers, for instance, led the cooperative movement in Maharashtra from the 1920s and they also led farmers' movements in Maharashtra and elsewhere from the 1970s. In Uttar Pradesh, under the flag of the Bharatiya Kisan Union, farmer-activists made headlines in 1988, when they stormed Meerut to demand higher sugarcane prices, lower input prices, a waiver on loan repayments, more rural investment, and lower rates for electricity and water. Whereas the old-style peasant movements focused on land rights, the new farmer movements that arose in Tamil Nadu, Punjab, Maharashtra, Uttar Pradesh, Karnataka, and Gujarat in the 1970s and 1980s have used roadblocks, marches, and votes to demand better prices and to assert village interests against the entrenched urban bias of development policies. As we have seen, the Anandapur Sahib resolution anchors Sikh cultural politics in Punjab farmers' economic interests.

Regional disparities in economic development and regional alliances among urban and rural politicians steadily increased the prominence of regional political parties that brought the public identities of regionally prominent social groups into the political foreground. Activists organized groups along ethnic, religious, and caste lines in the context of a universal adult franchise and of a national state that promised equality for all citizens. By 1975, when India's Home Ministry warned of the 'explosion' in rural India that could result from state failures to tackle rural inequality, the success of high caste groups in capturing the benefits of national development had become obvious to many observers. One of these was an elderly leader of the untouchable movement in Punjab, Mangoo Ram. Decades before, he had formed a political sect for Chamars, called the Adi Dharm, which struggled to put an end to untouchability. In 1971, Mangoo Ram told a colleague that despite his movement's success and despite government help, 'our people . . . are still treated like slaves . . . [by] their superiors and high caste people'. He proclaimed at an Adi Dharm conference, in 1970, that 'Hinduism is a fraud to us. Adi Dharm is our only true religion.'

Disenchantment in many quarters became politically active as the Congress emergency regime weakened the party's claim to represent popular aspirations, in 1975–6. Movements for regional autonomy and federalism gained strength. New social movements mobilized women's groups, mountain peoples, farmers, and lower caste groups. In the context of the same kind of disruptive politics that spawned Sinhala Buddhist majoritarianism and state-sponsored Islamic traditionalism in other countries, Hindu nationalism (Hindutva) mobilized mass support in India.

We have seen that Hindu nationalist parties had local and regional roots in late nineteenth-century India, where Hindu public sentiment (as distinct from religious feeling) attained an urban middle class audience. Before 1947, the major Hindu nationalist organizations were the Arya Samaj, Cow Protection Societies, Rashtriya Swayamsevak Sangh (RSS), and Hindu Mahasabha. None had a large following and all distanced themselves from Congress, though members were often active in Congress. One Hindu nationalist assassinated Mohandas Gandhi in 1948 to express their general hatred of Gandhi for accepting partition. It became an article of faith among Hindu nationalists that Pakistan occupies land that belongs to Hindu India. The Hindu Mahasabha became a new electoral party in independent India, the Jana Sangh. It maintained the separate political identity of Hindu nationalists and won a small number of seats in the Lok Sabha, mostly in Uttar Pradesh, where it was influential among Brahmans. Led by paramilitary RSS cadres, Hindu nationalists developed strong local bases among Brahmans, particularly in Maharashtra and Uttar Pradesh. They proclaimed that Hindu India had been dominated by Muslim rulers for centuries, torn apart by the Muslim League and betrayed by the Congress Party, which gave Muslims Pakistan and placated Muslim minorities in India to maintain itself at the expense of the Hindu majority.

Attacking Congress in this way did not win over many voters during decades of Congress strength in the 1950s, 1960s, and 1970s. Many Congress leaders were nonetheless sympathetic and used Hindu nationalist ideas to garner political support. The most influential of these Congress men was Vallabhai 'Sardar' Patel. A major Congress figure from Gujarat, Sardar Patel sponsored the rebuilding of the temple at Somnath, in Saurashtra, which Mahmud of Ghazni was said to have destroyed. On the heels of partition and war with Pakistan, and positioned close to the Pakistan border, the Somnath reconstruction and re-consecration dramatized the Hindu nationalist message that Muslims had desecrated Hindu India.

By 1980, the number of people looking for political alternatives to Congress had grown substantially. Congress had lost a national election and was losing more seats in the state Assemblies with every new poll. In 1980, the Jan Sangh became the Bharatiya Janata Party and began aggressive national campaigns in alliance with a family of organizations, called the Sangh Parivar, led by the RSS. Since then, activists in the Sangh family have concentrated on specific Hindu nationalist (Hindutva) projects. The largest organization, the Vishwa Hindu Parishad (VHP), or World Hindu Council, has propagated Hindutva in a broad range of public endeavours, whereas the BJP has focused on winning elections. BJP strategy focused initially on Gujarat, Rajasthan, Uttar Pradesh, Bihar, Maharashtra, and Madhya Pradesh, where Brahmans were politically important and where no other parties had proved capable of beating Congress in elections on a regular basis. In southern states, West Bengal, and Punjab, regional parties were strong and BJP candidates had little chance.

The Sangh Parivar concentrated their energies on generating animosity toward Muslims and Congress. Anti-Muslim agitations defined the Sangh's Hindu national ideology (Hindutva) as attacks on Congress led voters to the BJP opposition. The anti-Muslim campaign centred on Ayodhya, a pilgrimage town in eastern Uttar Pradesh. Here, the Vaishnava god Rama – the hero of the *Ramayana* – was said to have been born. An old mosque in the town, the Babri Masjid, was said to have been built on the rubble of a temple to Rama, destroyed by Babur. The VHP and BJP launched a mass campaign to destroy the mosque and rebuild a new Rama temple in Ayodhya.

The Ayodhya campaign was combined with attacks on Congress policies. In 1984, Operation Bluestar was a national disaster that the Sangh blamed on Congress willingness to accommodate Sikh separatists; and Rajiv Gandhi's pact with Sant Longowal, accepting basic Anandpur Sahib demands, fuelled the public fire of Sangh attacks on Congress for pandering to minorities and weakening the Hindu nation. In 1986, the Sangh's watershed agitation sprang from a Supreme Court decision in favour of Shah Bano, a Muslim widow who sought support from her ex-husband, who had divorced her. Prime Minister Rajiv Gandhi pushed through Lok Sabha legislation to nullify the court's ruling that Shah Bano had rights to support. This legislation affirmed the opinion of conservative Muslim clerics, who argued that the court decision contravened Muslim law. Sangh Parivar agitations sought public support for the credible claim that Rajiv Gandhi had bowed to Muslim conservatives for political gain. Hindutva leaders later looked back on the Shah Bano case as a key moment in their political ascendancy.

By 1989, the Congress had lost sufficient public support that a coalition government had formed without its support under the Janata Dal, led by Prime Minister V.P. Singh. The BJP had won enough votes in northern states to allow it to become an external partner of the coalition, in opposition to Congress. This parliamentary position allowed the BJP to launch a major agitation against the Janata Dal's decision to implement the Mandal Commission Report, in 1989. The Mandal Commission had proposed a huge increase in reservations in government employment and education to include a very large group of so-called 'other backward castes'. These castes included many aspiring landed groups. Government support for Mandal proposals generated huge opposition from the upper castes whose votes the BJP coveted.

At the same time, the Sangh accelerated the drive to demolish the Babri Masjid to reclaim Rama's birthplace, *Ramjanambhoomi*, for Hindu India. After the BJP had won elections in Uttar Pradesh and increased its Lok Sabha seats to 185, VHP activists mobilized the attack. Holy men declared 6 December 1992 auspicious. Over three hundred thousand people gathered in Ayodhya. Most wore saffron cloth, the symbol of the Sangh, adopted from the attire of ascetic monks. At mid-day, a vanguard broke police barricades around the Babri Masjid. Cheering young men swarmed the domes of the old mosque (built in 1528), and in five hours, they hammered and axed it to the ground. Video cameras hummed. Reporters took notes for news services around the world. Sangh leaders, who had worked for this day since 1984, watched with satisfaction. Government officials looked on ineffectually. Riots ensued across India, Pakistan, and Bangladesh that killed 1700 people and injured 5500 more in the next four months.

BJP electoral support dipped in the aftermath of the violence. The Sangh became identified with communal hatred and killing. In addition, the BJP's anti-Mandal agitation and its hard core of high caste and especially Brahman leaders triggered doubts among many aspiring lower caste groups that the BJP represented a good political alternative to Congress. Various other opposition parties arose in north Indian states, representing upwardly mobile landed groups and middle castes of the kind that Mandal was intended to bring to Congress. Yet as Congress decline continued, the BJP formed ever larger contingents in the Lok Sabha, until in 1998, it formed a national coalition government in New Delhi in alliance with seventeen regional parties. That coalition government fell in 1999 and another version came to power in that same year. One of the Sangh leaders who helped to organize the destruction of the Babri mosque, L.K. Advani, has been India's Home Minister since 1998, in charge of law and order in the country.

As a result of the rise of the Sangh Parivar since 1980, Hindu identity has been stamped in public discourse around the world with the saffron colours of Hindutva. The term 'Hindu' itself has come to connote a Hindu nationalist majoritarianism that claims to represent all of Hindu culture. In India, however, the BJP is merely the largest of many parties in the national coalition government. Today, as in 1999, its capacity to rule depends on decisions by leaders of regional parties who hold the balance of power in New Delhi. Most supporters of regional parties are also Hindus, for whom Hindutva is merely the ideology of one of India's many contemporary movements. The great bulk of the BJP's support is also regional and concentrates today in the same northern states that the party targeted in its campaigns in the 1980s. BJP success has also modified official Hindutva, as the party has sought support from a wider array of groups, including Muslims, who now vote for the BJP when local political contests lead them in that direction. At the same time, BJP power in Delhi has strengthened the Sangh Parivar immeasurably. Sangh cadres occupy most influential positions in major ministries. The Sangh Parivar's struggle to make India a Hindu nation continues in the face of opposition from many quarters, not only from secular activists who oppose its drive to define India in religious terms, but also from Hindus who strive to maintain their own diverse religious identities in a secular, multi-cultural, and egalitarian national environment.

Country Profiles

BANGLADESH

People's Republic of Bangladesh. 2001 population 131,269,860. 55,126 square miles (142,776 km^2), bordering Myanmar and the Indian states of West Bengal, Assam, Meghalaya, Tripura, and Mizoram. Dhaka is the capital and largest city. Chittagong is the other major city and also the major port.

The alluvial plains of Bangladesh occupy the combined delta of the Ganges, Brahmaputra, and Meghna rivers. Except for the Chittagong hills bordering the Myanmar border, the land lies below three hundred feet (90 m), filled with waterways that form the main transport network plied by boats of all sizes. The south-western coast, the Sundarbans, is a mangrove swamp with alluvial islands. The average annual rainfall of eighty inches (203 cm) falls mostly after July, and Sylhet, in the north-east uplands, is the wettest region with 140 inches (356 cm) annually. Much of the country is subject to severe flooding from rains, cyclones, tidal waves, and overflowing rivers.

Most people are Bengali, although Biharis and several tribal groups are significant minority groups in the cities and mountains, respectively. About eighty-eight per cent of the population is classified as Sunni Muslim, and over ten per cent as Hindu. Bengali is the dominant and official language.

More than sixty per cent of the workforce is engaged in agriculture. Rice, jute, tea, sugarcane, tobacco, and wheat are major crops, as well as jute. Fishing is an important economic activity. Natural gas is abundant and there are also small quantities of oil, coal, and uranium. Chittagong is the main port and Dhaka and Chittagong are the major industrial centres. Jute products, cotton textiles, processed food, steel, and chemical fertilizers are manufactured. The main exports are jute and jute products, tea, leather, fish, shrimps, and textiles.

A constitutional government came into being in 1972 after independence from Pakistan. The presidency is mostly ceremonial and the prime minister is head of government. The 330-seat national assembly is mostly elected in open polls but thirty seats are reserved for women. The major political parties are the Awami League, the Jatiya Party, and the Bangladesh Nationalist Party. The nation is divided into sixty-four administrative districts.

In 1971, after the war for independence had raged for months in Dhaka, Chittagong, Comilla, Sylhet, Jessore, Barisal, Rangpur, and Khulna, and over a million Bengalis had died, India allied with Bangladesh to defeat Pakistan. The leader of the Awami League, Sheikh Mujibur Rahman, had been chosen president while in prison in West Pakistan, and when released, in January 1972, he set up a new government as premier. Bangladesh joined the Commonwealth of Nations in 1972 and was admitted to the United Nations in 1974.

In 1975, after becoming president under a new constitution, Sheikh Mujib was assassinated in a military coup; and after further coup attempts, Major General Zia ur-Rahman became military ruler. In 1981, Zia was assassinated, and in 1982 was replaced in another coup by Lieutenant General Hussain Mohammad Ershad, who formed the Jatiya Party as president. Ershad later resigned his military office and won a disputed election.

In 1990, a popular revolt deposed Ershad and elections followed in 1991, won by the Bangladesh Nationalist Party under Khaleda Zia, the widow of Zia ur-Rahman, who became prime minister. In 1994, Zia's opponents resigned from parliament and after a series of general strikes, parliament was dissolved, in 1995. In the 1996 elections, boycotted by most parties, Khaleda Zia was returned to power, but faced with mounting popular protests, she resigned. An interim government supervised new elections, in 1996, that resulted in victory for the Awami League, led by Hasina

Wazed, the daughter of Sheikh Mujib. The first full term of parliament in the country's history was completed in 2001 and an interim government was installed to oversee national elections, which were won by Khalida Zia's BNP.

BHUTAN

Kingdom of Bhutan. 2001 population 2,049,412. 18,147 square miles (47,000 km^2), in the eastern Himalayas. Thimphu is the official capital and largest city.

Himalayan ranges running north to south divide the country into forested valleys with pasture. Perpetually snow-covered peaks are inhabited by Buddhist monks in scattered monasteries. Drained by Himalayan rivers that flow into India, Bhutan has frequent torrential rains and rainfall averages from 200 to 250 inches (508–635 cm) on the southern plains, where the valleys are intensively cultivated.

Bhutan's people are mostly Bhotias who call themselves Drukpas ('dragon people'). They are ethnically related to the Tibetans and practise a form of Buddhism close to Tibetan Lamaism. Dzongka, the official language, is Tibetan. In the south, there is a sizable minority of Nepalese (about a third of the population), who practise Hinduism and speak various Nepali dialects. Large numbers of ethnic Nepalis have been expelled to Nepal since the late 1980s, and the government has pressured Nepalis to adopt Bhutanese dress, customs, religion, and language. In addition, some fifteen per cent of Bhutan's people are from indigenous or migrant tribal groups.

Small-scale farming employs over ninety per cent of the workforce, producing rice, corn, root crops, citrus fruit, barley, wheat, and potatoes; and raising yaks, cattle, sheep, pigs, and short, stocky tangun ponies prized for mountain transportation. Cement, metal, wood, leather, alcoholic beverages, calcium carbide, textiles, and handicrafts are also produced. Fuels, grain, machinery, and vehicles are the major imports. Cardamom, gypsum, timber, handicrafts, cement, and fruit are the primary exports. Hydroelectric power is a most important resource, with some electricity being exported to India. Tourism is significant though restricted and is the country's largest source of foreign exchange. Bhutan's economy is closely tied to that of India, through both trade and monetary links.

Bhutan's hereditary monarch, the Druk Gyalpo (Dragon King), is assisted by two advisory councils. In 1953, a national assembly (Tshogdu) was created; thirty-five of its 150 members are appointed by the king, ten monastic representatives are selected by the ecclesiastical bodies, and the rest are popularly elected; all serve three-year terms. The national assembly is empowered to select and remove the king and to veto his legislation. The assembly must also give the king a periodic vote of confidence. Political parties are banned. Bhutan is divided into eighteen administrative districts.

INDIA

Republic of India. 2001 population 1,029,991,145. 1,261,810 square miles (3,268,090 km²).

The republic contains twenty-six states: Andhra Pradesh, Arunachal Pradesh, Assam, Bihar, Delhi, Goa, Gujarat, Haryana, Himachal Pradesh, Jammu and Kashmir, Karnataka, Kerala, Madhya Pradesh, Maharashtra, Manipur, Meghalaya, Mizoram, Nagaland, Orissa, Punjab, Rajasthan, Sikkim, Tamil Nadu, Tripura, Uttar Pradesh, and West Bengal. There are also six union territories, administered by the federal government: Andaman and Nicobar Islands, Chandigarh, Dadra and Nagar-Haveli, Daman and Diu, Lakshadweep, and Pondicherry.

In 1991, India had twenty-three cities with urban areas of more than one million people: Ahmadabad, Bangalore, Bhopal, Bombay, Calcutta, Coimbatore, Delhi, Hyderabad, Indore, Jaipur, Kanpur, Kochi (Cochin), Lucknow, Ludhiana, Madras, Madurai, Nagpur, Patna, Pune, Surat, Vadodara (Baroda), Varanasi, and Vishakhapatnam. In 2001, its three largest cities, Mumbai (Bombay), Calcutta, and Delhi, ranked third, ninth, and fourteenth, respectively, among the world's largest cities.

India's cultural diversity is indicated by its more than fifteen hundred languages and dialects. The constitution recognizes fifteen regional languages (Assamese, Bengali, Gujarati, Hindi, Kannada, Kashmiri, Malayalam, Marathi, Oriya, Punjabi, Sanskrit, Sindhi, Tamil, Telugu, and Urdu). Ten of the major states of India are generally organized along linguistic lines.

About eighty per cent of the population is classified as Hindu, fourteen per cent as Muslim, and most of the remainder as Christian, Sikh, and Buddhist. There is no state religion.

About fifty-five per cent of the land is arable. Agriculture produces about thirty per cent of gross domestic product and employs almost seventy per cent of the workforce. The Chota Nagpur plateau of Southern Bihar and the hill lands of south-western West Bengal, northern Orissa, and eastern Madhya Pradesh are the most important mining areas for coal, iron, mica, and copper.

Industry employs about fifteen per cent of the workforce. There are large textile works at Bombay and Ahmadabad, a huge iron and steel complex at Jamshedpur, and steel plants at Rourkela, Bhilainagar, Durgapur, and Bokaro. Bangalore has electronics and armaments industries. India also produces machine tools, transportation equipment, and chemicals and has a growing computer software industry.

India is a federal state with a parliamentary government under the 1950 constitution. The President of India is elected for a five-year term by elected members of the federal and state parliaments. The President's official executive powers are exercised by the Prime Minister (head of the majority party in the federal parliament) and council of ministers (which includes the cabinet). The ministers are responsible to the lower house of parliament (Lok Sabha) and must be members of parliament.

The federal parliament is bicameral. The upper house, the council of states (Rajya Sabha), consists of a maximum of 250 members elected by state assemblies, appointed by the President, and one representing Pondicherry. The lower house is elected every five years and may be dissolved earlier by the President. It is composed of no more than 545 members apportioned among the states. The Supreme Court is appointed by the President.

State governors are appointed by the President for five-year terms. States have either unicameral or bicameral parliaments and have jurisdiction over police and public order, agriculture, education, public health, and local government. The federal government has jurisdiction over any matter not specifically reserved for the states. In addition the President may intervene in state affairs during emergencies and may even suspend a state's government.

MALDIVES

Republic of Maldives. 2001 population 310,764. 115 square miles (298 km²), off the coast of South Asia in the northern Indian Ocean. Malé Island (1995 population 62,937) is the capital and the largest island.

The Maldives stretch five hundred miles (800 km) from north to south in the Indian Ocean south-west of Sri Lanka. Its twenty-five atolls include over one thousand coral islands, of which about two hundred are inhabited, some having freshwater lagoons. There are nineteen administrative divisions plus the capital area.

The people are a mixture of Sinhalese, south Indian, Arab, and African, almost all Sunni Muslims. The major language is Divehi, a Sinhala dialect, and English is spoken widely. Tourism, fishing, shipping, and coconut products are the economic mainstays. Most food must be imported. Industry includes fish and coconut processing, boat building, and garment and handicraft production.

Under the 1968 constitution, the president is head of state and elected by the legislature for a five-year term. The Majlis, the legislative body, has forty-eight members, forty elected and eight appointed by the president; all serve five-year terms.

NEPAL

Kingdom of Nepal. 2001 population 25,715,463. *Circa* 54,000 square miles (139,860 km²). Bordered by India and Tibet. Kathmandu is the capital.

Nepal has three major areas. The south, the Terai, is a low region of cultivable land, swamps, and forests. The north lies in the Himalayas, including Mount Everest (29,035 feet/8856 m) and deep Himalayan gorges. Central Nepal contains the Kathmandu valley, the country's most densely populated region and its administrative, economic, and cultural centre. Nepal's railways, connecting with lines in India, do not reach the valley, which is served by a highway and a bridgelike cable line.

The population is the result of a long intermingling of Mongolians, who migrated from the north (especially Tibet), and peoples who came from the Ganges plain in the south. The chief ethnic group, Newars, may be original inhabitants of the

Kathmandu valley. Several ethnic groups are classified together as Bhotias; among them are the Sherpas, famous for guiding mountain-climbing expeditions, and Gurkhas, a term loosely applied to fighting castes who achieved fame in the British Indian army and continue to serve in India's army and in the British overseas forces.

Nepali, the country's official language, is an Indo-European language and has similarities to Hindi. Tibeto-Burman and Munda languages and various Indo-Aryan dialects are also spoken.

About ninety per cent of the people are classified as Hindu and most of the remainder as Tibetan Buddhists and Muslims. Tribal and caste distinctions are officially maintained by the state and Brahmans retain great political influence.

Most people work in agriculture, which accounts for forty per cent of national product. The Terai is the main agricultural region, where rice is the chief crop and pulses, wheat, barley, oilseeds, jute, tobacco, cotton, indigo, and opium are also grown, and forests provide sal wood and commercial bamboo and rattan. In mountain valleys, rice is grown in the summer, and wheat, barley, oilseeds, potatoes, and vegetables in the winter. At higher altitudes, corn, wheat, and potatoes are raised on terraced farms. Livestock is second to farming in Nepal's economy: oxen predominate in the lower valleys; yaks in the higher valleys; and sheep, goats, and poultry are raised almost everywhere.

Biratnagar and Birganj, in the Terai, are the main manufacturing towns, and Kathmandu has some industry. Products include carpets, textiles, shoes, cigarettes, cement, and bricks; there are rice, jute, sugar, and oilseed mills. Wood and metal handicrafts are also important. Mica and small deposits of ochre, copper, iron, lignite, and cobalt are mined in the hills.

The reign of the Rana kings ended in 1950 with a popular revolt led by the Congress Party of Nepal. In 1959 a new constitution led to parliamentary elections that gave the Congress a majority. In 1960, the new constitutional king Mahendra dissolved parliament and, in 1962, instituted 'basic democracy' based on elected village councils (panchayats) and an indirectly elected national panchayat. Under the Panchayat System, political parties were banned. Crown Prince Birenda succeeded to the throne (1972) and like his father married a member of the Rana family.

In 1990, protests and general strikes forced King Birenda to proclaim a new constitution that legalized political parties, abolished the Panchayat System, and vastly reduced the king's power. Since 1991, parliamentary elections have produced a series of short-lived governments. A Maoist guerrilla movement that began in the countryside in 1996 has grown steadily in strength since then. In 2001, the reigning king and most of his close family were assassinated in the palace.

PAKISTAN

Islamic Republic of Pakistan. 2001 population 144,616,639. 310,403 square miles (803,944 km^2), bordered by India, Iran, Afghanistan, and China. Islamabad is the capital and Karachi is the largest city.

Pakistan has eight administrative divisions: Baluchistan, North-West Frontier Province, Punjab, Sind, Federally Administered Tribal Areas, Northern Areas, Islamabad Capital Territory, and Azadkashmir. Until 1971, Pakistan also included East Pakistan, which then became the independent state of Bangladesh.

The Indus is the chief river and flows the length of the country, fed by three of the five rivers of Punjab: Chenab, Jhelum, and Ravi. Most of the population live along the Indus, which waters most agricultural land and provides hydroelectric power.

Baluchistan is arid but a bit wetter in the north. Much of the province is unfit for agriculture, and nomadic sheep grazing is the principal activity. Coal, chromite, and natural gas are found here. On the rocky Makran coast of the Arabian Sea, fishing and salt trading are important. Quetta is the main city on the railway line between Afghanistan and the Indus valley.

Sind and Punjab are vast alluvial plains fed by the Indus. Sind shades in the east into the Thar desert. Extensive irrigation makes the arid Indus basin extremely rich agricultural land filled with wheat, rice, and cotton and containing the major cities of Lahore, Faisalabad (formerly Lyallpur), Hyderabad, and Multan. The sprawling port city of Karachi is west of the irrigated land on a site more accessible to ships than the Indus delta.

The North-West Frontier Province has low hills, plateaus, and fertile valleys. Its trunk road to Afghanistan runs up the Hindu

Kush. Wheat is the main crop and fruit trees and livestock are abundant. Peshawar and Rawalpindi are the major cities and major manufacturing centres. Northern parts of the North-West Frontier Province and Azad Kashmir contain the mountain peaks of the Hindu Kush, Himalaya, and Karakorum ranges.

The population includes many ethnic groups, almost all (about 97%) Muslim. Urdu is the official language, but Punjabi, Sindhi, Paxtu, Baluchi, and Brahui are also spoken, along with English.

Until 1999, Pakistan was governed by the constitution of 1973 as amended in 1985, which provides for a federal parliamentary form of government. Under the constitution, there was a bicameral parliament, comprising a 217-member national assembly (207 of whom represent Muslims and ten represent non-Muslims) elected by popular vote, and an eighty-seven-member senate indirectly elected by provincial assemblies. The president was the head of state, and the prime minister the chief executive. The constitution was suspended following a coup in 1999 and parliament was to be replaced by a national security council.

Four years after Pakistan's creation in 1947, its original statement of constitutional principles was abandoned (in 1951) when Prime Minister Liaquat Ali Khan was assassinated. An autonomy movement in East Bengal gained force in 1952. In 1954, government dissolved the constituent assembly and declared a state of emergency. In 1956, a constitution was adopted and Pakistan formally became a republic within the Commonwealth of Nations. In 1958, President Mirza abrogated the constitution and granted power to the army under General Muhammad Ayub Khan, who assumed presidential powers and in 1960 was elected to a five-year term, after which he abolished the office of prime minister and ruled by decree. In 1965, Ayub was re-elected. Following riots in 1968 and early 1969, Ayub resigned and handed power to General Agha Muhammad Yahya Khan, the head of the army, who declared martial law.

Elections in 1970 produced a National Assembly to draft a new constitution. The East Pakistan Awami League party won an overwhelming majority in the National Assembly by taking 153 of the 163 seats allotted to East Pakistan. The opening session of the National Assembly was twice postponed by Yahya Khan and then cancelled. Yahya Khan banned the Awami League and imprisoned its leader, Sheikh Mujib, in West Pakistan on charges of treason for the League's declaration of East Pakistan autonomy. The Awami League then declared the independence of Bangladesh on 26 March 1971, whereupon East Pakistan was placed under martial law and occupied by the Pakistani army, composed entirely of troops from West Pakistan. In the ensuing civil war, some ten million refugees fled to India and between one and three million were killed. On 16 December 1971, Bangladesh became independent following the defeat of Pakistan's army by India.

In 1972, Zulfikar Ali Bhutto, the deputy prime minister and foreign minister, came to power in West Pakistan. Sheikh Mujib was released from prison and allowed to return to Bangladesh. Bhutto's 1977 election victory was challenged by the opposition and the army chief of staff, General Mohammed Zia ul-Haq, deposed Bhutto in a military coup. Zia was declared president in September, and Bhutto, convicted of ordering the murder of political opponents, was hanged in 1979. In 1985, Zia announced the end of martial law after amending the constitution to strengthen his power as president.

In 1986, Benazir Bhutto, daughter of Zulfikar Ali Bhutto and his heir as head of the Pakistan People's Party (PPP), returned to the country. In May, 1988, Zia dismissed parliament, charging it with widespread corruption, and announced general elections for November. In August, Zia died in a mysterious plane crash. The PPP won the November elections, and Bhutto became prime minister. In 1990, President Ghulam Ishaq Khan dismissed Bhutto and her cabinet and elections brought to power a coalition government headed by Nawaz Sharif. In 1991 the parliament approved legislation raising the status of Islamic law. When Nawaz Sharif moved to reduce presidential power, he was dismissed (1993) by President Ishaq Khan; the ensuing crisis was resolved with the resignations of both men. Bhutto's party won the most seats in new elections later in 1993, and she once again became prime minister, heading a coalition government. Farooq Leghari, a Bhutto ally, was elected president. In 1995, some three dozen military officers were arrested, reportedly for plotting an Islamic revolution in Pakistan. Bhutto was again dismissed in 1996 on charges of corruption by President Leghari. In 1997, Leghari established a Council for Defence and National Security, which gave a key role in political decision-making to the heads of the armed forces.

Nawaz Sharif's Pakistan Muslim League won a huge majority in the 1997 elections and he once again became prime minister. Sharif soon moved to enact legislation curbing the president's power to dismiss elected governments and to appoint armed forces chiefs; the Supreme Court blocked these moves and reinstated a corruption inquiry against Sharif. In an apparent victory for Sharif, President Leghari resigned in December 1997, and the chief justice of the Supreme Court was dismissed. Mohammad Rafiq Tarar became president in 1998. In 1999, a bloodless military coup led by General Pervez Musharraf ousted Sharif, suspended the constitution, and declared martial law.

SRI LANKA

Democratic Socialist Republic of Sri Lanka. 2001 population 19,404,635. 25,332 square miles (65,610 km^2). The capital and largest city is Colombo.

Eighty per cent of the island is flat or gently rolling land ringing central mountains that rise to Pidurutalagal (8291 feet/2527 m). Administratively, the country is divided into eight provinces. In addition to Colombo, other important cities are Dehiwala–Mount Lavinia, Kandy, Galle, and Jaffna.

The population is seventy-five per cent Sinhalese, mostly Theravada Buddhists. Tamils who are mostly Hindu comprise eighteen per cent. There are also smaller groups of Muslim Moors, Burghers (mixed Dutch and Portuguese descendants), and Eurasians (mixed British descendants). The official language is Sinhalese (Sinhala). Tamil is a second national language, and English is commonly used in government. Education is free through to the university level and the literacy rate is about ninety per cent.

The country's economy is primarily agricultural; the emphasis is on export crops such as tea, rubber, and coconut (all plantation grown). Cocoa, coffee, cinnamon, cardamom, pepper, cloves, nutmeg, citronella, and tobacco are also exported. Rice, fruit, and vegetables are grown for local consumption. Sri Lanka is an exporter of amorphous graphite, its principal mineral industry.

Petroleum refining is also important, and precious and semi-precious gems, mineral sands, clays, and limestones are mined. Substantial deposits of iron ore have not yet been exploited. The island's swift rivers have considerable hydroelectric potential.

Industry has been centred chiefly around the processing of agricultural products, especially the cash crops – tea, rubber, and coconut. By the mid-1980s, however, textiles and garments had become Sri Lanka's biggest export. A great variety of consumer goods are also manufactured. Sri Lanka opened itself to foreign banks in 1979 and has developed an offshore insurance and banking industry. It has a persistent balance-of-trade problem, however, and the country is dependent on large amounts of foreign aid. Although coastal lagoons provide many sheltered harbours, only southern Sri Lanka lies on the main world shipping routes. The port of Colombo, on which most of the country's railways converge, handles most foreign trade.

Sri Lanka is governed under the constitution of 1978. The president, who is popularly elected for a six-year term, is both the chief of state and head of government. Members of the 225-seat unicameral parliament are also elected by popular vote for six-year terms. A movement for independence arose during World War One. The constitution of 1931 granted universal adult suffrage to the inhabitants; demands for independence continued, and, in 1946, a more liberal constitution was enacted.

Sri Lanka became independent on 4 February 1948, with dominion status in the Commonwealth of Nations. In 1950 delegates of eight countries of the Commonwealth met in Colombo and adopted the Colombo Plan for economic aid to South and South-East Asia. Riots occurred in 1958 between Sinhalese and Tamils over Tamil demands for official recognition of their language and for the establishment of a separate Tamil state under a federal system. In 1959, Prime Minister S.W.R.D. Bandaranaike was assassinated, and in 1960 his widow, Sirimavo Bandaranaike, became prime minister. The Federal Party of the Tamils was outlawed in 1961. Elections in 1965 gave a parliamentary plurality once more to the United National Party (UNP) of Dudley Senanayake, who became prime minister with a multi-party coalition. In 1970, Mrs Bandaranaike and her three-party coalition won a landslide victory. She launched social welfare programmes, including rice subsidies and free hospitalization. An armed rebellion by the People's Liberation Front was crushed in 1971 with Soviet, British, and Indian aid. In 1972 the country adopted a new constitution, declared itself a republic though retaining membership in the Commonwealth of Nations, and changed its name to Sri Lanka. Tamil demands for federal government were continuously denied and eventually produced sustained violence pitting the army against Tamil guerilla fighters. 1981 was a turning point, when the army burned to the ground the Jaffna library that contained centuries of Tamil literary heritage. A civil war has raged ever since, pitting the army against the Liberation Tigers of Tamil Eelam.

Selected Readings

GENERAL REFERENCE

Online internet sources are important. Searching for authors, topics, and places will often yield good results. The quote from Madhu Kishwar in the Introduction comes from one of her essays at http://members.aol.com/Critchicks/articles.html. The Anandpur Sahib Resolution text is at http://www.satp.org/India/Documents/Punjab_Anandpur%20Sahib%20Resolution.htm and http://www.sikhmediawatch.org/resources/political_information/anandpur_sahib_resolution.htm. Numerous scholars and institutions have useful online reference sites: one general access page to many others is the author's own site, http://www.sas.upenn.edu/~dludden/index.html. Country Profiles draw on material available online from various sources, including *The Columbia Encyclopedia*, Sixth Edition. New York: Columbia University Press, 2001, at http://www.bartleby.com/65/.

For geographical information, dynastic chronologies, and place references see: *A Historical Atlas of South Asia*. Ed. J.E. Schwartzberg. 2nd edn, New York: Oxford University Press, 1992 (1st edn, Chicago: University of Chicago Press, 1978). For texts and authors see: *Sources of Indian Tradition. Volume One. From the Beginning to 1800*. Ed. and rev. Anislee T. Embree. New York: Columbia Univesity Press, 1988 and *Volume Two, Modern India and Pakistan*. Ed. Stephen Hay. New York: Columbia University Press, 1988.

GENERAL SURVEY

De Silva, C.R., *Sri Lanka, a History*. New Delhi: Vikas Publishing House, 1997.
Stein, Burton, *A History of India*. London: Blackwell, 1998.

ANCIENT HISTORY

Thapar, Romila, *A History of India, Volume One*. Baltimore: Penguin Paperback, 1966.
——, *From Lineage to State: Social Formation in the Mid-First Millennium B.C. in the Ganges Valley*. Delhi: Oxford University Press, 1996.
——, (ed.), *Recent Perspectives on Early Indian History*. Bombay: Popular Prakashan, 1995.

EARLY MEDIEVAL HISTORY

Chattopadhyaya, Brajadulal, *The Making of Early Medieval India*. Delhi: Oxford University Press, 1994.
Gunawardana, R.A.L.H., *Robe and Plough: Monasticism and Economic Interest in Early Medieval Sri Lanka*. Tucson: Published for the Association for Asian Studies by the University of Arizona Press, c.1979.
Regmi, D.R., *Medieval Nepal*, 4 vols. Calcutta: Firma K. L. Mukhopadhyay, 1965–66.

LATER MEDIEVAL HISTORY

Ikram, Sheikh Mohamad, *Muslim Civilization in India*. New York: Columbia University Press, 1964.
Rizvi, S.A.A., *The Wonder that was India, Part II, A Survey of the History and Culture of the Indian Subcontinent from the Coming of the Muslims to the British Conquest, 1200–1700*. Calcutta: Runa and Co., 1987.
Wink, Andre, *Al-Hind, the Making of the Indo-Islamic World*, 2 vols. Leiden: E.J. Brill, 1990.

MUGHAL HISTORY

Habib, Irfan, *The Agrarian System of Mughal India: (1556–1707)*. Bombay & New York: Asia Publishing House, 1963.
——, *An Atlas of Mughal Empire: Political and Economic Maps with Notes, Bibliography and Index*. Delhi: Oxford University Press, 1982.
——, *Interpreting Indian History*. Shillong: North-Eastern Hill University Publications, 1988.
—— (ed.), *Medieval India 1: Researches in the History of India, 1200–1750*. Delhi: Oxford University Press, 1992.

Raychaudhuri, Tapan and Irfan Habib (eds), *The Cambridge Economic History of India*. Cambridge: Cambridge University Press, 1982.

MODERN SURVEY

Bose, Sugata and Ayesha Jalal, *Modern South Asia: History, Culture, Political Economy*. London & New York: Routledge, 1997.

BRITISH EMPIRE

Bayly, C.A., *Imperial Meridian : the British Empire and the World, 1780–1830*. London: Longman, 1989.
Lloyd, T.O., *The British Empire, 1558–1983*. Oxford: Oxford University Press, 1984.

BRITISH INDIA

Bayly, C.A., *Indian Society and the Making of the British Empire*. Cambridge: Cambridge University Press, 1988.
—— (gen. ed.), *The Raj: India and the British, 1600–1947*. London: National Portrait Gallery, 1990.
Metcalf, Thomas R., *Ideologies of the Raj*. Cambridge: Cambridge University Press, 1994.

ECONOMIC HISTORY

Kumar, Dharma and Meghnad Desai (eds), *The Cambridge Economic History of India, Volume 2: c.1750–c.1970*. Cambridge: Cambridge University Press, 1983.
Roy, Tirthankar, *The Economic History of India, 1857–1947*. Delhi: Oxford University Press. 2000.
Tomlinson, B.R., *The Economy of Modern India, 1860–1970*. Cambridge: Cambridge University Press, 1998.

NATIONALITY

Aloysius, G., *Nationalism without a Nation in India*. Delhi: Oxford University Press, 1997.
Brown, Judith, *Modern India: The Origins of an Asian Democracy*. Oxford: Oxford University Press, 1985.
Bayly, C.A., *Origins of Nationality in South Asia: Patriotism and Ethical Government in the Making of Modern India*. Delhi: Oxford University Press, 1998.
Chandra, Bipan, *Nationalism and Colonialism in Modern India*. New Delhi: Orient Longman, 1979.
——, *The Rise and Growth of Economic Nationalism in India: Economic Policies of Indian National Leadership*. New Delhi: People's Publishing House, 1966.

Guha, Ranajit (ed.), *A Subaltern Studies Reader, 1986–1995*. Minneapolis: University of Minnesota Press, 1997

Hardy, Peter, *The Muslims of British India*. Cambridge: Cambridge University Press, 1972.

Hasan, Mushirul (ed.), *Communal and Pan-Islamic Trends in Colonial India*. New Delhi: Manohar, 1985.

Hashmi, Taj ul-Islam, *Pakistan as a Peasant Utopia : the Communalization of Class Politics in East Bengal, 1920–1947*. Boulder: Westview Press, 1992.

Greenstreet, Denis K., *Ethnic and Elective Problems of Sri Lanka*. London: Sasor, 1982.

McLane, J.R., *Indian Nationalism and the Early Congress*. Princeton: Princeton University Press, 1977.

Regmi, D.R., *A Century of Family Autocracy in Nepal: Being the Account of the Condition and History of Nepal During the Last Hundred Years of Rana Autocracy, 1846–1949*. Nepal: Nepali National Congress, 1958.

NATIONAL ENVIRONMENTS

Bartholomeusz, Tessa J. and Chandra R. de Silva (eds), *Buddhist Fundamentalism and Minority Identities in Sri Lanka*. Albany, NY: State University of New York Press, c.1998.

Brass, Paul R., *The Politics of India Since Independence*. Cambridge: Cambridge University Press, 1994.

Frankel, Francine R. and M.S.A. Rao (eds), *Dominance and State Power in India. Decline of a Social Order*. New York: Oxford University Press, 1990.

Hasan, Mushirul (ed.), *India Partitioned: the Other Face of Freedom*. New Delhi: Lotus Collection, 1995.

Kumar, Dhruba (ed.), *Domestic Conflict and the Crisis of Governability in Nepal*. Kathmandu: Centre for Nepal and Asian Studies, 2000.

Kumar, Radha, *The History of Doing. An Illustrated Account of Movements for Women's Rights and Feminism in India, 1800–1990*. London: Verso, 1997.

Ludden, David, *Reading Subaltern Studies: Critical History, Contested Meaning, and the Globalisation of South Asia*. Delhi: Permanent Black, 2002.

Omvedt, Gail, *Reinventing Revolution: New Social Movements and the Socialist Tradition in India*. Armonk: M.E. Sharpe, 1993.

Index